Daniel Bell
and the
Agony of
Modern Liberalism

Recent Titles in
Contributions in Political Science
Series Editor: Bernard K. Johnpoll

Power and Policy in Transition: Essays Presented on the Tenth Anniversary
of the National Committee on American Foreign Policy in Honor of Its
Founder, Hans J. Morgenthau
Vojtech Mastny, editor

Ideology and Soviet Industrialization
Timothy W. Luke

Administrative Rulemaking: Politics and Processes
William F. West

Recovering from Catastrophes: Federal Disaster Relief Policy and Politics
Peter J. May

Judges, Bureaucrats, and the Question of Independence: A Study of the
Social Security Administration Hearing Process
Donna Price Cofer

Party Identification, Political Behavior, and the American Electorate
Sheldon Kamieniecki

Without Justice for All: The Constitutional Rights of Aliens
Elizabeth Hull

Neighborhood Organizations: Seeds of a New Urban Life
Michael R. Williams

The State Politics of Judicial and Congressional Reform: Legitimizing
Criminal Justice Policies
Thomas Carlyle Dalton

With Dignity: The Search for Medicare and Medicaid
Sheri I. David

American Prince, American Pauper: The Contemporary Vice-Presidency
in Perspective
Marie D. Natoli

Shadow Justice: The Ideology and Institutionalization of Alternatives to Court
Christine B. Harrington

Daniel Bell and the Agony of Modern Liberalism

NATHAN LIEBOWITZ

Contributions in Political Science, Number 124

Greenwood Press
Westport, Connecticut • London, England

Library of Congress Cataloging in Publication Data

Liebowitz, Nathan.
  Daniel Bell and the agony of modern liberalism.

  (Contributions in political science, ISSN 0147-1066 ;
no. 124)
  Bibliography: p.
  Includes index.
  1. Bell, Daniel. 2. Conservatism—United States.
3. Liberalism—United States. I. Title. II. Series.
H59.B42L54 1985   300′.92′4   84-15690
ISBN 0-313-24279-8 (lib. bdg.)

Library of Congress Catalog Card Number: 84-15690
ISBN: 0-313-24279-8
ISSN: 0147-1066

First published in 1985

Greenwood Press
A division of Congressional Information Service, Inc.
88 Post Road West, Westport, Connecticut 06881

Printed in the United States of America

10 9 8 7 6 5 4 3 2 1

Copyright Acknowledgments

  The author and publisher are grateful for permission to reprint from the following works.
  From *The Coming of Post-Industrial Society* by Daniel Bell. © 1973 by Daniel Bell. Re-
printed by permission of Basic Books, Inc., Publishers.
  From *The Cultural Contradictions of Capitalism* by Daniel Bell. © 1976 by Daniel Bell.
Reprinted by permission of Basic Books, Inc., Publishers.
  From *Confrontation: The Student Rebellion and the Universities*, ed. by Daniel Bell and
Irving Kristol. © 1968 by National Affairs, Inc. Reprinted by permission of Basic Books, Inc.,
Publishers.
  "For This Relief Much Thanks." Reprinted with permission from *The New Leader*, 30
May 1936.
  "Social Democratic Federation: Statement of Principles." Reprinted with permission from
The New Leader, 30 May 1936.
  Daniel Bell, "The Real Issue." Reprinted with permission from *The New Leader*, 18
January 1936.
  Daniel Bell, Review of *Patents for Hitler* by Guenter Reimann. Reprinted with permission
from *The New Leader*, 7 November 1942.
  Daniel Bell, Review of *Dated Socialist-Liberalism* by Stuart Chase. Reprinted with permis-
sion from *The New Leader*, 5 December 1942.
  C. Wright Mills, "Collectivism and Freedom." Reprinted with permission from *The New
Leader*, 19 December 1942.

Daniel Bell, "Two Steps toward Monopoly State." Reprinted with permission from *The New Leader*, 26 February 1944.

Daniel Bell, "Washington '44—Prelude to the Monopoly State." Reprinted with permission from *The New Leader*, 29 January 1944.

Daniel Bell, "The Balance Sheet of the War." Reprinted with permission from *The New Leader*, 21 October 1944.

Daniel Bell, "A Parable of Alienation," *Jewish Frontier*, November 1946.

Andrew Hacker, Review of *Political Man* by Seymour Martin Lipset, *Commentary*, June 1961.

Daniel Bell, "Adjusting Men to Machines," *Commentary*, January 1947.

Daniel Bell, "Ideology—A Debate." Reprinted from *Commentary*, October 1964, by permission; all rights reserved.

Will Herberg, "From Marxism to Judaism," *Commentary*, January 1947.

Judd L. Teller, "A Critique of the New Jewish Theology," *Commentary*, March 1958.

Irving Howe, "The Lost Young Intellectuals," *Commentary*, October 1946.

Daniel Bell, "Screening Leaders in a Democracy," *Commentary*, April 1948.

Daniel Bell, Review of *The Coming Crisis* by Fritz Sternberg, *Commentary*, May 1947.

Daniel Bell, Review of *Strategy for Liberals* by Irwin Ross, *Commentary*, December 1949.

Daniel Bell, Review of *Reveille for Radicals* by Saul Alinsky, *Commentary*, March 1946.

Daniel Bell, "America's Un-Marxist Revolution," *Commentary*, March 1949.

Daniel Bell, "The Moral Vision of *The New Leader*." Reprinted with permission from *The New Leader*, 24 December 1973.

For my mother and father
Sarah and Harry Liebowitz

To be superficial means to consider neither the characteristics of a contradiction in its totality nor the characteristics of each of its aspects; it means to deny the necessity for probing deeply into a thing and minutely studying the characteristics of its contradiction, but instead merely to look from afar and, after glimpsing the rough outline, immediately to try to resolve the contradiction.

Mao Tse Tung
"On Contradiction," *Selected Works*

Give us serenity to accept what cannot be changed, courage to change what should be changed, and wisdom to distinguish the one from the other.

Reinhold Niebuhr, 1934

Man doesn't really exist until he is fighting against his own limits.

Ignazio Silone
Bread and Wine

If I am not for myself, who will be for me?
If I am for myself only, what am I?
If not now – when?

Talmudic Saying
Mishnah, Abot

Contents

Acknowledgments

This study owes a great deal to two men: Dr. Joseph Bensman and Dr. Daniel Bell. Dr. Bensman first suggested the topic as a dissertation project. However, my gratitude to him goes beyond appreciation for the initial stimulus. Dr. Bensman provided an intellectual environment characterized by the freedom to explore an important and essentially Weberian notion: the greatest gains in the social sciences are won by critiquing concept constructions. In this environment, Dr. Bensman encouraged me to investigate Daniel Bell's work to the point of challenging the conventional wisdom and constructions of the Left.

Besides a rich and deep canon of work to explore, Daniel Bell set a tone of intellectual honesty which I tried to emulate, and which I deeply admire. Specifically, Dr. Bell raises issues -- the functions and limits of planning in a democratic society; creating a distributive mechanism predicated on fairness; establishing a workable balance between tradition and reform which were not always popular or palatable to the Left or the Right, and not easily solved by rhetoric. Rather than cant, they demand honesty; rather than the expertise of technocrats, they demand Hillel's passion for a just solution.

My debt to Daniel Bell extends to his generosity in granting the very lengthy interview which contributed to the completion of this study. I will also remember Dr. Bell serving soup to a cold and nervous interviewer on a snowy Cambridge day.

It is at this point that an author usually acknowledges the support of friends and colleagues. That seems hardly sufficient recognition to those mentioned here. One can only hope that as they read their names, they will know that simple words are never enough. Jan Zyniewski, Jay Fleishman, Alan Edelstein, Marty Shaw, Jack Krakowsky, Nancy Allen, and Brigit Marcuse continue to be good friends after I hopelessly overdrew on my account of their patience and encouragement. Ellen Pettit gave me belief and special friendship when I needed it most. Gita Voivodas seemed to have an unending fund of efficiency, awareness of detail, and humor as she typed the manuscript. For Jacqueline Lofaro, I hold the special respect reserved for a scholar of deep passion and firm conviction, and the affection for a friend whose sense of life gave a greater meaning to mine. My aunt and uncle, Joe and Adele Liebowitz, and my sister and brother-in-law, Gloria and Joseph DeLisi, were real family to me. Ike, a stray cat, who adopted me during the book's hectic production stages, was, and remains, a source of calming distraction.

**Daniel Bell
and the
Agony of
Modern Liberalism**

Introduction

Daniel Bell fashioned the notion of the "postindustrial society" in an unpublished but widely circulated paper he presented in 1963. It was quickly adopted as the term of reference in discussions about the form of the "new society" into which the United States and other technologically advanced societies seemed to be evolving in the early 1970s. These discussions centered on the displacement of the traditional market economy, the growing preeminence of the public sector, and the increasing reliance on planning and new modes of forecasting in the planning process by technologically advanced administrators and scientists in both the public and private sectors.

In his study of Bell and other "neoconservatives," Benjamin S. Kleinberg argues that Bell's efforts to develop a theory of the postindustrial society should be of interest to all those concerned with where our society is going. Kleinberg reasons that the main themes introduced by this theory have "since been incorporated into informal political discussions as well as into the outlook of many social scientists, and are already influential in the shaping of new perspectives on American society."[1]

This book is an analysis of Bell's efforts to construct a theory of the postindustrial society. A central problem at hand is the charge raised by Kleinberg and other critics of Bell that he is an ideologist of the "end of ideology" who is attempting, through the development of the theory of the postindustrial society, to rationalize the ideological perspectives embedded in the end of ideology. These perspectives include the disavowal of the ideological politics of the left in favor of a kind of administrative or technical rationality that requires that no action be undertaken unless its costs and benefits are specified in advance. They also include an assessment of social conditions in the United States that obviates the need for radical reform or socialism, namely, the view that the fundamental political problems of the industrial revolution have been solved.

The charge made against Bell by Kleinberg is an important one. There are several reasons why it warrants serious attention, not the least of which is that, if true, this charge serves to discredit a body of work that purports to be scientific. In making this charge, Kleinberg questions the credibility of Bell's efforts to construct a philosophy of the public household, that is, a new philosophy of Welfare State liberalism.

Kleinberg has every right to question the scientific credibility of Bell's work. During the late 1960s and early 1970s, Bell worked consecutively on developing a theory of the postindustrial society and establishing, on the foundations of that work, the conceptual framework upon which a new consensual basis for liberalism in the United States could emerge. Because of this circumstance, it was inevitable that questions were raised about the ends that guided Bell's efforts at theory construction. It also was inevitable that concerned individuals should ask if the theory of the postindustrial society was constructed to justify the ends and values embodied in the philosophy of the public household, investing those ends with a greater authority than they might otherwise have.

Moreover, if Bell is an ideologist, then his efforts to develop a theory of modern liberalism can be viewed, must be viewed, with some healthy skepticism. By the same token, one can hardly be expected to take very seriously his efforts to develop a theory of the postindustrial society. The ends espoused by an ideologist are generally very different from those of the philosopher. Ideology, while it has come to have a variety of meanings and uses since it was first used during the French Revolution by Antoine Destutt de Tracy, does not mean the same thing as philosophy, nor does it specify the same things.

Philosophy is generally viewed as a system of thought that seeks to postulate an ultimate order to

the world. It is a system that tries to unify human
experience by seeking to determine the principles that
regulate the universe and underlie all knowledge. In
contrast, ideology is part of an effort to promote a
specific image of the world; one that conceals a calculated, predetermined ultimate end. While the images
promoted by different ideologies vary, the basic intentions that underpin the construction of those images
resist experience. Rarely are those intentions amena-
ble to the knowledge gained from experience. As such,
the images promoted by ideologists seek either to guide
men's actions on the basis of the articulator's class-
bound interests or his political, social, or professional interests; or to rationalize his particular
predetermined point of view.

In investigating the merits of Kleinberg's charge,
we trace the main themes and ideas in Bell's work. The
question of whether Bell is an ideologist is an empirical one. No ready formula crafted on the left or the
right can substitute for the actual work that a solution to this problem requires. No analysis exists that
has come to terms with the contradictions and tensions
that frame Bell's work. Most seem to obscure them.

What makes Bell's work worth serious attention is
less the conclusions he reaches than the contradictions
and tensions that one finds in those conclusions. This
is not to suggest a dismissal of those conclusions.
Ultimately, the conclusions Bell reaches on issues like
the limits of democratic planning and political policy
have great value. Bell has often been charged with
being a neoconservative. While the term is fuzzy,
there is common agreement among accusers and accused
that, unlike ideologues whose work legitimated the
French Revolution, the neoconservatives are not intellectuals who lack experience in the everyday affairs of
the state. The question concerns the extent to which
their tendency to generalize on that experience prevents them from exploring new solutions to old problems. That problem, in and of itself, would not be
serious were it not for one fact: intellectuals who
define political thoughts and ideas have played a dis-
tinctive role in defining public policy. One need not
look beyond de Tocqueville's study of the French Revolution to realize that intellectuals can serve as legitimators of new ideas; ideas that often are drown upon
by makers of political policy to distinguish the possible from the impossible. Ultimately, then, if politics

is the art of the possible, it is they who define the possible.

Why the emphasis on the contradictions and tensions in Bell's work? Kenneth Burke once remarked about a book he was reviewing that what distinguished it from others of its genre was the wealth of its contradictions. The contradictions that permeate Bell's work run deep. They reflect the Weltanshauung of the 1940s and 1950s, the age that spawned them. Like the 1970s, it was an age very much preoccupied with the limits of science, politics, and ideology in providing solutions to what John Dewey called the "quest for certainty."

The contradictions and tensions in Bell's work are less those of an intellectual who is a "liberal in politics, a conservative in culture, and a socialist in economics," that those of a man caught between two conflicting worldviews: Hellenism and Hebraism.2 The ultimate questions posed by Kleinberg rest in relating Bell's efforts to develop a theory of the postindustrial society to the kinds of contradictions and tensions that arise when one seriously tries to reconcile certain parochial identities such as Hebraism with the universal aspirations embodied in Hellenism. These are the same contradictions and tensions that are endemic to the Jewish socialist tradition from which Bell emerged: they are contradictions and tensions that emerge when one seeks to temper the radical idea with the conservative impulse.

One first finds these contradictions and tensions in Bell's work on the end of ideology and later in his construction and use of the concept of the postindustrial society. They have served to make Bell's intellectual and professional passages "winding passages," for they are nothing less than the contradictions and tensions of the prodigal son, who, in the manner of the Jewish socialist Moses Hess, has gone beyond the pale, but is caught somewhere between his own Rome and his own Jerusalem.

These very contradictions and tensions in Bell's work give it universality and contemporary relevance. Any Catholic, Islamic, or Jewish political theorist, socialized by the orthodoxy of his or her youth, yet inspired by a belief in human equality, the preeminence of reason over dogma and particularism, and the democratic creed, could experience the same set of contradictions and tensions. The experience of Central

America, Iran, and Israel are, seen from this perspective, germane. But there is something else that gives Bell's work its contemporary relevance: the current American economic crisis.

At first glance, it appears that Bell's efforts to construct a theory of the postindustrial society and build on the foundations of that theory a new philosophy of Welfare State liberalism were made irrelevant by the election of Ronald Reagan and the relative success of Reagonomics in dismantling the New Deal Welfare State. However, several interrelated factors have contributed to making Bell's work appropriate for consideration today, not the least of which is the impact of Lester Thurow's study of American political economy, _The Zero-Sum Society_.

The success of Thurow's books is due to the fact that its prescriptions for a full-employment, managed economy buttressed by the creation of a national investment board suggest an alternative to the economic policies of Reagan with their return to the homilies and assumptions of the 1920s. However, the program for America to solve its economic problems suggested by Thurow is not a complete one.

While one can be easily seduced by the call for a managed economy that can allocate losses intelligently without appeal to secondary political and personal interests through its recognition of the zero-sum element in economic decision making, the call for a managed economy is not enough. Thurow himself would not suggest it was. _The Zero-Sum Society_ achieves its intellectual authority when it finally calls for the creation of a public philosophy that can explicitly specify the equitable distribution of rewards and losses and curb the tendency toward inflation promoted by increased productivity without resorting to tight monetary policies that result in idle industrial capacity and systemic unemployment. This, however, is precisely the same call made by Bell in the early 1970s.

Seen from this viewpoint, Bells' efforts to construct a philosophy of the public household anticipated Thurow's work. Given both the persistence of America's economic problems and the Democratic party's search for a viable alternative to the policies of Reagan from which it can mount a successful electoral challenge in 1984, Thurow's work, with its emphasis on centralized economic planning, may grow in importance. The architects of that Democratic alternative will have to wrestle with the same problems subsumed in Bell's efforts to develop a philosophy of the public household. The still prevalent crisis in liberal political theory will demand no less.

Since this book's initial writing, Daniel Bell has published two collections of essays, The Winding Passage and The Crisis in Economic Theory. Both elaborate on the same thesis and tendency described in this study: Bell's cogent analysis of the crisis in American liberalism and contemporary political theory born out of his ongoing struggle to reconcile and balance the worldviews of Hellenism and Hebraism.

In The Crisis in Economic Theory, Bell continues to focus on the inability of contemporary liberal political theory to manage the contradictions inherent in the relationship between liberalism and managerial capitalism--an uncomfortable relationship described by John Dewey as early as 1935 in Liberalism and Social Action. Bell tries to develop a theory of the post-industrial society--in essence a theory of social change--that is more substance than abstraction. In order to experience the nuances of Bell's personal struggle to construct a theory of the postindustrial society, one must read The Winding Passage as a companion piece to The Crisis in Economic Theory because it is almost an intellectual diary, a candid account of the professional situations that exacerbated and defined Bell's struggle to reconcile his two worldviews in order to produce a theory of modern liberalism that could satisfy him and attend to the stresses in American society.

Bell recounts his association with the socialist New Leader and that bastion of American capitalism, Fortune magazine, two very different publications. Clearly, these two professional relationships identify the opposing poles of Bell's intellectual struggle in a vivid way. Also, the very fact of these associations gives credence to Bell's critique of academicians who experience no professional life outside the university. Without the demands to confront and perhaps solve the real life dilemmas facing society and its policy-makers, such academicians are forced to rely on abstractions and dogma to the exclusion of the human dimension that permeates all corporate and political constructs. It is in the university classroom that this paucity of life experience becomes most evident.

Those of us who have endured lectures on political life that rely more on dogma than on scholarship motivated and guided by real life issues welcome Bell's sentiments:

> I regret the loss of such opportunity (opportunity to change careers) today for young people. When I listen to some of my colleagues today who have been in the lockstep of student, graduate student, young instructor, and then tenured professor without the crosshatch of experience that might leaven their large generalizations about "the State," "capitalism," "revolution," I regret not only the loss to themselves but even more to their students for whom such abstractions take on the "reified consciousness" of reality with no sense of what the world is about.3

Underlying all Bell's attempts to deal with his intellectual traditions as played out in his dedication to constructing a viable theory of modern liberalism is the nearly unspoken recognition of the caveats and clarion calls by Max Weber, a not so different sociologist who may have experienced pulls and pushes similar to Bell in trying to define a role for the social sciences outside the university. Weber saw the social sciences as the tool for fashioning social policy alternatives that can guide public policy decision making. This combination of warning and invitation emphasizes the substantive and discourages the pull toward reification much in evidence in today's sociology and economics: imputing to the theoretical, the abstract construction of the theorist (e.g., "the social system," the "laws" of economics) a life and permanence of their own.

Another element in the Weberian tradition brings us full circle to the question—though not the most important—dealt with in this book: is or is not Bell merely an ideologist? Weber recognized that no science can conceptually grasp reality without, in the process, transforming it. These transformations are conditioned by the theoretical purposes that underlie each science's efforts to gain knowledge of the empirical world. Recasting the question of Bell as ideologist in

these terms makes it look like this: does he, by virtue
of the very concepts he employs, exclude possible explanations of events and problems that somewhat different constructions would make accessible? The answer
becomes obvious if we accept Weber's, and, later,
Thomas Kuhn's notion that progress in science is marked
by the tension between the desire for new knowledge and
established paradigms that correspond to the state of
the field's current level of knowledge and focus of
interest.

Max Weber gives us some very good reasons to
consider seriously Bell and the canon of his work to
date. No easy solution is sufficient substitute for
the hard empirical and intellectual work that today's
economic, political, and social problems raise. To
attend completely to our tasks, we must comprehensively
analyze the ideas and values that have guided Bell's
efforts to develop a theory of the postindustrial society. They are nearly a mirror of American intellectual
history for the past 40 years. And, as both George
Santanyana and Karl Marx would say, we are condemned to
repeat a history we don't know or understand.

Notes

1.   Benjamin S. Kleinberg, American Society in
the Post-Industrial Age (Columbus, Ohio: Charles E.
Merrill Publishing Co., 1973), p. 1.
2.   Daniel Bell, Foreword to The Cultural Contradictions of Capitalism (New York: Basic Books,
1978), p. xi.
3.   Daniel Bell, The Winding Passage (New York:
Basic Books, 1980), p. xiii.

1

The End of Ideology

With the publication in 1960 of Daniel Bell's
The End of Ideology and Seymour Martin Lipset's
Political Man, a controversy was touched off in the
social sciences that has barely subsided. Generating
the controversy is a particular conception of the end
of ideology, one that was first formally developed by
the French political writer Raymond Aron and the American sociologist Edward Shils in the mid-1950s. Emphasizing the declining appeal of socialism and the relative success of Welfare State liberalism in Western
societies, the Aron-Shils conception of the end of
ideology received its sharpest phrasing from Bell and
Lipset.

The Aron-Shils conception of the end of ideology
varies dramatically from the conception of the end of
ideology that was suggested by Karl Mannheim in his
book _Ideology and Utopia_. It also varies from the
conceptions of the end of ideology that can be derived
from Georg Hegel's and Karl Marx's writings. The distinction is basic.

In the writings of Hegel, Marx and Mannheim, the
end of ideology emerges as an image of an abstract
social order. It is implied in their work as the
projection of some distant emergent reality. In Aron's
and Shils's works the term is used to capture the
spirit, the intellectual and political mood, of the
West during the post-World War II period. In their
writings it is used to describe a gradually emerging
phenomenon. It remained for Bell and Lipset to take
their descriptions one step further.

Before considering Bell's and Lipset's works on

the subject, we shall trace the philosophical origins
of the end of ideology. In tracing the origins of this
concept we shall be laying the foundations for a discussion of the controversy that their work on the end
of ideology triggered. Such an overview provides the
context by which we can discern the meaning of certain
terms that are central to that controversy.

The Philosophical Origins of the End of Ideology

While they presented different visions of the end
of ideology in a curious way, one that reflects Marx's
substitution of the material for the spiritual, Hegel's
and Marx's conceptions of the end of ideology overlap.
While they differ dramatically on the underlying dynamics, the motivational force of history, both Hegel and
Marx produce a vision of the end of ideology from a
mutually shared conception of the meaning of ideology.
Both Hegel and Marx see ideology as representing imperfect modes of thought which, in obscuring the ultimate
purposes and ends of history, produced false consciousness, the inability of observers to comprehend the real
relationship between reality and appearance and between
man and reason. Similarly, their visions of the end of
ideology are the product of a mutually shared view of
history as constituting a rational system whose ultimate purpose would be grasped by humanity through a
"true" understanding of history. For each of them such
a history was one that was free from the distortions of
ideological thought and the false consciousness of
people laboring under these distortions.
In Hegel's writings the vision of the end of
ideology emerges as a product of his efforts to define
the conditions upon which a true understanding, its
purposes, and inevitable direction can be derived
through conscious mental activity. Comprehension of
the "true" content of history, of its objective
meaning, presupposes for Hegel the philosopher's
ability to understand and summarize the spirit, the
Weltanschauung, of an epoch.
This presumption that history has an a priori
objective meaning was based on two ideas that underlie
Hegel's whole philosophical system. The first is that
the Absolute Mind, the Universal Spirit, objectifies
itself in material forms so that it may gain a true
comprehension of its essential nature as both a cre-

ative and unifying force. It is the notion that mind actualizes itself through a dialectical process that embodies the overcoming of oppositional forces that it itself creates as a condition for its coming to know itself. This is a process that, in its entirety, involves the self-alienation of the Absolute Mind as a precondition for its attaining true self-consciousness, true knowledge of itself as "being in itself." Ultimately, it is a process that enables the Absolute Mind to recognize that it has an existence that is logically prior to that of human comprehension of its existence. The second idea is that the whole process of self-consciousness is a cognitive process, one that presupposes that the Absolute Mind realizes itself cognitively in man through thought. What underlies this idea is the notion that thought constitutes the highest and purest form by which Absolute Mind actualizes itself.[1]

History as the progress of the Absolute Mind's overcoming of its own alienation from itself is a dominant theme of Hegel's philosophy of history. That theme is the basis of his vision of the end of ideology and his doctrine of the end of history.[2]

For Hegel the overcoming of Absolute Mind's alienation in historical reflection, in thought, is a task that involves the overcoming of ideological thought. Thus, ideology in Hegel's philosophical system always represents a barrier that temporarily prevents man's achievement of true self-consciousness. The problem of ideology thus emerges as a problem of false consciousness.

False consciousness in Hegelian philosophy refers to the failure of humanity to grasp the objective meaning, the true content of history. That failure is understood by Hegel to represent humanity's failure to comprehend the ultimate purpose to which history, as the successive unfolding of Reason, has directed itself.[3]

The presumption that men can grasp the true content of history, that they can grasp its objective meaning, is for Hegel the product of faith. It is the product of his faith in the philosopher's capacity to overcome the imperfect consciousness that underlies humanity's past failures to come to terms with the directions that history has taken. For Hegel the ability to come to such terms requires more than a comprehension of history. It requires a comprehension of the

role that certain individuals and nations serve as the
instruments of a process made known through history.
But this process is one whose meaning is always con-
cealed from the actors. The meaning of this process
only becomes "self-conscious post festum in the philosopher who sums up the sense of the epoch."4

To the extent that Hegel's philosophy of history
promotes the view that such self-consciousness is possible, it promotes a vision of the end of ideology. In
this vision philosophy constitutes a solution to the
problem of ideology and false consciousness.

The vision of the end of ideology promoted by Marx
flows from an idea that also underlies his philosophy
of history. This idea, simply put, is that once capitalism has been superseded the profit motive will cease
to dictate events. When the profit motive is no longer
a factor, the need for ideologies will no longer exist.
In short, Marx's vision rests on the idea that with the
inevitable emergence of communism the structural
sources of ideological thought will be removed and then
all ideological thought will cease.

Marx's vision of the end of ideology rests on a
very large presumption: that all ideologies can be
understood as systems of thought that serve one universal function. This function is one of obscuring the
material forces that make ideologies the intellectual
instruments through which conditions necessary to the
interests of one economic class are rationalized, that
is, treated as historically necessary and therefore
inevitable.5

Mannheim locates the end of ideology in the expected rise of the socially unattached intellectuals.
Bounded by a common intellectual heritage, a heritage
that would predominate over class and ethnic loyalties,
these intellectuals would constitute a relatively
classless stratum dedicated to transforming conflicts
of interest into conflicts of ideas. For Mannheim the
success of their intellectual labors would produce a
series of time-bound, relative syntheses of partial
truths (that is, ideologically conditioned truths) that
would ultimately serve to eliminate ideology as a mis-
leading mode of thought. Thought not guided by the
kinds of tenuous assumptions that characterized both
Hegel's and Marx's vision of the end of ideology,
Mannheim's is also questionable.6

Mannheim's significance, however, for the discussion of the end of ideology far outweighs the substan-

tive and theoretical limitations of his vision of the
end of ideology. While both his vision of the end of
ideology and the theory from which it emerged (the
theory of socially unattached intellectuals) failed to
generate much enthusiasm, Mannheim, nonetheless, held a
prominent place in Western intellectual circles during
the late 1950s and early 1960s.

Mannheim's significance can be understood to have
derived from his definition of ideology and the distinction that he made between ideological and utopian
thought. Mannheim elaborates his definition of ideology as thought "which conceals the present by attempting to comprehend it in terms of the past."[7] In so
doing he made significant contributions to the latter
day discussion of the end of ideology. His first
contribution was that of laying the groundwork from
which Shils and later Bell and Lipset in their reformulation of Aron's work would develop their particular
conception of the end of ideology. A second contribution made by Mannheim is that he provides some of the
critics of the latter day conception of the end of
ideology with the conceptual grounds against which they
would develop their arguments. In short, Mannheim's
efforts to elaborate upon his definition of ideology
serves on a formal level to define the parameters of
the end of ideology debate.

Mannheim's Conception of Ideological and Utopian Thought

Mannheim's definition of ideology is fashioned by
his analysis of the functions and limits of ideological
analysis in politics. In the course of his analysis
Mannheim makes the distinction between two different
concepts of ideology: the particular and the total.

By the particular conception of ideology Mannheim
refers to a method of analyzing ideas in which the
content of a particular set of ideas is viewed as a
distortion of a factual situation. The ideas are
branded as ideologies by those who occupy an adversary
position to the individual or individuals who propagate
them. The form of analysis generated by the particular
conception of ideology is a mode of analysis that is
conducted on the psychological level. It designates
part of an opponent's assertions as ideologies by
treating them as a function of his particular position
in the social milieu. The particular conception of

ideology thus refers to the function of ideas in obscuring or masking the real intentions and motives of an adversary in claiming truth for one idea or set of ideas over another.

By the total conception of ideology Mannheim refers to a more comprehensive form of analysis, one that critically invades the entire worldview of an adversary. Less concerned with the actual content of an opponent's ideas, the ideological analyst seeks to discredit an opponent's total Weltanschauung, including the methods and concepts by which he constructs a view of the world. The analyst seeks to accomplish this goal by relating the ideas to the socio-existential situation that the analyst views as producing them. The analyst views all of the opponent's mental products as being the functions of the collective life in which the opponent participates. Total ideological analysis exchanges the psychological for the theoretical. It makes this exchange by interpreting the content, as well as the conceptual structure of thought styles as functions of social conditions that determine intellectual production. Thus, ideologies are not just interpreted as subjective, deliberate disguises concealing particular interests, as in the case of the particular conception of ideology. They are interpreted as the cognitive reflections of the objective socioeconomic conditions that produce them. In both cases, the manifest content of the ideas are devalued.

The major distinction that Mannheim draws between the particular and the total conceptions of ideology is that where the particular acknowledges a common standard of truth and validity between the ideological analyst and the opponent, the total conception denies the existence of an objective standard. This is because the total conception of ideology embodies a clash between totally different thought systems, totally different ways of looking at the world. The particular conception of ideology permits for some dialogue between adversaries in that both can refer to the same theoretical frame of reference to substantiate their respective claims. The total conception does not.

The distinction that Mannheim makes between the particular and the total conceptions of ideology figures prominently in the debate over the merits of the end of ideology "thesis" propagated by Aron, Shils, Bell, and Lipset. Critics like Dennis Wrong and C. Wright Mills, among others, would, as we shall see

later in this chapter, question the end of ideology
thesis in terms of the narrowness of its proponents'
definitions of ideology and the ambiguities contained
within those definitions. Behind much of this criticism was an expression of the need to preserve the
conceptual distinctions embodied in Mannheim's analysis
of the particular and the total conceptions of
ideology.

But, while Mannheim's distinction between the
particular and the total conceptions of ideology figures predominantly in the "end of ideology debate," the
distinction that he makes between ideological and utopian thought has in fact a far greater place in defining the structure of the debate. This was because
much of that debate centered on whether the proponents
of the end of ideology thesis, in their enthusiasm over
the decline in political strength of Marxism and socialism in the West, were actually describing the end
of ideological and utopian thought in general.

For Mannheim both ideological and utopian thought
represent categories of thought that are incongruous
with reality in the sense that they each claim to
transcend the social and historical realities prevalent
at the time of their emergence. Yet, for Mannheim,
ideologies and utopias are very different: they embody
very different orientations to the world and they serve
to fulfill different functions.

For Mannheim utopias are not merely representative
of a state of mind that is incongruous with the order
of things and the state of reality in which it develops: utopias are only those situationally transcendental orientations to the world that, when they become
converted into action, have a transforming effect on
history in that they disrupt the status quo, shattering
stagnant structures.

In contrast to utopias, ideologies are reflective
of a state of mind that, even though oriented to goals
that transcend an existing order, nonetheless have the
effect of maintaining the existing order of things.
This conservative function is based upon the recognition that throughout history representatives of different social orders have been able to use situationally
transcendental ideas to protect their own interests.
Such representatives, Mannheim explains, have always
been reductionalists. Their aim has always been to
reduce ideas and social programs, whose successful
implementation would require major structural changes,

to the completely unrealizable. By rendering them socially impotent they confine those ideas and programs to a place somewhere beyond the Pale. They confine them to a place somewhere "beyond history and society," they confine those ideas and programs to a world "where they could not effect the status quo."[8]

Every period in history has contained ideas that transcend existing social orders. But, as Mannheim notes, very few of them have functioned as utopias. Rather, most ideas functioned as the "appropriate ideologies" of the times in which they emerged just as long as "they were organically and harmoniously integrated into the worldview characteristic of the period (i.e., did not offer revolutionary possibilities)."[9] The idea of Christian brotherly love in the medieval world offered a case in point. For Mannheim it represents a leading example of how a potentially revolutionary idea, the idea of paradise, could serve as an ideology and thus become the mechanism by which the status quo is preserved. It was this idea that sustained the idea of Christian brotherly love in the medieval world.

The fact that the incongruity of Christian brotherly love in a society founded on serfdom did not provoke conflict was a function of the ability of the medieval order to promote its own self-serving image of paradise. It was within this context that Mannheim noted that just as long as the clerically and feudally organized medieval order was able to locate its paradise outside of society (that is, in some otherworldly sphere), the idea of paradise remained an integral part of medieval society. The location of paradise in some otherworldly sphere transcending history "dulled its revolutionary edge."[10]

The idea of Christian brotherly love in the medieval world demonstrated two features characteristic of all ideologies. The first is that ideologies are situationally transcendent ideas "which never succeed de facto in the realization of their projected contents."[11] The second is that although these ideas often function to provide individuals with good intentions, something happens to them when they are put to work. Their meanings frequently become distorted.

That situationally transcendental ideas could function as ideologies was thus for Mannheim not a phenomenon reducible to the content of the idea itself. It was contingent on what function such ideas could be made to serve. Situationally transcendental ideas can serve both as ideologies and utopias.

Similarly, it must be stressed that in Mannheim's thought any idea can pass from being an ideology into a utopia. A prominent example of this in Western history was the Chiliastic idea of the dawn of a millennial kingdom on earth. This idea always contained a revolutionary tendency, one that the Catholic Church had long committed itself to undermining. The idea became utopian only when, through the revolutionary activities of Thomas Munzer and the Anabaptists, an oppressed strata, tried to put it into practice.12 Thus, only when an oppressed and potentially ascending group seeks to transform the wish images embodied in situationally transcendental ideas into conduct do ideologies become utopias. But, it is not always clear when a situationally transcendental idea ceases to be an ideology and becomes utopian.

The difficulty in determining whether an ideas is, at a given point in history, ideological or utopian is compounded by the fact that invariably the designation of situationally transcendental ideas as utopian always involves the interplay of subjective values and standards. In elaborating on this point Mannheim stresses that what in a given case appears as utopian or ideological is always dependent on the stage and degree of reality to which one applies those standards and values. He also stresses that "the representatives of a given order will label as utopian all conceptions of existence which from their point of view can in principle never be realized."13

While conceding that there were certainly some situationally transcendental ideas which in principle could never be realized, Mannheim stresses that the recognition of this fact ought not prohibit us from recognizing something equally true. This is that people who have a vested interest in preserving an existing social or political structure will invariably designate ideas and programs that may be unrealizable when implemented within that existing structure as absolutely utopian.14

Mannheim's identification of this tendency did not go unnoticed: it figured heavily in some of the criticisms leveled at the proponents of the end of ideology. For Mannheim this tendency requires that a distinction be made between two types of utopias: the absolute and the relative. By the absolute type Mannheim means those situationally transcendental ideas that are completely unrealizable in any social order. By the relative type Mannheim means situationally transcendental ideas that are only unrealizable in a given political order.

Consistent with his emphasis on the subjective forces that shape the designation of a particular situationally transcendental idea as utopian, Mannheim stresses that the labeling of an idea as utopian can fulfill a distinct ideological function. A reluctance to transcend the status quo can push one to regard "something that is unrealizable merely in the given order as completely unrealizable in any order."[15] This blurring of distinctions has its rewards. One benefit is that it enables one to "suppress the validity of the claims of the relative utopias."[16] Another benefit is that it enables one to enjoy a sense of security. "By calling everything utopian that goes beyond the present existing order, one sets at rest the anxiety that might arise from the relative utopias that are realizable in another order."[17]

Mannheim also notes the existence of other factors that served to complicate even further the determination of whether at a given period a situationally transcendental idea can be regarded as a utopia or as a ideology. A first factor was social position. While the designation of ideologies as illusory ideas ill adapted to the present order is generally the work of "representatives of an order which is still in process of emergence," the labeling of an idea as utopian rests with another group. It is usually the work of representatives "of an epoch that has already passed."[18] In other words, while it is always the groups that have a vested interest in preserving the status quo that designate new ideas, political initiatives, and programs as being "utopian" it becomes the province--the working agenda--of ascending groups that are in conflict with the status quo that ultimately "determines what is regarded as ideological."[19] A second complication was the fact that utopian and ideological elements generally do not occur separately in the historical process. Rather, the utopias of the ascendant classes "are often, to a large extent, permeated with ideological elements."[20] In order to explain this seemingly contradictory tendency Mannheim focused on the utopia of the nascent bourgeoisie.

The sixteenth-century idea of freedom represented a real utopia to the ascendant bourgeoisie because it

contained elements that were both instrumental to the
disintegration of the feudal social order as well as
those that became realizable with the ascent of the
bourgeoisie.   This idea, nonetheless, contained ideological elements.   For Mannheim an understanding of the
ideological elements embodied in this idea requires us
to recognize that "wherever the idea of freedom had to
make concessions to the concomitant idea of equality,
it was setting up goals which were in contradiction to
the social order which it demanded and which was later
realized."21

Against this background Mannheim argues that the
only adequate criterion that could be used to judge
what is truly utopian and what is ideological in the
outlook of a rising class is the realization of the
ideas embodied in that outlook.   The realization of
those ideas serves, then, as a "retroactive standard,"
one that puts to an end what under any other circumstance would be an unresolvable "conflict of
opinion."22

No review of Mannheim's efforts to distinguish
utopias from ideologies would be complete if it did not
stress what for Mannheim is the single most crucial
difference between these two reality-transcending modes
of thought.   That difference is the difference in what
the complete disappearance of utopias would mean.
Noting that the "end of ideology" would represent a
crisis for certain groups only, Mannheim argues that
the complete absence of the "utopian element" from
intellectual discussion and social action would alter
the flow of history and change the progressive course
of human development.23

The disappearance of utopia would bring about "a
static state of affairs in which man himself becomes no
more than a thing."24 We would then be faced with the
"greatest paradox imaginable": just when history has
ceased to become "blind fate," just when science and
reason are triumphing over superstition and sublime
ignorance, the delegation of utopias and the concomitant absence of ideals produced by that condition would
make man, again, just a creature of impulse. "With the
relinquishment of utopias man would lose his will to
shape history and therewith his ability to understand
it."25

One thing that is very clear about this argument
is that Mannheim's own vision of the end of ideology is
not one that promotes an image of a static society.

Whether the same can be said for the conception of the end of ideology developed initially by Aron and Shils and later elaborated by Bell and Lipset is another matter.

The Modern Conception of the End of Ideology

The conception of the end of ideology that emerged in the 1950s has little or nothing in common with those projected in the writings of Mannheim, Marx, or Hegel. Absent from the writing of Shils, Aron, Bell, and Lipset is any distant vision of the end of ideology. Absent too, is the assignment of the intellectual with the historic mission of transforming society.

In place of some distant vision of the end of ideology, Aron and Shils held that the end of ideology was by the mid-1950s well on the way to being achieved in the Western world. Writing from the vantage point of the late 1950s, Bell and Lipset went one step further: for them the end of ideology had already been achieved in the West. Like Aron and Shils, they equate the end of ideology with the decline of socialism in advanced industrial societies. But the similarities do not end here.

Aron, Shils, Bell, and Lipset each develop their views on the end of ideology very much in the broader context of a discussion of the role of the intellectual in modern society. Each of them define that discussion in terms of intellectuals as proponents of left-wing ideologies. Moreover, each of them frame their discussion of this issue as a response to the problem of alienation. Their discussion emerges out of what amounted to an emotionally charged polemic against left-wing intellectuals, intellectuals who did not share with them the conviction that ideological politics no longer had a firm or credible basis in the modern world.

Directed almost exclusively against Marxism and communism, their polemic is especially noteworthy in its origins. To a large extent this polemic originated with and became the dominant theme of the 1955 Congress of Cultural Freedom meetings in Milan.

What also makes their polemic noteworthy is that it was developed by men who, save Aron, had at one point or another been largely identified with various segments of the political left. Not unrelated to this

was the fact that in the 1930s Shils had been a registered communist, and both Bell and Lipset in the 1930s
and early 1940s had been involved in the socialist
movement.

The fact that Aron had no history as a disillusioned radical is of little consequence in accessing
the role he played in shaping the end of ideology
thesis elaborated by Bell and Lipset. His book The
Opium of the Intellectuals is the blueprint upon which
they would build their work on the end of ideology. It
is a book that was written as a critique of the left,
one that is dedicated to repudiating the assumptions
and claims of Marxism.

Aron's critique is one that links ideology with
intellectuals and defines ideology as a secular religion. It is an attack on left-wing French intellectuals for their emphasis on the credibility and contemporary relevance of Marxism as the logical fulfillment
of rationalist philosophy and bourgeois aspirations.
It is an attack that specifies the failure of the
French left-wing intellectuals to recognize that the
moral excesses of communism as manifested by the Moscow
trials and the purges of the 1930s represented more
than Stalin's decadence: they reflect the inherent
weaknesses of Marxism as a political creed. And finally, Aron's attack singled out the intellectuals for
allowing their need for ideologies to blind them to the
success of Welfare State policies in mitigating the
need for Marxism in advanced industrial societies.

While Aron provides the blueprint for the end of
ideology, Shils gives that thesis its distinctly "cele-
brationist" tone. That tone reflects the mood of the
1955 Milan Congress of Cultural Freedom meetings.

Representing little more than a summary of Aron's
presentation to the Congress, Shils's paper "The End of
Ideology" praises the participants for their maturity
and scholarly wisdom. He equates their absence of
ideological fervor with a growing recognition of the
substantive deficiencies of Marxism. That recognition
was reflected in their willingness to abandon the
search for universal truths in favor of political moderation and independent thought. The failure of Marxism to generate amongst Western intellectuals the kind
of enthusiasm that it evoked in the 1930s confirmed
both the success of Welfare State liberalism and the
maturity of the intellectuals. Shils, however, stops
short of declaring that the end of ideology had been

reached.

In both the Milan paper and later in a paper delivered in 1958, "Ideology and Civility," Shils cautions his audiences not to impute too much to the apparent decline of Marxism in the West.26 He cautions them not to invest the temporal with permanence. The old ideologies were being transcended but the elimination of newer ones could only be achieved by eliminating conditions favorable to their emergence. Required was the establishment of a suitable alternative to ideological politics. Such an alternative is a system of politics that could incorporate the intellectual's passion for ideals with civility, that is, with a commitment to the ideal of the common good and a binding respect for tradition and moderation. Embodied in the politics of civility is an orientation to politics that specifies the legitimacy of the equalitarianism championed by the left but tempers its enthusiasm for those ideals with the view that no theoretical system is ever realizable in practice.

Bell's analysis is very similar to Shil's analysis. Bell equates ideology with the intellectual's need for passion. Like Shils, he examines the conditions upon which civil politics could be adopted in place of ideology and concludes with Shils that society cannot discount the legitimacy of the progressive ideals of the left. He also concludes with Shils that intellectuals must realize that no theoretical system is ever realizable in practice. Yet, Bell's analysis generated a heated controversy in Western intellectual circles, while Shil's analysis went barely noticed.

Why the uproar over Bell's analysis? Part of the reason is that while Shils exercises caution and restraint in discussing the decline of socialism in the West, Bell exercises no such restraint. Socialism was not just declining in its ability to fuse the passions of the intellectuals and stir the imagination of the workers, the end of ideology had been achieved. It was a fait accompli.

While Bell does not go as far as Lipset in declaring that "democracy is the good society in operation," Bell's essay on the end of ideology, "The End of Ideology in the West: An Epilogue," is provocative.27 It is not just provocative in its declaration about the end of ideology. The essay is provocative in the way it arrives at that judgment.

The chief measure that Bell appeals to is plan-

ning. He charges that "few serious minds would believe
it was possible to set down blueprints and through
'social engineering' bring about a new utopia of social
harmony."28 That charge, given its faith in reason and
science, attacks the very foundations of socialism.

Bell's essay is also provocative when it locates
the source of ideology in the intellectual's need for
passion. The intellectual's unrest was branded as an
evil. The conditions generating that unrest were minimized. The inference was something that it took Lipset
to spell out: "the fundamental political problems of
the industrial revolution have been solved."29 Distinctions were drawn between the intellectual and the
scholar. Behind those distinctions the charge was
pressed that those intellectuals still searching for
ideologies to believe in lacked a "meaningful memory"
of the ideological debates that had consumed the passions of an older generation of intellectuals. They
were also charged with embarking on a faith ladder
"which in its vision of the future cannot distinguish
possibilities from probabilities, and converts the
latter into certainties."30

And finally, Bell's essay is provocative in the
constraints that it places upon reform movements.
Reform movements were needed. Utopias were still
needed. They were needed because humans need "some
vision of their potential, some manner of fusing passion with intelligence."31 The end of ideology "is
not--and should not be--the end of utopia."32 But
utopias could be pursued only in a certain way. They
could not be pursued with the same passion that had
guided humanity in the 1930s. Passion would have to
give way to reasonableness, order, and empiricism. The
lessons of the 1930s dictated that "the ladder to the
City of Heaven can no longer be a faith ladder, but an
empirical one: a utopia has to specify where one wants
to go, how to get there, the costs of the enterprise,
and some realization of, and justification for the
determination of who is to pay."33

The controversy that surrounded "the End of Ideology in the West" did not escape Bell. But four years
would pass before he would fully elaborate his views on
the end of ideology and choose to support Lipset's
conclusions about democracy while at the same time
minimizing the disagreement between him and his
critics.34

For Bell the "end of ideology debate" did not

involve a conflict of intellectual positions. It involved a "conflict of contrasting temperaments."35 In
support of this argument Bell proceeds in his debate
with Henry David Aiken to provide a resume of his
political philosophy and affinities. The construction
of this resume was prompted by Aiken's charge that the
outright effect of the end of ideology thesis "is to
reinforce acceptance of our institutional status quo,
and to declass those intellectuals who seek to modify
in any radical way the fundamental structures of Western political life."36 In response to this charge Bell
declares himself to be a democratic socialist. In
support of this claim Bell sets down the following list
of political principles and affinities:

> I wish to see a change in the fundamental
> structures of our economic life. I de-
> plore the social and economic power of
> the corporation. I detest the cult of
> efficiency which sacrifices the worker to
> the norms of productivity. I favor na-
> tional planning in the economy. I want
> to see more public enterprise. And I
> want to introduce other criteria than
> those of the market or the private profit
> motive as means of allocating resources
> in the society.37

Whether the end of ideology debate involved just a
conflict of contrasting temperaments is a complex problem. The solution to it can be established only following a review of some of the criticisms that were
directed at Bell and other proponents of the end of
ideology thesis. Tentatively, the solution to this
problem would seem to rest on an understanding of the
substantive and theoretical issues involved in the end
of ideology debate as well as on an understanding of
where the proponents of the end of ideology thesis
stand on those issues.

Criticisms of the End of Ideology Thesis

Generally, critics of the end of ideology thesis
have tended to view it as an argument that serves to
rationalize the status quo, that is, the prevailing
socioeconomic and political pattern of postwar Western

industrial society.   In developing this point of view
some critics have argued that the thesis is, itself, an
ideology, one that makes a fetish of empiricism in
order to justify its own ideologically derived image of
the world.   This image is one of American society as a
Welfare State, as a society that has successfully
solved the larger class-oriented problems that once
legitimately stirred the left.   It is an image of a
society that has institutionalized a set of mechanisms
through which solutions to racial discrimination,
poverty, or unemployment can be administratively
secured.

Commenting on the relationship between their past
and more recent work, one critic has argued that the
end of ideology thesis stands as a point of departure
upon which Bell and Lipset are currently seeking to
develop a revised liberal-pluralist theory of interest
group politics.   The purpose of that theory, according
to Benjamin S. Kleinberg, would be to legitimate the
institutionalization of a kind of statist liberalism,
one that since the 1930s has evolved into an active
interventionist state capitalism.[38]

Characteristically, what underlay much of the
criticism of the end of ideology thesis was a concern
over the political and cultural implications of the
developments that Bell and Lipset had looked so favor-
ably upon, namely, the decline of ideological politics
in the United States, and the institutionalization of
technical-administrative orientations to the political
process.

A survey of the literature shows that, by the time
that Henry David Aiken had advanced his argument that
the effect of the end of ideology thesis was one of
reinforcing a New Deal Welfare State status quo, that
argument had already become the standard thesis of a
small core of American and British commentators.

The origins of the argument can be traced back to
a 1959 essay written by Dennis Wrong titled "The Perils
of Political Moderation: Our Self-Defeating Party System."[39]   The basic thrust of this essay is that the
fear of totalitarianism current in the West had introduced a new consideration into the debate between the
defenders of the American two-party system and the
proponents of the European party system.   Wrong makes
no secret of his concern about the effect this development would have on future debates.

Wrong sharply objects to the way in which certain

defenders of the American two-party system have seized
upon this fear to rationalize the politics of moderation into a fixed ideological position.   He objects to
the way in which they were, in effect, "raising a
mindless moderation based on loose party coalitions
into a political principle."40   For Wrong this is the
result of an overreaction to the political dictum that
the end justifies the means.   Wrong argues that "the
exponents of moderatism ignore ends altogether in their
preoccupation with the use of power, i.e., legal and
constitutional means."41   The result, adds Wrong, is
the legitimation of "a political formalism which cele-
brates the institutional process through which decisions are reached while ignoring the content of the
decisions."42

For Wrong moderation of this kind was hardening
into a new conservative ideology.   Wrong argues that
"the compulsive bi-partisanship of the 50s owes less to
the alleged need so frequently invoked by neo-conserva-
tives, to compromise the demands of rival blocs and
interest groups in American society than to the spread
of the ideology of moderatism itself in a period of
prosperity and international crisis."43   Such ideology,
stresses Wrong, is one that serves to rationalize "a
retreat from politics under the guise of offering a new
philosophy of politics."44

The association of the politics of moderation with
the end of ideology would remain a persistent theme for
Wrong.45   But no one pursued this theme with greater
vigor and force than C. Wright Mills.   Mills' critique
of the end of ideology thesis was simple, concrete, and
polemical.

In his "Letter to the New Left," Mills argues that
the end of ideology thesis had a very limited relevance
to the modern world.46   Mills claims that the origins
of this thesis could be located in a disillusionment of
its proponents with any real commitment to socialism
that resulted from their own personal and political
frustrations.

Against this background Mills asserts that "if the
phrase the end of ideology has any meaning at all, it
pertains to self-selected circles of intellectuals in
the richer countries."47   The end of ideology serves as
a "slogan of complacency, circulating among the prema-
turely middle aged, [and] centered in the present."48
He also asserts that the end of ideology is itself an
ideology.   It is an ideology of "the ending of politi-

cal reflection itself as a public fact."49 Expanding
on this point, Mills concludes that the end of ideology
is "an ideology of complacency which seems the only way
now open for many writers to acquiesce in or to justify
the status quo."50

It is obvious from these comments that Mills was
not just reacting to the idea that the West was experiencing an end to ideological politics. Like Wrong,
Mills was reacting much more to the positive interpretation given to this development by the proponents of
the end of ideology thesis. But Mills and Wrong were
not alone.

Andrew Hacker, for instance, in an otherwise
favorable review of Lipset's book Political_Man took
Lipset to task for minimizing the contributions made by
ideologies. His criticism is simple and to the point:
"if the end of ideology is, in fact, the case, then we
have the best explanation of why we in the West are
standing still."51

Underlying Hacker's criticism, and for that matter
most of the criticism that focused on Bell's and
Lipset's positive interpretation of the end of ideology, was a deeply rooted concern over the consequences
that would result from the uncritical acceptance of the
end of ideology thesis. This concern was largely generated by the view that the uncritical reader would not
realize that when Bell and Lipset spoke of the end of
ideology what they meant was "the end of utopian
thought."52 Such a misunderstanding, reasoned their
critics, would be the result of Bell's and Lipset's
inconsistent use of the terms ideology and ideological
politics.

In developing this point, Stephen Rousseas and
James Farganis in their essay "American Politics and
the End of Ideology" rely on the distinction that
Mannheim makes between ideology and utopia. That distinction is between ideologies as the ideas and thought
patterns of interest-bound ruling classes that serve to
rationalize the status quo and utopias as the intellectual stimulus provided by oppressed groups who, in
challenging the established order, seek to transform it
into their own image of the good society.

Rousseas and Farganis hold that when Bell and
Lipset spoke of the end of ideology what they really
mean is that the end of utopian thought. There could
be no mistaking this point since both Bell and Lipset,
when talking about the end of ideology, are "clearly

referring to the decline of socialist or Marxian ideas within the context of an affluent Western Society."53 This misuse of terms constituted a serious error. When the interpretation of the decline of Marxian ideas embodied in the end of ideology was pushed farther by Lipset through his declaration that democracy "is the good society in operation" it "obliterated" the distinction between the empirical and the normative, the political and the ethical.

For Rousseas and Farganis the obliteration of this distinction means that the "traditional role of the intellectual as social critic is no longer logically possible."54 "For if what ought to be," they explain, "already is, then the intellectual has no other function than to describe and to celebrate the arrival of utopia."55   This had one major consequence.

By invalidating the critical role of the intellectual, the proponents of the end of ideology thesis served to distort the meaning of much of the intellectual discontent with the established order of things reflected in literature and in films throughout the postwar period. True, Bell and Lipset recognize the alienation underlying this discontent; but by failing to understand that this discontent was political, the proponents of the end of ideology thesis, argue Rousseas and Farganis, had distorted its meaning not only as a cultural but as a political phenomena. That Bell and Lipset could fail to grasp the political nature of such growing discontent with American society was a function of their conception of politics, one which was limited to the evaluation of voting behavior and welfare measures.   To this criticism, Rousseas and Farganis add that "if traditional idea of political philosophy is maintained, there is yet some small contribution that intellectuals can make, which will be something other than a justification, tacit or overt, for whatever is."56

Such a contribution, they argue, can only be predicated on an awareness of the functions that the end of ideology thesis has in promoting a self-defeating image of Western industrial society. This is an image that serves to transform modern democracy into a system or set of techniques.   It is an image that serves to reduce democratic politics to a "constellation of self-seeking pressure groups peacefully engaged in a power struggle to determine the allocation of privilege and particular advantage."57

It was against the background of this general
criticism that Rousseas and Farganis identify two negative functions of the end of ideology thesis. The
first is that it served to legitimate the view that
there was no room for ideological politics since compromise and evolution represent the only possible
means, given the agreed upon rules of the game that
characterize the modern democratic political system,
for achieving "the few second order goals which continue to remain in an otherwise near perfect society."[58]
In serving this function the end of ideology thesis
also served to further rationalize the currently
acceptable role of the modern politician as the "man
who understands who to manipulate and how to operate in
a Machiavellian world which divorces ethics from politics."[59] This is its second function. Like the first
it serves to "defend the status quo in the name of
democracy" while failing to recognize what Max Weber
was able to come to terms with when he wrote that
"certainly all historical experience confirms the truth
--that man would not have attained the possible unless
time and again he had reached out for the
impossible."[60]

Rousseas and Farganis also argue that if the
intellectual was to make a meaningful contribution as a
social critic he or she must not accept the choice
outlined by the proponents of the end of ideology
thesis as absolute. They must not accept the choice
between "the wide-eyed fanatic and the cool, uncommit-
ted pragmatist who is willing to take his progress
piecemeal, if at all."[61] The intellectual need not,
they argue, equate ideology with Chiliastic fanaticism.
Rather, the intellectual must recognize that ideology
still has a valid role, one of fusing passion with
critical reason in response to the problems of the
modern world. As such, the intellectual, they reason,
must recognize in ideology that which distinguished
progress from mere change, namely, that progress can be
"defined meaningfully only in terms of some vision."[62]

It was against this background that Rousseas and
Farganis argue that it is irrelevant whether one agrees
with the vision of a particular ideology. The important thing is that one recognize that intellectual
freedom "and a social commitment which transcends the
status quo are interrelated and interdependent."[63]

This last argument is a very powerful one. What
makes the argument so powerful is that it represents a

clear extension of Mannheim's thesis that the disappearance of utopia would bring about "a static state of
affairs in which man becomes no more than a thing."64
But this was certainly not a thesis that Bell was
unfamiliar with.

It is to be remembered that Bell went to great
lengths to stress that the end of ideology did not mean
the abandonment of utopia. But it is very clear that
Bell had a very different conception of the nature of
utopian thought than the one Rousseas and Farganis
derive from their interpretation of Mannheim.

Toward a Reappraisal of the End of Ideology

The notion of utopias that specify their "costs"
represents a very rational image of what, if we follow
Mannheim's thinking, never is a completely rational
mode of thought. Indeed, it is very understandable
why, given the atrocities perpetrated the name of the
Nazi and Soviet "utopias," Bell would be apprehensive
about utopias that did not specify their "costs." But
to insist that future utopias should only be "empirical" imposes a somewhat arbitrary set of boundaries on
a phenomenon that, historically at least, has always
defied conventional rules. This insistence would seem
to reflect the articulation of boundaries that, as
William Delaney briefly notes, were firmly embodied in
the values of managerialism, namely, a preference for
utilizing administrative rather than political means to
secure solutions to fundamentally political problems.65
Closely related to this criticism was the criticism made by C. Wright Mills that, in the name of truth
and science, the proponents of the end of ideology made
a "fetish of empiricism" in order to rationalize their
own ideologically derived image of the world. Criticizing Bell, Lipset, and others for failing to examine
their own ideological assumptions, Mills in his "Letter
to the New Left" refers to the end of ideology as "an
intellectual celebration of apathy" that in its selective reconstruction of the world collapses "reasoning
into reasonableness."66
The broad outlines of this less than systematic,
but nonetheless important criticism was developed by
Mills when, in noting that the end of ideology thesis
embodied a highly stylized form of thought, he argues
that it is a "journalistic fashion," one in which "the

facts are duly weighed, carefully balanced, [and] always hedged."67 For Mills, the employment of this technique had one common result, namely, that the power of facts to "outrage, their power to truly enlighten in a political way, their power to aid decision, even their power to clarify some situation" all became blunted or destroyed.68 Mills makes no secret about how he arrived at this conclusion.

Mills believes that the proponents of the end of ideology thesis suffered from a marked tendency. They would always acknowledge facts and arguments that suggested that the Western democracies have resolved their major political problems. But they would always fail to integrate those facts and arguments in a way that would relate them to the changing institutions of Western society.

Mills is equally blunt about the consequences that he sees arising from that failure. The failure of the proponents of the end of ideology thesis to properly integrate the facts they worked with into the larger picture "make it impossible to understand the structural realities which these facts might reveal; the longer run trends of which they might be tokens."69 The result is that "the real questions are not even raised, and the analysis of the meaning of facts not even begun."70

The crux of Mill's argument is that, having made a "fetish of empiricism," the proponents of the end of ideology have served to delimit artificially and devitalize the functions of sociological analysis. In essence, what Mills is accusing them of is their failure to recognize the nature and limits of scientific knowledge, that is, the fact that "facts" are themselves the product of viewing "reality" through theoretical preconceptions. These preconceptions are always grounded in the perception of the problematic and the evaluation of what is significant. Such perceptions are of course never value free. How significant was this failure? Does that failure provide an adequate basis for concluding, as Rousseas and Farganis have in their interpretation of Mills' critique, that the proponents of the end of ideology in their preoccupation with "pure facts" were indulging in "an ideological positivism which amounts to nothing more than an unthinking apologia for whatever is?"71 These are questions that require close examination.

Such an examination must be prepared to deal with

the end of ideology thesis in terms of the interplay of
a specific set of overlapping theoretical and substantive considerations. With regard to the former, such
an examination must be prepared to determine the connection between the kind of empiricism specified by
Bell and Lipset and the pragmatism of John Dewey. The
necessity of establishing this connection is suggested
by Bell's acknowledgment of Dewey as one of his principal intellectual "masters."72 It is also suggested by
Bell's acknowledgment of the influence of Dewey's student and leading interpreter Sidney Hook on his intellectual development. Hook was the man to whom Bell
dedicated the book The End of Ideology.73

Also, such an examination, as noted earlier, must
aim to develop an understanding of where the proponents
of the end of ideology stood on the issues raised by
their critics. Specifically, such an examination must
seek to determine where they stood on such key issues
as the place of utopian or radical politics, the functions and limits of empiricism and science in politics
and the alienation of the intellectual and its roots.
Similarly, the examination of the merits of this charge
of empiricism must first determine the grounds upon
which the end of ideology thesis can be understood as
establishing a conceptual framework through which the
then, and still, existent preeminence of New Deal
pluralism and liberal statism in the American political
system can be justified and maintained. It must, then,
determine whether Bell's framework has its foundations
in Dewey's pragmatic approach to social problems and
policymaking or in Bell's interpretation of that
approach.

Such an analysis may enable us to determine if
Bell's image of the postindustrial society is based, as
Kleinberg has argued, on an ideologically derived construction of the world, one that is grounded in the
image of American society projected in the end of
ideology thesis. To make this determination we must
first understand the groundwork out of which Bell's
approach to the end of ideology emerged. This means
that we must seek to get a sense of the underlying
values that conditioned his approach.

Such a project is one that must start with an
examination of Bell's earlier work as the summary of a
variety of intersecting and converging factors. These
factors may allow us to understand the development of
that work within the intellectual and historical con-

text from which it emerged. An understanding of them may allow us to gain some measure of the kinds of values and assumptions that framed Bell's efforts to develop a theory of the postindustrial society. The nature of Bell's ideas and intellectual concerns as a member of a once radical generation of intellectuals, his involvement in the Congress of Cultural Freedom, his affinity for Deweyian pragmatism, his long-standing interest in the subject of alienation, particularly the alienation of the Jewish intellectual, are the factors to which we refer.

The necessity of adopting this approach is dictated by the fact that Bell's essay "The End of Ideology in the West: An Epilogue" is just that, an epilogue. The views and formulations expressed in that essay must therefore be examined and ultimately understood in relation to what that essay was an epilogue to. More than just an epilogue to 15 often diverse sometimes highly schematic, essays, it served as an epilogue to the political struggles and moral conflicts that expressed the mood of Bell's generation of intellectuals. Bell, in a highly autobiographical essay, "The Mood of Three Generations," characterizes that generation as "twice born." This was a generation of intellectuals that once having revelled in the political struggles of the 1930s was to find in the 1950s, to quote Bell, "its wisdom in pessimism, evil, tragedy, and despair."[74]

"A deep-seated sense of malaise, a feeling that times are profoundly out of joint, a realization that mass industrial society for all its material achievements is not a utopia," nor can it ever be, combined with the belief that "somehow man has lost his moral bearings," are, as James P. Young observes, all characteristic of that mood.[75] Infusing much of the social and political thought of the 1950s with its sense of pessimism concerning the basic nature of humanity and the limits of democracy in providing solutions to deep-seated moral and social problems was an intellectual mood that did more than just shape Bell's positive interpretation of the end of ideology. More than anything else, it helped to shape his views on the alienation of the modern intellectual and the problems of mass society in almost exclusively cultural terms. In part, it also served to underlay his reaction to the social unrest and tensions of the 1960s. As will be shown later in this study, this intellectual mood also underlay Bell's efforts to develop a theory of the postindustrial society based upon the social and political problems confronting American society.

The end of ideology essay represents only one stage in an intellectual development that has meaning only in relation to the experiences within which it was grounded, that is, the experiences of Bell as a member of the "twice born" generation. It must also be understood in relation to the debates and converging theories that, along with those experiences, ultimately served to determine arguments and guide the directions that Bell would take in his more recent writings. In short, "The End of Ideology in the West: An Epilogue" is an epilogue to the events, experiences, and perceptions that shaped Bell's life up until its writing. His essay indicates the end of both a personal and intellectual era, but it contains both the seeds and the problems for his later work.

Notes

1. There is in Hegel as there is in the historical school in general the presumption that the world is a unity that is conceivable only with reference to the knowing subject. In affirming the governing principle of the idealist faith, the notion that matter is organized by mind, Hegel held that reason is at once general and particular. It was, he argued, a concrete universal that differentiates itself into particular thinking minds.

2. Common to both Hegel's and Marx's dialectical view of history is this notion that once the objective purpose of history is realized, history as humanity has known it will come to an end. The common assumption was that history was a succession of events that underscored the failure of humanity to comprehend its ultimate purposes.

3. This is Hegel's cunning of reason thesis. Historically, its significance is that it has been used to justify the totalitarian state. Behind this thesis is the notion that a concrete manifestation of Absolute Mind was provided through the national state. In the 1930s this philosophy was used to support the Nazi state and invest it with legitimacy.

4. George Lichtheim, The Concept of Ideology and Other Essays (New York: Vintage Books, 1967),

p. 15.

5. Especially important in this regard is
Marx's critique of Adam Smith.   Marx's argument against
Smith was that in defining all wealth in terms of
industrial wealth (and thus failing to distinguish
labor from industry) Smith provided capitalism with an
ideology that constituted the political-economic basis
for humanity to be conceived of as private property,
that is, as a commodity or as a thing.   In Capital (8th
ed., ed. Frederick Engels, trans. Samuel Moore and
Edward Aveling; London: Swan Sonnenschein, 1902) Marx
extended this argument into a thorough-going critique
of commodity fetishism.   For Marx's argument see Karl
Marx, Economic and Philosophic Manuscripts of 1844, ed.
Dirk J. Struik (New York: International Publishers,
1964), p. 45.   Also important in explicating this point
is Georg Lukacs's History and Class Consciousness:
Studies in Marxist Dialectics (Cambridge, Mass.: M.I.T.
Press, 1968).   In extending Marx's argument and developing his theory of reification around it, Lukacs argues that the objective dimension of reification is the
emergence of a society conditioned by a commodity
structure where the laws governing the movement and the
relation of objects "confront men as invisible forces
that generate their own power."   Lukacs, History and
Class Consciousness, p. 87.

6.   It is important to understand that when
Mannheim argues that the unattached intellectual can
integrate the particular interest-bound ideologies that
are based on a multitude of interests into an emerging
objective set of truths that are universally binding he
was making certain untestable claims.   He is asserting
that the intellectual because of his detachedness can
achieve a higher objectivity.   He is also asserting
that it is possible to create a value-free (interest-
free) set of ideas that are different from ideologies.
Both of these propositions are extremely problematic.
It is relatively easy to imagine detached intellectuals
being alienated from all previously existing interest
groups.   But intellectuals, in achieving the consensus
necessary, in Mannheim's terms, to arrive at objectivity, may also develop interests as intellectuals.   These
interests may be in jobs, in prestige, and in power,
especially the power to impose their thought and their
interests upon a society that from the standpoint of
its distributive interests may not be predisposed to
accept the claims of the intellectual.   Mannheim's

second proposition is even more problematic. The assumption that the intellectuals, in their objectivity, their knowledge, and their wisdom, can create a unified consistent system of thought independent of particular values is open to question. What Mannheim asserts is the possibility of a value-free social theory. Yet long before Mannheim raises this implicit possibility, the possibility of such a social theory was called into question by, among others, Max Weber, through his concept of value relevance. So far as we know nobody has disproven Weber's notion that ultimate values are not ascertainable by objective inquiry. In order for Mannheim to suggest the possibility of a unified intellectual consensus based on the study of the empirical "law of history," it is necessary for him to assume that it is possible to reach a stage of intellectual development where ultimate values become the basis of a higher objectivity. The argument that the objectivity is the emerging product of a growing consensus based on scientific inquiry requires that one accept the notion of progressive consensus. So far as we know this consensus has not occurred. In fact, the history of knowledge, at least until now, demonstrates, as Mannheim himself concedes, the emergence of continuous new forms of dissension that occur either because of changes in the structure of society or because of change in the priority given to ultimate values at a given time or place by a particular group of intellectuals. Finally, every scientific or intellectual discovery tends to disturb or upset the established consensus of a given time or place. On the subject of Mannheim's views on dissension see Karl Mannheim, _Ideology and Utopia_, trans. Louis Wirth and Edward Shils (New York: Harcourt, Brace and World, 1936), p. 81.

7.   Ibid., p. 67.
8.   Ibid., p. 193.
9.   Ibid.
10. Ibid.
11. Ibid., p. 194.
12. Ibid., p. 211.
13. Ibid., p. 196.
14. Ibid.
15. Ibid., p. 197.
16. Ibid.
17. Ibid.
18. Ibid., p. 203.
19. Ibid.

20.   Ibid.

21.   Ibid., p. 204.

22.   Ibid.

23.   Ibid., p. 262.

24.   Ibid., pp. 262-63.

25.   Ibid., p. 263.

26.   The full title of the essay is "Ideology and Civility: On the Politics of the Intellectual." The essay was presented originally as a series of lectures at the University of the South to commemorate its centennial. The essay was published in the _Sewanee Review_, Summer 1958.

27.   Seymour Martin Lipset, _Political Man_ (New York: Anchor Books, 1960), p. 442.

28.   Daniel Bell, "The End of Ideology in the West: An Epilogue," in Daniel Bell, _The End of Ideology_ (New York: Free Press, 1960), p. 402.

29.   Lipset, _Political Man_, p. 442.

30.   Bell, "The End of Ideology," p. 402.

31.   Ibid., p. 405.

32.   Ibid.

33.   Ibid.

34.   Bell first responded to his critics in 1961. See his debate with Dennis Wrong in the Winter 1961 issue of _Dissent_, pp. 75-77.

35.   Daniel Bell and Henry David Aiken, "Ideology --A Debate," in _The End of Ideology Debate_, ed. Chaim X. Waxman (New York: Funk and Wagnalls, 1968), p. 267.

36.   Ibid., p. 265.

37.   Ibid.

38.   See Benjamin S. Kleinberg, _American Society in the Post-Industrial Age_ (Columbus, Ohio: Charles E. Merrill Publishing Co., 1973), pp. 25-42.

39.   Dennis Wrong, "The Perils of Political Moderation: Our Self-Defeating Party System," _Commentary_, January 1959, pp. 1-8.

40.   Job Leonard Dittberner, "The End of Ideology and American Social Thought, 1930-1960" (Ph.D. dissertation, Columbia University, 1974), p. 201.

41.   Wrong, "The Perils of Political Moderation," p. 6.

42.   Ibid., p. 8.

43.   Ibid.

44.   Ibid.

45.   Wrong continued to elaborate on this point in "Reflections on the End of Ideology," _Dissent_, November 1960, pp. 286-291.

46. Mill's "Letter to the New Left" originally appeared in the New Left Review, November 1960. It was included in Waxman, ed., The End of Ideology Debate.
47. Ibid., p. 128.
48. Ibid.
49. Ibid., p. 129.
50. Ibid., p. 131.
51. Andrew Hacker, review of Political Man by Seymour Martin Lipset, in Commentary, June 1961, p. 550.
52. Stephen W. Rousseas and James Farganis, "American Politics and the End of Ideology," in Chaim X. Waxman, ed., The End of Ideology Debate, p. 212.
53. Ibid.
54. Ibid., p. 313.
55. Ibid.
56. Ibid.
57. Ibid., p. 210.
58. Ibid., p. 211.
59. Ibid., p. 210.
60. Ibid., pp. 211-12.
61. Ibid., p. 216.
62. Ibid.
63. Ibid.
64. Mannheim, Ideology and Utopia, pp. 262-63.
65. William Delaney, "The Role of Ideology: A Summation" in Waxman, ed., The End of Ideology Debate, pp. 312-13.
66. Mills, "Letter to the New Left" in Waxman, ed., The End of Ideology Debate, p. 127.
67. Ibid.
68. Ibid.
69. Ibid.
70. Ibid.
71. Ibid.
72. In the beginning of The End of Ideology Bell acknowledges his intellectual debt to both Karl Marx and John Dewey. Of all Bell's critics the only one who discusses the link between Bell and Dewey is Henry David Aiken in his debate with Bell. In his rather brief discussion Aiken argues that while Dewey's doctrine of the continuum of means and ends provides a significant contribution to moral philosophy Bell makes no real use of it in his work. He only makes the claim that he does. Aiken also argues that not only did Bell and "his 'socialist' friends" fail to use Dewey's doctrine they fashioned in their distorted view of Dewey's

work an "ideal, sentimental socialism, untouched by the slightest hesitation about what socialist aspirations can mean in a historical context in which no determinate program exists for realizing it." Bell and Aiken, "Ideology--A Debate" in Waxman, ed., The End of Ideology, p. 275. Aiken also went on to attack the notion advanced by Bell that "values like any empirical proposition, can be tested on the basis of their claims." He concluded that this notion "is one of the weirdest attempts at reduction of the Dewey-Hook theory regarding the empirical, or even scientific verifiability of value judgments that I have yet seen." As suggested earlier, the connection between Bell and Dewey is a subject that we shall have a great deal more to say about later in this study.

73. In his acknowledgment of Hook's influence Bell credits Hook with being "one of the great teachers of the generation"; a man who taught "him the appreciation of ideas." Bell, The End of Ideology, p. 409.

74. Daniel Bell, "The Mood of Three Generations," in The End of Ideology, p. 300.

75. James P. Young, The Politics of Affluence (San Francisco: Chandler, 1968), p. 29.

2

Toward the Development
of a Worldview

Webster's New World Dictionary of the American Language defines the word epilogue as a "short speech or poem spoken to the audience by one of the actors at the end of a play."[1]

The image of Daniel Bell as an actor so speaking to his audience is an appropriate one. Appropriate, because it is an actor in a historical drama that he spoke of the end of ideology. The drama is of the radical as the prodigal son. It unfolds over nearly a decade and a half.

Whatever else "The End of Ideology in the West: An Epilogue" is, it is an epilogue to a drama that Bell participated in and studied with keen and by no means detached interest. For many who had participated in the radical movement of the 1930s the drama had a profound and lasting effect on their lives. In Bell's words, their participation involved "the loss of inno-cence" by a generation of intellectuals and radicals who would come to bear "as on invisible frontlets, the stamp of those years on their foreheads."[2] This gener-ation, the "twice born" would soon come to find its "wisdom in pessimism, evil, tragedy, and despair."[3]

The Depression, the rise of Hitler, the violent suppression of socialism in Austria and Germany, the Moscow trials, the Nazi-Soviet Pact, the Holocaust were the leading events against which their personal drama was played out. But the stage, the scenes, and the cast of characters were drawn from the streets of New York's lower East Side, the Bronx, the college campuses

of America's Northeast, and the small socialist week-
lies that grew in number during the 1930s.

Daniel Bell was one of those characters, one of
the less than 20 thousand college and high school age
youths who took part in radical political activities
during the 1930s.4

The radical movement of the 1930s is a subject
that Bell took a keen interest in. As a journalist for
the right-wing socialist weekly the New Leader, Bell by
the early 1940s had established a reputation as a
knowledgeable and astute commentator of both the student radical and American labor movements. His study
Marxian Socialism in the United States, a work that was
written in 1952, still stands as one of the most ex-
haustive and knowledgeable studies on the subject. But
in none of his writings on the subject, including the
somewhat biographical essay that appeared in The End of
Ideology called "The Mood of Three Generations," do we
ever get any real sense of Bell's personal involvement
in that period of American history.5

Instead, what emerges from these works is an in-
terpretative framework. It is a framework against
which both the failure of Marxian socialism to sustain
itself as an active political movement in the United
States and the complexities of political life in an
immoral world are detailed. Through it Marxian socialism is likened to a religious movement, one that because of its messianic and ecstatic faith in the
"transforming moment" always stands outside of the real
world.

The framework developed by Bell is an important
one. It is analytical framework, a conceptual prism,
through which Bell would rely and build upon in much of
his later work on ideological politics and political
movements in Western societies. It was derived from
two sources. It was derived from Karl Mannheim's perceptions about the "orgiastic Chiliasm" of Thomas
Munzer and the Anabaptists of the sixteenth century.6
The second source was Max Weber's discussion of the
tensions between the "ethics of responsibility" and the
"ethics of conscience."7 The tensions are between the
acceptance of the limits and constraints imposed on a
political group by the world as it is and the dedication of that group to a set of absolute or moral ends.

The framework that Bell developed had a clear-cut
set of functions. It permitted Bell to define the
failure of Marxian socialism as being the result of its

inability to exist in the real world. It was also a
framework that permitted him to define the failure of
Marxian socialism in terms of its inability to make
hard and pragmatic decisions about whether it should
accept capitalist society and seek to work within that
society in order to transform it, as the labor movement
had done. In short, it was a framework that permitted
Bell to locate the failure of Marxian socialism to, in
effect, resolve the tension between the "ethics of
responsibility" and the "ethics of conscience" to its
being like the Anabaptists of the sixteenth century; a
movement that was of but not in this world.

That Bell came to adopt this framework as a way of
conceptualizing the failure of Marxian socialism is no
accident; for just as "no generation can be denied an
experience, even a negative one" no generation can ever
completely spare its members of the experiences that
define and significantly shape its collective consciousness, its historically specific Weltanschauung or
worldview. No style of intellectual thought, no worldview or conceptual framework can ever be, as Karl
Mannheim once remarked, completely free from the events
and experiences that serve to shape the lives of its
creators and its carriers.8 Thus, it is important that
we take notice of some of the events and of some of the
turning points in Bell's life and in his intellectual
development.

The Making of a Right-Wing Socialist

Born in Brooklyn in 1919 to Jewish immigrant parents, Daniel Bolotsky was raised in New York City's
lower East Side. When he changed his name is somewhat
unclear.9 What is clear is that the early years of his
life were not easy ones. Bell's father died when he
was six months old. His mother, who spoke only Yiddish, found work in a factory. As a result Bell spend
considerable time in a day orphanage.

This is the bare outline of a childhood spent in a
world surrounded by poverty and filled with the hopes
and frustrations of a Jewish immigrant population drawn
largely from Eastern and Central Europe, a population
that for a variety of historical and sociological reasons maintained a clear and persistent association with
socialist politics.

The then Daniel Bolotsky was only 13 when in 1932

he joined the Young People's Socialist League (YPSL)--
the youth organization of the Socialist party.

During the Depression it was not uncommon for the
sons and daughters of Jewish immigrants to be attracted
to the local branches of the League.10 Typically, they
served as meeting places that fulfilled both political
and social functions. They offered opportunities for
young men and women to meet, to exchange ideas, and to
listen to lectures and readings on Marxist and socialist literature. Factionalism and heated debates over
political tactics and philosophy were characteristic of
the YPSL meetings.

If Marxism and socialism were of secondary importance to some who were drawn to the YPSL meetings, they
were not for Bell. Subject, like other YPSL members,
to the pressures and pulls of the Young Communist
League with whom they held frequent debates and, driven
by the rise of Hitler in Germany and the violent suppression of the Austrian Socialist party in 1933, Bell
had begun to think seriously about becoming a communist.

Doubt always nourishes the drive toward conversion. For Bell the summer of 1933 was one filled with
intense doubts; doubts that sprung from his work that
summer with the International Ladies Garment Workers
Union (ILGWU). A volunteer union organizer, Bell
learned that the ILGWU was hiring strong-arm men to
harass and beat up scabs. Revolted by the news, Bell
and a small group of YPSLs offered their services.
What followed was a near comic episode. As Bell tells
it:

> The next morning, an assistant manager of
> the union took us to a building on West
> 35th Street, and when a scab came down,
> clutching a paper bag to his coat, the
> ILGER said, "Go, quickly, give a knyock."
> Someone stepped forward, but, as a Yipsel
> is invariably wont to do, he began making
> a speech: "You're a scab, you're taking
> the bread from a worker's table, the milk
> from a worker's child." The man immedi-
> ately began to scream loudly, "Help,
> Police." In a panic, the Yipsel turned
> and ran, inexplicably grabbing the bag
> the scab had been clutching. The police
> came and arrested him for petty larceny.

> The ILGWU went back, I think, to using
> strong-arm men for beating up scabs.11

What emerged from this episode was a lasting lesson; "a
lesson in the moral perplexities of action"--a lesson
that resulted in a loss of innocence.12
    Troubled by this episode, Bell now felt, by his
own account, vulnerable when debating members of the
Young Communist League. The use of violence by the
ILGWU represented a betrayal of his faith in the prospects of a socialist society being achieved through the
nonviolent efforts of the trade unionist movement.
When confronted by the communist charge that the socialists were naive in believing that socialism could
be achieved without armed insurrection and revolutionary terror, Bell could no longer turn to the ILGWU to
justify his faith.
    Caught in the tension between wanting a socialist
society and an active disdain for violence, Bell turned
to reading Leon Trotsky's Terror and Communism, a book
written in response to German Social Democrat Karl
Kautsky's attack against the Bolsheviks for their use
of violence. Trotsky, who was then the head of the Red
Army, had not hedged on the issue:

> . . . in what way do your tactics differ
> from the tactics of Tsarism? we are asked
> by the high priests of Liberalism and
> Kautskyism.
>   You do not understand this, holy
> men. We shall explain to you. The ter-
> ror of Tsarism was directed against the
> proletariat. . . . Our Extraordinary
> Commissions shoot landlords, capitalists
> and generals who are striving to restore
> the capitalist order. Do you grasp this
> distinction? Yes? For us Communists it
> is quite sufficient.13

Bell had discussed Trotsky's answer to the problem
of violence with a cousin of his, a Russian anarchist
who had lived through the Russian Revolution. This
cousin was one of several anarchist cousins on his
mother's side of the family who in their concern over
Bell's interest in Communism sought to blunt that
interest.
    But this cousin's technique was subtle. Instead

of answering him directly he placed in his hands a copy of Alexander Berkman's book <u>The Bolshevik Myth</u>. The book was the diary of an anarchist who had shot Henry Clay Frick during the Homestead strike; was imprisoned in the United States for 14 years; and then along with another Russian anarchist Emma Goldman was deported to Russia. What concerned Bell were the entries labeled "Kronstadt." These entries along with two pamphlets given to him by his other cousins, Berkman's "The Truth about the Bolshevki" and Goldman's "The Kronstadt Rebellion," made a lasting impression on Bell.

All these works dealt with the uprising of Russian sailors at the Kronstadt naval base, which was located near what is now the city of Leningrad. This was an event that took place shortly before the Tenth Party Congress in 1921. They described the background of the Kronstadt uprising: the pressing of the Kronstadt sailors' demands for freedom of speech, press, and assembly for all working men along with the liberation of all arrested socialists and nonpartisan working men. The writings also described in detail Trotsky's role in this incident, that is, his ordering with the approval of Lenin and the Communist party, the Russian Army to open fire upon the dissident Kronstadt sailors who on February 28, 1921, had participated in a strike that would last until March 17 of that year. The writings raised serious questions over the lack of parliamentary democracy in Russian, the harshness of the regime, and the unwillingness of that regime to tolerate political opposition from within the radical movement.

But what especially impressed Bell about these writings were the pictures they contained of Lenin and Trotsky. Evident from them was the cynicism of the Soviet leadership; their willingness to compromise the moral principles of the Russian Revolution in favor of political expediency. Memorable, then, were the following entries from Berkman's diary:

> March 4. An official manifesto appeared today signed by Lenin and Trotsky. They declare the Kronstadt sailors guilty of mutiny and the demand for free Soviets a counterrevolutionary conspiracy. The Moscow radio broadcast this message:
> "Just at this moment, when in America a new Republican regime is assuming

the reins of government and showing an
inclination to take up business relations
with Soviet Russia, the organization of
disturbances in Kronstadt have the sole
purpose of influencing the American President and changing his policy toward
Russia. . . . The rebellion of the Petro-
pavlovsk crew is undoubtedly part of a
great conspiracy to create trouble within
Soviet Russia. . . ."

March 5. Trotksy has issued an
official ultimatum decreeing that "Kronstadt and the rebellious ships must immediately submit. . . ." The city is on
the verge of panic. Threats against Jews
are becoming audible. Military forces
continue to flow into Petrograd. Trotsky
has sent another demand to Kronstadt to
surrender, the order containing the
threat: "I'll shoot you like pheasants."

March 7. It is 6 P.M. Kronstadt has
been attacked.

March 17. Kronstadt has fallen
today. Thousands of sailors and workers
lie dead. Summary execution of prisoners
and hostages continues.

March 18. The victors are celebra-
ting the anniversary of the Commune of
1871. Trotsky and Zinoviev denounce
Theirs and Gallifet for the slaughter of
the Paris rebels. . . .14

The symbolic significance of Kronstadt was not
lost on Bell. Armed by the knowledge that these very
same sailors who at the last moment swung the October
Revolution in the Bolsheviks' favor were betrayed by
Trotsky and Lenin and by the passionate indignation
that can accompany such knowledge, Bell confronted his
tormentors. At debates with members of the Young Communist League Bell would angrily ask them to explain
what happened at Kronstadt. Their answer was "Where is
Kronstadt?"15

These debates provided Bell with a crucial lesson.
The evident obliviousness of the young communists to
the moral perplexities of action was no accident.
There was no innocence involved. "The young Communists
had their faith, and they were armed against all ques-

tions and resolute against all doubts."[16]

The experiences as a volunteer union organizer, the awareness of the Kronstadt rebellion and the moral cynicism of Trotsky and Lenin, the debates with the Young Communist League, and the lessons that he would derive from them all led Bell to become fiercely anti-communist. They led Bell to move to the right wing of the Socialist party. They also led him to align himself, following the 1936 split in the Socialist party, with the "old guard" in its formation of the Social Democratic Federation (SDF).[17]

In the Social Democratic Federation, Bell found a political organization that supported both his strong anti-communist stance and his interest in the labor movement. Like Bell, the Social Democratic Federation saw itself as part of the political left but was firmly anti-communist in its orientation to political and social problems. Also, like Bell, the Social Democratic Federation had a keen interest in bringing socialism into the labor movement. It sought to do this through exclusively democratic means. From the standpoint of his experiences as a volunteer union organizer and the lessons that he derived from news of the Kronstadt rebellion, it was no accident that Bell would identify with the principles and aims of the Social Democratic Federation.

The Social Democratic Federation was very explicit about what those principles and aims included as the following statement issued by it on the eve of its birth in May 1936 demonstrates:

> The party which we now launch stands for the long accepted purposes and methods of the International Socialist movement. . . .
> The goal at which we aim is the social owner ship and democratic control of all productive wealth which, under private ownership, serves as a source of profit to its owners at the expense of the toiling masses. . . .
> With this goal in view, we strive for every possible betterment of the condition of the masses through extension of private ownership and through social and labor legislation to relieve the workers from poverty, overwork, unemploy-

ment and other evils resulting from the
system of private ownership and production for profit.
      We stand shoulder to shoulder with
the organized wage workers and working
farmers in their economic struggle and we
call upon them to sever their connections
with parties which uphold the capitalist
system and to organize themselves to use
political as well as economic action for
the advancement of their interests and
for ultimate universal emancipation.
      We rely for the attainment of our
aims upon the use of democratic methods.
In the United States there is no justification for any open or veiled propaganda
in favor of our preparation for such
action.18

Apart from its significance in providing Bell with
an intellectual and political outlet from which to
develop his thinking on socialism and politics, the
Social Democratic Federation was also significant because it provided him with an opportunity to get into
journalism. The SDF youth section was so small that,
as Bell puts it, "everyone knew everybody else."19 One
person closely associated with the youth section of the
Social Democratic Federation was Victor Reisel, then
managing editor of the socialist weekly the New Leader.
Impressed by Bell, Reisel in 1938 asked him to write a
report on the American Student Union Convention.
      This was a real opportunity for Bell because it
allowed him to continue what he liked doing best,
"intellectual work."20 At that time, a good part of
Bell's intellectual work consisted of debating other
politically active students at the City College of New
York.
      Though Bell was not a radical at City College,
where he was a member of the class of 1939, he had
learned to move skillfully in student radical circles,
especially amongst the Trotskyite section of the City
College lunchroom. That faction was affectionately
referred to by Irving Kristol as Alcove no. 1.
      In his lively and nostalgic New York Times piece
on 1930s City College student politics, Kristol, who
was then a Trotskyite, offers an interesting picture of
Bell and his standing in the radical student movement.

He [Bell] was that rarity in the
30s: an honest-to-goodness social-demo-
cratic intellectual who believed in a
"mixed economy," a two party system based
on the British model and other liberal
heresies. His evident skepticism toward
all our ideologies would ordinarily have
disqualified him from membership in Alcove No. 1. But he had an immense intellectual curiosity, a kind of amused fond-
ness for sectarian dialectics, knew his
radical texts as thoroughly as the most
learned among us and enjoyed "a good
theoretical discussion" the way some of
us enjoy a Turkish bath--so we counted
him in. Over the years, his political
views have probably changed less than
those of the rest of us, with the result
that, whereas his former classmates used
to criticize him from the left, they now
criticize him from all points of the
ideological compass.[21]

Bell's skepticism was grounded in a deeply rooted
anti-dogmatic temperament, one that was nurtured by his
strong affinity for John Dewey's writings. Ironically,
Bell was able to shape that temperament into a political and intellectual stance while he was a student at
City College, and there a member of the John Dewey
Society. A small society popularly known on the City
College campus as the "Hopefully Confused Liberals,"
their motto (which, according to Bell, they "proudly
flaunted" when they were confronted by some of their
"baiting adversaries") was: "If you think, you can't be
dogmatic; if you're not dogmatic, you're not definite;
not being definite, you're uncertain; and if you're
uncertain, you're confused--but we have the courage of
our confusion."[22]
Converting uncertainty and confusion into a political stance and into a positive intellectual perspective is at best ironic. At the worst it is sophistic.
But somewhere in between the ironic and the sophistic
was the conversion of these two emotional attitudes
into an intellectual stance that represents both an
understandable and intellectually defensible reaction
to the Kronstadt rebellion and the Stalin purges. Be-

lief would have been more indefensible.

If Bell's skepticism and his fierce anti-communism were out of place on the City College campus, they were not in the small and crowded New Leader offices. By the time that he joined the New Leader staff in 1940 he more than matched that publication's anti-communist stance. In doing so he fashioned a niche for himself as a serious and knowledgeable commentator, one who knew the ins and outs of the student movement.23

The New Leader provided a platform for several young writers to formulate ideas and perspectives that would give coherence to their hopes, doubts, frustrations, and anger. Among these were the hopes of a socialist-labor coalition; the doubts about Marxism and messianism as reflected by the writings of Reinhold Niebuhr and Sidney Hook, intellectuals who by the end of the 1930s were turning away from socialism; and the frustrations and anger over the Moscow trials and the penetration of communists into American socialist politics. Bell, first as a staff writer and later as an editor, used that platform to lay the groundwork for a theory of the monopoly state. Bell's efforts to develop such a theory grew out of a basically Marxist orientation to the problems that would confront the United States in its movement from peace to a war time economy.

Bell's Marxist orientation to issues like managerial capitalism, planning, and the role of business and the government in the planning of America's future belies Kristol's recollection of him as a strong advocate of the British two-party system and of mixed economies. Similarly, Bell's basically Marxist orientation might also appear to stand in sharp contradiction to his acknowledged faith in Dewey whose pragmatic philosophy, and the worldview embodied in it, is generally not associated with socialism or Marxism. The test rests with an understanding of Dewey and the relationship of his ideas to socialism.

Socialism and John Dewey

It was not unusual for Bell and many American socialists to both admire England's mixed economy and its two-party system and to adjust their commitment to Marxism in the light of the British experience with socialism. It was also not unusual for socialists to have viewed Dewey and Marx as not inconsistent and to derive from American pragmatism, with its emphasis on instrumentalism, certain principles that were logically consistent with democratic socialism.[24]   Both were fairly commonplace in socialist circles by the middle of the 1930s.

Both the British two-party system and the British mixed economy were very different from their American counterparts.   Given its peculiarities, the British political system favored the development of socialism in England during the early part of the twentieth century.[25]   Similarly, the mixed economy that England had come to adopt in the 1930s was fashioned by strong socialist and collectivist interests and tendencies that were unique to that country.   While planning was a virtually revolutionary idea in the United States before the New Deal, by the 1930s that idea was already an established tradition in England.   This difference was largely the result of the successes of Fabian socialism, the trade union movement, and of the British Labour party in promoting a wide-scale acceptance of the necessity of planning well before the Depression made Keynesian economics, with its emphasis on fiscal planning, a reasonable alternative to laissez-faire capitalism in the United States.   In short, the British mixed economy reflected the relative success of the English socialist and labor movements and allowed the British Labour party to develop along lines that have long been the subject of intense debate and conflict within the ranks of socialism.[26]

Socialism in England following the successes of the Labour party in the 1920s was far less revolutionary than it was reformist.   The British Labour party was largely a trade union movement that, having absorbed principles of Fabian socialism, based its claim to being a socialist party on the idea that if socialism were to be successful in a particular country then socialist leaders must be prepared to modify their programs to satisfy the conditions as well as the national character unique to that country.[27]

In regard to the relationship between Dewey and Marx, there is a line of continuity between pragmatism and Marxism around common philosophical principles that extends back to 1913.   In that year William English Walling published his book The Larger Aspects of Socialism.

Walling, an English socialist of some international prominence, found Dewey's philosophy of instrumentalism, with its emphasis on knowledge as being essentially experimental and truth as being something that was to be realized in practice, to be a radically new technique of inquiry. He also found that this technique was embodied in a rudimentary form in the philosophical writings of both Karl Marx and Friedrich Engels. Both the idea that all philosophy must evolve just as science does, as well as the idea that moral ends can be scientifically tested through the consequences they may produce, Walling argues, were principles that Marx and Engels shared with Dewey.28 In stressing this point, Walling calls upon socialists to recognize that American pragmatism was a socially radical philosophy that embodied the true spirit of socialism. In turn, he calls upon socialists to swallow their prejudices and not reject American pragmatism even though it had not been created by the founders of socialism.

Walling's argument was very straightforward. Socialism "is constantly assimilating new elements from all quarters, and it is just as significant if science and philosophy evolve toward Socialism as it would be if Socialism itself should produce the scientific philosophy."29 Moreover, even though Marx and Engels had made a decided beginning in the direction of pragmatism, they could not have been expected to develop this new philosophy since they were limited by the science and society of their day.

While other attempts to establish a line of continuity between American pragmatism and Marxism were made by Walter Lippman and Max Eastman in their defense of Walling's book, the most noteworthy attempt at such a reconciliation, if not from an intellectual standpoint then certainly from the point of view of its timing, is the one made by Sidney Hook.30 Hook, an American social philosopher whose works Bell has variously acknowledged, was an influential voice in the late 1930s amongst the growing number of student radicals and left-wing socialists who, in reaction to the Moscow trials, became suspicious of the kind of Marxism practiced by Joseph Stalin and the Bolsheviks. The reason for this was that, as a long-standing veteran of radical politics and defender of the intellectual merits of Marxism, Hook had already established himself as a knowledgeable and articulate spokesman, one who could properly give vent to their frustrations and growing sense of disillusionment with communism.

Having described Dewey's <u>Liberalism and Social Action</u>, a work that was first published in 1936, as a "book that could well be for the twentieth century what Marx and Engels Communist Manifesto was to the nineteenth," Hook proceeds in his intellectual biography of John Dewey to argue that Dewey's social philosophy represented the best elements of Marxism without the ideological trappings of Bolshevik-Leninism. Hook repeats this assertion in an extended critique on the relevance of Marxism that is a part of his book <u>Reason, Social Myths, and Democracy</u>. There he also asserts that "if ever a democratic socialist movement succeeds in striking roots in American soil, it will have to derive one of its chief sources of nourishment from the philosophy of John Dewey."[31]

Though he never systematically elaborates this thesis, Hook did state that, allowing for differences in idiom and terminology, the broad philosophical positions of Marx and Dewey were the same. Moreover, Hook, in distinguishing Marxism from the Russian communism of the 1930s takes the position that "were realistic Marxists prepared to submit their methods of achieving democratic socialism to serious scientific criticism, and were Dewey prepared to work out a more detailed program of political action with reference to the social and economic relations of the current scene, their positions would converge on a set of common hypotheses leading to common activities."[32]

While Hook never succeeded in elaborating a systematic exegesis on the convergence between Marx and Dewey, he did note one overriding similarity in their way of thinking. Both of them had a common faith in humanity's capacity to overcome the limits of ideological thought and habit through the use of intelligence as a method of social reconstruction and authority. Similarly, he notes that the use of intelligence as a method required the recognition that ethical ideals could and should be made the subject of scientific criticism. In this vein, Hook argues that what was common to both Marx and Dewey was the belief that ethical ideals--the good and the right, the better and the more just--should be evaluations that were based upon knowledge and experimentation rather than on intuition, revelation, habit, authority, or deduction from purely formal laws as preponderantly had been the case throughout history. But the similarities did not end there.

Convergence could be demonstrated because each in their own fashion stressed that ethical ideals must be evaluations and commitments to action that are based upon "knowledge of (i) all the relevant interests involved in a particular situation, (ii) how they are related to the state of productive forces and relations, (iii) the alternatives of action open to men, and (iv) the consequences of the respective actions."[33]

While Walling's and Hook's works provide some basis for understanding the sources of Dewey's appeal to some democratic socialists, a better source is provided by Dewey himself. Here we need only understand that Dewey's Liberalism and Social Action is a radical critique of liberalism; a critique that locates the "crisis of capitalism" within liberalism itself. This is a theme that Bell would, along lines initiated by Dewey, develop nearly 40 years later in The Cultural Contradictions of Capitalism.

By the crisis of liberalism Dewey means that liberalism in the 1930s was experiencing a crisis in belief and action, one that rendered it wholly inadequate to develop and legitimate the kind of social organization required to provide direction for the creative forces that the success of a capitalist culture had produced in the nineteenth century.

The overriding problem was that liberalism had become frozen. It had become frozen in its disregard for history.34 Their reliance on an absolutist conception of history instead of a relativistic one (a relativistic conception that recognizes that "effective liberty is a function of the social conditions existing at any time") forced nineteenth century liberals into an intellectually untenable and socially disastrous position.35 It forced them to blind themselves "to the fact that their own special interpretations of liberty, individuality, and intelligence were themselves historically conditioned, and were relevant only to their own time."[36]

Liberalism's disregard for history had other, even more profound, consequences. It permitted liberalism to legitimate and prescribe along doctrinal lines a fixed view of social change. The view that it legitimated was that "social change can come about in but one way, the way of private economic enterprise, socially undirected, based upon and resulting in the sanctity of private property--that is to say, freedom from social control."37

But even more importantly, liberalism's disregard
for history blinded it to its own false panaceas. The
reality was that while the rise of national politics in
the nineteenth and twentieth centuries pretended to
represent the order, discipline, and spiritual authority required to counteract the social disintegration
produced by nineteenth-century capitalism, it was a
tragic pretense. What made it tragic was that it
proved wholly inadequate to the task. If anything, the
rise of national politics provided "a tragic comment
upon the unpreparedness of older liberalism to deal
with the new problem which its very success precipitated."38   This new problem was the problem of legitimacy. This was the very same problem whose resolution
Bell would devote himself to in his post-end of ideology writings, especially "The Public Household." It is
the problem of how to establish upon a set of democratic principles the moral foundations for a new integrating philosophy, one that would give direction to the
creative energies unleashed by the success of nineteenth-century capitalism.

It was in his call for a "renascent liberalism"
that Dewey addresses the problem of legitimacy and with
it the evils of laissez-faire capitalism. His call is
fashioned by both a commitment to democracy and an
openness to socialist principles and values. This is
an openness that led him to argue that if humanity is
to escape from the present and future regimentation of
human beings and preserve the values dear to liberalism
(the values of freed intelligence, of liberty, of opportunity for the realization of individual potential
to its fullest), then the relationship between humans
and machines, capital and person must be reversed.
Liberals must recognize that such a reversal can only
be accomplished by regimenting the mechanical and productive forces of society. In short, they must recognize the necessity for centralized social planning.
"Organized social planning, put into effect for the
creation of an order in which industry and finance are
socially directed in behalf of institutions that provide the material basis for the cultural liberation and
growth of individuals, is now the sole method of social
action by which liberalism can realize its professed
aims."39

But such planning imposes its own demands and
preconditions. Centralized social planning, Dewey con-

cludes, demands a "new conception and logic of freed
intelligence as a social force"--one that gives as much
weight to preserving and extending civil and cultural
liberties as to increasing production norms.[40]

This faith in humanity's conscious capacity to
reverse traditional conceptions of thought and practice
provides a clue to the ultimate basis of Dewey's appeal
to democratic socialists: the utopianism that is implicit in his educational thought.

Like ideology, the word _utopianism_ has been subject to a variety of different uses and interpretations
since the nineteenth century.[41]   When we speak of
Dewey's utopianism we are speaking of a liberal utopia,
one that projects a vision of society in which war,
superstition, disease, and poverty would be eliminated
by the inevitable progress of science and education.
Dewey's utopianism is a utopianism of method, one that
projects a fluid rather than fixed image of the world.
It is a utopianism that advocates the reconciliation
between the present and the past; it is, in the final
analysis, a worldview that locates progress in a dia-
lectic fashioned by humanity through the pursuit of
knowledge. It is a worldview in which knowledge is
viewed as a continuous process, one in which the
achieved end is always viewed as the outcome of the
consequences produced by the means used in the pursuit
of a stated goal.[42]

Richard Hofstadter, in his assessment of Dewey's
contribution to American education, characterizes the
nature of Dewey's utopianism very well when he says
that

> Dewey's utopianism was not based upon
> some portrait of an ideal educational
> system. He was too wise to draw a blue-
> print for a finished world, and the very
> nature of his thesis that education is
> the continuous reconstruction of experi-
> ence argued against it. His utopianism
> was one of method: he believed that the
> old polarities and dualisms were not, so
> to speak, qualities in reality that must
> be resisted, minimized, managed, and
> confined; but were miscalculations de-
> rived from the false way of conceiving
> the world that had prevailed in the past.
> One could do better than merely resolve

> these polarities in various limited and
> inevitably unsatisfactory ways; in a
> higher synthesis one could overcome them
> altogether.43

This emphasis on synthesis, that is, on effecting
a reconciliation between the polarities and dualisms of
the past (the dualism between theory and action)
through the present in order to create the future, is
one that places Dewey within a very distinct, although
sometimes neglected, liberal tradition. This liberal
tradition might be understood to have its philosophical
and intellectual grounding in the work of Matthew
Arnold, a nineteenth-century English social critic,
who, like Dewey, dedicated himself to effecting a reconciliation between the present and the past, between
the Hellenistic and the Hebraic.44 It is a tradition
that Bell would come to operate out of in his efforts
to temper the radical idea (the Enlightenment idea of
individual freedom and the inevitability of progress
through science and reason) with the conservative impulse (the impulse to go slow and to reject untried
solutions) and, in the process, formulate an answer to
the problem of legitimacy posed by Dewey. This liberal
tradition is one that Bell would make himself a part of
after an intellectual odyssey that would begin with his
employment at the New Leader.

The New Leader Period

When Bell first started writing for it in 1938,
the New Leader had lost its largely Marxist orientation, although traces of it remained. It no longer
billed itself as "a Socialist Party publication devoted
to the interests of the Socialist and Labor Movement"
as it had done up to May of 1936, but when Bell joined
it it projected itself through its new masthead as "an
official organ of the Social Democratic Federation
devoted to the interests of the Socialist and Labor
Movement."45 This change in wording grew out of the
1936 Socialist party convention, where the national
leadership refused to seat the "old guard" New York
State delegation because of the tensions that surrounded Norman Thomas's nomination as the Socialist party
presidential candidate. The change, thus, was a reflection of the political and ideological factionalism

and the uneasy alliances that characterized American
socialism during the mid-1930s.

The explanation given to its readers for the
change in masthead was brief. The editorial comment
simply read: "An incidental but for us important result
of the Cleveland Convention is that after next week the
New Leader will not have to give so much space as
hitherto to interparty controversy. If many of our
readers and all our sub-getters rejoice in this let
them rest assured that the editors rejoice with
them."[46]

While this comment provided little hint of the
underlying issues and of the intense ideological and
often personal nature of the conflicts that surrounded
the change, the editorial staff understandably could be
excused for not going into more detail. This is because for some time preceding the Cleveland convention
the issues had been widely discussed in the New Leader.

By January of 1936 the issues and antagonisms
confronting the American socialist movement had been
reduced by the editorial staff of the New Leader to one
central and overriding issue: whether the establishment
of a working alliance, a partial united front, with the
American Communist party, as Norman Thomas and others
of the left and more moderate segments of the Socialist
party had advocated, would compromise its integrity and
undermine its viability as an independent political
organization. Such a policy, they believed would limit
its ability to adapt its strategies and aims to the
social and political exigencies of American society. A
January 18 editorial summed up the issue: "shall the
Socialist Party go Bolshevik or shall we remain a
Socialist Party?"[47]

In its formulation of this issue there was a deep-
seated suspicion of communists stemming from a variety
of events, of which many were prominently featured in
the New Leader long before the 1936 split in the movement. Many of these events concerned communist infiltration of unions and Stalin's purges. While no admir-
er of Leon Trotsky, Trotsky's views concerning Stalin
and the Moscow purges were often cited in articles by
New Leader staff writers to demonstrate the corruptabi-
lity of the Soviet dictatorship and the pitfalls of
bureaucratic collectivism. Similarly, it defended its
opposition to the efforts of the Socialist party to
develop an ad hoc united front with the communists in
the 1936 presidential election. Its opposition reflec-

ted a deep-seated faith in the virtues of both democracy and socialism.

Relentlessly anti-communist, the New Leader was at the same time relentlessly anti-big business and anti-fascist during the period that Bell was associated with it, first as a staff writer, then, in 1942, as its managing editor.

As indicated earlier, Bell used his time at the New Leader to develop the framework for a theory of the monopoly state. Spurred by government investigations into the business activities of Standard Oil of New Jersey, ALCOA, and Sterling Products, Bell attacked American capitalism. Collusion and profit making at the expense of the war effort were the subjects of a number of his war time articles. Convinced that many American businesses were planning for victory no matter which side won the war, Bell repeatedly called for a full federal investigation of American firms that retained through third parties large investments in German businesses like I. G. Farben. Highlighted in many of his articles were the names of corporations that either continued to sell their products to the Nazis or who severly retarded American war production by engaging in strategies designed to eliminate competition.48

Bell's war time articles were unified by two themes: the absence of public responsibility of corporate capitalism and the dangers inherent in the continued institutionalization of managerial capitalism under the impetus of a war economy. Bell repeatedly lectured his readers on the evils of managerial capitalism; evils generated by the changing structure of American capitalism itself and by the greed of its new power brokers. These were the faceless, colorless men, the representatives of absentee capital who thrived on their anonymity. Protected by their anonymity, these were the men who, with the system of trusts, patents, and other legal devices that by the 1930s had become the trademarks of managerial capitalism, could allow a Rockefeller to separate his personal views from the policies of his own company, Standard Oil of New Jersey. Their use of these devices could permit the Rockefellers to justify the complex network of patent agreements initiated by the managers of Standard Oil with the German munitions conglomerate I. G. Farben with the words "business is business."49

The framework that Bell developed consisted of a set of fears and projections. That the corporate mana-

gers could under the ideological banner of free enterprise and its attendant myths develop an economic policy modeled after Nazi Germany was its most pronounced
fear. That the separation between ownership and control documented by A. A. Berle and G. Means in their
now classic study The Modern Corporation and Private Property could result in the United States becoming a monopoly state and an imperialistic power was its
leading projection.

Modeled on Guenther Reimann's book Patents for
Hitler, with its image of Hitler and the German capitalists each using the other to further their own ends,
the framework that Bell developed embodied a defense of
the socialist critique of capitalism. Bell's defense
was fashioned in response to Stuart Chase's charge that
socialism was no longer relevant to the modern world
because the problem confronting industrial societies
was not capitalism but managerialism and statism; a
charge that Chase suggested was confirmed by the emergence of Nazism.50

Bell's response was quick and to the point.
Nazism, managerialism, and statism all worked to eliminate private property. But, the strength of the socialist critique of capitalism did not exclusively rest
on the ownership of property. It rested on property
relations, on the antagonism between the productive
forces and the social conditions of production. Therefore, it mattered little whether control was in the
hands of those who owned the means of production. The
contradictions of capitalism, "the fetters of production," are not effected by managerial shifts.51
What was really important and what still made socialism
relevant was that neither managerialism in the United
States nor statism in Nazi Germany had changed property
relations.

The thrust of Bell's argument is that Chase in his
enthusiasm over the Berle and Means thesis had neglected the fact that the exploitation of the industrial
worker was the product of the role that the capitalist
assumes in relation to the worker. The managers,
argues Bell, were just as capable as the capitalists in
adopting capitalist ideology to suit their needs. In
failing to recognize these constancies and in underestimating the extent of the real power held by the
capitalists in American and Germany, Chase had produced
a warped analysis.

"Facts," Bell retorts, "are stubborn masters."52

Chase had neglected facts that served to put Nazism, managerialism, and statism into proper perspective. The facts, Bell argues, were contained in Franz Neumann's study of the German economy, <u>Behemoth</u>.

Neumann had shown that it was the capitalists who had successfully developed strategies that resulted in monopoly groups gaining control of German industries. Another fact established by Neumann, notes Bell, was that Germany's monopolistic structure was not maintained solely by the managers; it was maintained just as much by owner-capitalists as by general managers. Otto Wolff, Friedrich Flick, and Gunther Quandt were not managers but powerful capitalists; not rentiers who just cut the coupons at the end of the year. Also, the managers who helped maintain the monopolistic structure were not themselves simply managers; they were not salaried employees. They had for some time assumed the role of capitalists by investing in their company's shares and often by speculating with the funds of their own corporation. They thereby strengthened their own financial power and stake within those corporations.

No, the capitalists were not without power in Nazi Germany. Still the absence of an autonomous, uncontrolled market in the German economy raised the problem of whether that economy could still be considered capitalistic. Perhaps, as an economic system, Germany's war economy was not, by strict classical or Marxian economic standards, capitalism. But this was of little consequence.

It was the war economy and not the Nazi political system that had given the German state its noncapitalistic twist. Therefore, it is important, Bell stresses, not to impute to Nazism credit for a series of economic changes that were primarily the product of a war economy, as Chase had done, nor to imply that those changes are inevitable in all war economies, as Chase had also done. The war economy, even in a capitalist system, reasons Bell, "may solve the 'contradiction' by creating full employment via subordinating the profit motive and restricted production to the 'use' dictates of the war."[53]

Bell concludes his polemic on a sharp note. The socialist critique of capitalism was still relevant because serious attention to it could prevent the kind of conspiracy between big business and government that had occurred in Germany from happening in the United States. Socialism could help Americans to sharpen

their thinking about the role of property and ownership, class alignments, democratic controls, and administrative techniques.   In the face of the inevitability
of collectivist planning brought on by the necessity of
the war economy in the United States, the problems of
both statism and of increased governmental controls
were very real problems as Chase had properly noted.
But Chase's efforts to reject socialism only served to
hinder the development of the kinds of approaches and
perspectives such problems required.

Foreshadowed in Bell's defense of socialism were
his misgivings about the mixed economy.   Ultimately,
Bell's fear of the mixed economy led him to call for
its elimination in favor of strong government regulation and comprehensive social planning.   It led him to
align himself with C. Wright Mills, Carl Dreher, and
other New Leader contributors who expressed the fear
that the United States was being dominated by an in-
transigent military-industrial complex dedicated to a
policy of finance-imperialism.54   That fear also led
Bell to search for new evidence; evidence that America,
under the prodding and manipulation of big business,
was moving toward a monopoly state and to the adoption
of a foreign policy aimed at worldwide domination.

Bell found evidence to support his suspicions from
a variety of sources, the most significant of which was
the Wall Street Journal.   In an article written at the
end of 1943 bearing the headline "Monopoly Groups Seek
to Smash Anti-trust Laws after the War," Bell cites a
December 20 Wall Street Journal article as evidence of
business's plans to control the American postwar economy.   That article, notes Bell, had vigorously endorsed
an alleged administration proposal that would call for
a two-year suspension of anti-trust laws and a carteli-
zation of industries to stabilize the economy after the
war.   While Bell was critical of the accuracy of the
implication of this article that that proposal was
reflective of the administration's thinking, he wanted
to cast light on what he considered to be a campaign
that "monopoly elements" were working to move America
closer to becoming a "monopoly state."   The Wall
Street Journal's endorsement of this proposal was a
part of that campaign, but only a part.   This campaign
was designed to produced a cartelized economy that
would ultimately result in "a permanent merger between
government and business and the creation of a huge
administrative bureaucracy."55

In a January 29, 1944, article ominously titled
"Washington '44--Prelude to the Monopoly State?" Bell
found other sources that seemed to confirm his suspicions that business was seeking to move the United
States toward a monopoly state. The most notable was a
speech made by General Motors' Charles E. Wilson. The
speech was one that Wilson, in his capacity as the
executive head of the War Production Board, gave before
members of the Army Ordinance Association. In it,
Wilson urged that the United States be continually
prepared for war, since future wars were inevitable.
He then proceeded to outline two postwar programs that
would involve an ongoing partnership between business
and government. One was a huge armament production
program, the other an ongoing research program that
would involve leading government and private agencies.
Both programs would require unity between the government, industry, and the army.

The fact that Wilson gave his speech in the setting that he did, was, to Bell, appropriate. What made
it so was that the Army Ordinance Association was not
an official body of Army officers but, rather, a private group made up of leading steel and armament execu-
tives, as well as key Army officers who deal with
ordinance and munitions production.[56]

In the same article Bell also refers to the text
of an address given by William L. Batt, the American
members of the Allied Combined Raw Materials Board.
Batt, like Wilson, was a leading industrialist. Bell
stresses that Batt's speech contained a proposal for a
foreign trade and a raw material stockpiling program
that would lead to an extension of the Allied Combined
Raw Materials Board: that Board was a joint war time
project of the United States, British, and Canadian
governments. Such as proposal and others like it
would, Bell warns, lead the Board to form an international cartel that would police the world's supply of
raw materials.

For Bell, the Wilson and Batt speeches were omi-
nous signs of business's efforts to integrate industry
with government in the direction of a corporate economy
dominated by the huge monopolies. But they were also
something more. Bell saw those speeches as a clear
sign of big business's efforts to develop a new language and set of ideas that would act to justify the
necessity of a monopoly state. Phrases like the permanent war economy, power politics, and balance of power,

phrases that were a consistent part of Wilson's and Batt's speeches, were noteworthy. They were absorbed into the language of American journalism. That language was not a part of the ideological substructure of big business's "efforts to impose a monopoly state within the formal constraints of a democratic capitalist society."[57] Collectively, "what we have here," concludes Bell in his January 29 article, "is the industrial facade of the corporative state, without the brutal political connotations of a fascist party--which might get out of hand and dominate industry."[58]

Until he left the New Leader in December of 1944, Bell continued to write articles that elaborated his views on America's movement toward a monopoly state. These were hard-hitting articles. One article, written in October, concluded with the observation that American industrialists were fighting a different war than were other Americans. The war they were fighting was a selfish one. The industrialists were fighting a war to restore nineteenth-century capitalism and to extend, under the ideological banner of "free enterprise," the American business "drive to supplant Great Britain as the directing force of a world economy."[59] Another article specifically singled out Standard Oil of New Jersey. In that article Bell locates in the government's Petroleum Reserves Corporation's plans for the construction of a one thousand-mile oil pipeline through the Middle East, a design fostered by Standard Oil to develop a new imperialistic policy and calculated to provide protection for the American oil monopolies in their attempt to control foreign markets.[60] But all of this fell short of the mark.

In none of his articles is Bell able to build substantially on the theoretical framework that he had established in his earlier writings on monopoly state capitalism. He focuses primarily upon documenting his initial thesis.

Eager to expand that framework into a full scale theory of the monopoly state, Bell left the New Leader to devote his time fully to that task. But this was a task that he would never complete. Instead, the period that he spent working on this project seems to have produced, in part, a distinct and lasting shift in Bell's thinking, one that would deepen and lead him away from his starting point. This shift was characterized by a movement away from the type of Marxism evidenced in his New Leader writings to a growing skepticism of the rationalistic claim that, by eliminating the economic basis of exploitation, socialism would solve basic social problems. This was a shift that led one analyst, Job Leonard Dittberner, to characterize this period of Bell's life as one marked by a "conversion experience."[61] This is a moot point.

In commenting on this period, 1944 through 1945, Bell has been very candid.

> You see, a young man who's very ambitious, such as I was, wants to write a book. In '44-'45 I began a book and had a contract with John Day for a book called the Monopoly State. . . . I began sitting daily in the New York Public Library in that famous room 315, and reading and reading and I suddenly thought: all this is silly. I only know this second hand; I know this by imputation: I'm using some mechanical categories; I'm making comments on them, and it's all silly. I suddenly realized I was educated in a vulgar Marxist framework, if you want to put it that way, making imputations about corporate behavior and I never really knew what was going on. And I suddenly felt that all this was silly. I had a manuscript that was about 300 to 400 pages and I looked at it and I said to myself: this is really nonsense.[62]

Bell's rejection of the "vulgar Marxist framework" that he worked from in his short-lived efforts to develop a theory of the monopoly state was one part of an intensely complicated and personal experience. But that experience can scarcely be characterized as a conversion experience.

On the Nature of Bell's "Conversion"

It is tempting to see Bell's rejection of "vulgar" Marxism as a conversion experience since that interpretation gains support from the argument of C. Wright Mills and others concerning the end of ideology. That argument, as was noted earlier, was that the end of

ideology thesis was based on the disillusionment of
Bell, Lipset, and Shils, all ex-socialists, with socialism. Similarly, this viewpoint gains support from
Peter Gay's argument that the end of ideology thesis
was shaped by ex-radicals who were expressing through
it a self-hatred of their radical past.[63] What made
Dittberner's viewpoint even more plausible is the fact
that it provides an explanation for Bell's employment
in 1949 as a labor editor for Fortune Magazine, a
publication that continues to be regarded as the
spokesperson for American big business. In short, on
the surface it provides an explanation for what would
appear to be a radical shift in perspectives and loyalties.

The only problem with Dittberner's interpretation
is that it is factually wrong. A conversion experience
is generally an intense, highly emotionally charged
experience. Doubt, disillusionment, and crisis are the
conditions that produce conversions. Conversions are
also generally accompanied by a total rejection of the
ideas and beliefs around which the convert built his
image of the world in favor of a new set of ideas and
beliefs. Because they are total, all-encompassing
experiences, conversions allow for little if any balance between the new and the rejected religious or
political faiths.[64]

There were, to be sure, definite shifts in Bell's
thinking from the time that he left the New Leader to
the time that he joined the Fortune staff. But those
shifts were less dramatic, less extreme, than one might
imagine given Fortune's reputation; a reputation that,
ironically enough, Bell helped to encourage when some
time earlier he called it "the dollar-a-month spokesman
of big-business."[65]

It is true, as Dittberner notes, that the animus
toward big business that was clearly a part of Bell's
writings for the New Leader was far less in evidence
during this interim period. Yet nowhere was Bell's
loyalty to the radical spirit common to Marx and Dewey
as much in evidence as in his 1947 essay "Adjusting Men
to Machines."

It was in this essay that Bell charges industrial
sociologists with being "technicians" who work within a
fixed ideological framework that serves to rationalize
the claims and objectives of management. They, charges
Bell, serve to preserve existing work relations in the
factory by imputing to those relations a measure of

permanence and historical necessity that is no more
than a methodological fiction.

> Being scientists, they are concerned with
> "what is" and are not inclined to involve
> themselves in questions of moral values
> or larger social issues. They operate as
> technicians, approaching the problem as
> it is given to them and keeping within
> the framework set by those who hire them.
> Many conceive of themselves as "human
> engineers," counterparts to the indus-
> trial engineers: where the industrial
> engineer plans a flow of work in order to
> assure greater mechanical efficiency, the
> "human engineer" tries to "adjust" the
> worker to his job so that the human equa-
> tion will match the industrial equation.
> To effect this, the sociologists seek
> "laws" of human behavior analogous to the
> laws of the physical world, and by and
> large they give little thought to the
> fact that they are not operating in the
> physical world. And almost none among
> them seem to be interested in the possi-
> bility that one of the functions of so-
> cial science may be to explore alterna-
> tive (and better, i.e., more human) modes
> of human combinations, not merely to make
> more effective those that already
> exist.[66]

Bell repeats this charge when he argues that:

> Despite their claims to scientific
> objectivity, these researchers rest on
> the unstated assumption that mechanical
> efficiency and high output are the sole
> tests of achievement--of "good" results.
> There are under way no studies to see
> what kinds of jobs can best stimulate the
> spontaneity and freedom of the worker,
> and how we can alter our industrial meth-
> ods to assure such jobs. The present
> organization of industrial organization,
> inhuman as it may be, is accepted as an
> inalterable "given." Sociologists tend

> to work on the behaviorist assumption
> that the human being is a bundle of con-
> ditioned reflexes--equally malleable,
> psychologically, to any situation. But
> it is possible that the increasing
> "rationalization" of living (its organi-
> zation for greater efficiency), pervading
> all areas and narrowing all choices, is
> itself the root cause of the stresses and
> breakdown in social living that everybody
> decries.67

Bell would later repeat this argument in 1956 in his book Work and Its Discontents and again in 1960 through The End of Ideology.

In general, it is difficult to characterize Bell's intellectual development between the time that he left the New Leader and the time he joined Fortune as being part of a genuine "conversion" experience. The major difficulty with this characterization is that Bell was never, despite his efforts to develop a theory of the monopoly state, an advocate of Marxian socialism. Nor, for that matter, was his method of analysis restricted exclusively to "vulgar" materialism. Bell's sophisti-cation, his ability to recognize the limits of Marxist analysis in understanding the complexities of the modern world, was, for all intents and purposes, demon-strated by several book reviews that he wrote during the same time he was attempting to put together his theory of the monopoly state. Each of these book reviews were sharply critical of what Bell saw as the authors' neglect of noneconomic factors in explaining the rise of fascism. In a review of Business as a System of Power, Bell took its author, Robert Brady, to task for neglecting, in favor of categories of analysis sanctioned by "mechanical Marxism," the psychological mechanisms that in addition to economic factors condi-tioned the development of German fascism.68

The point here is a simple one. It is only by neglecting or minimizing the significance of both these book reviews and his essay "Adjusting Men to Machines" that one can characterize the changes that took place in Bell's writings after he left the New Leader as being part of a genuine conversion experience.

In total, there was one fundamental, clear-cut change that took place in Bell's writings from the time that he left the New Leader to roughly the time that he joined the staff of _Fortune_ in 1949. This was his complete rejection of the finance-imperialism, "military-industrial complex" idea that was so much a part of the framework that he shared with C. Wright Mills in favor of a pluralistic theory of power.

This change, along with the particularly strong anti-ideological stance that he adopted toward Marxian socialism after 1945, cannot be minimized. They were important changes. They were suggestive not only of a shift in Bell's thinking but also of a fundamental and often overriding shift in the thinking of many socialists and communists of his generation. This shift was away from radicalism in politics to moderation, particularly as embodied in the Welfare State liberalism of the 1940s. This was less of a shift in ends and means for Bell than it was for others since, as both his and Irving Kristol's comments suggest, his basic impulse was to move cautiously, "to move slowly."69 More than any thing else, this shift seems to be the product of a young man given to operating on different levels. It also seems to be the product of the intellectual mood that permeated the United States in the postwar period.

While there was some relief and happiness in 1945 and 1946 because the allied forces had stemmed the tide of Nazi terror, it was not an entirely happy period. Rather, for many intellectuals it was a period of unrest and crisis. It as in Arthur Schlesinger's words "an age of anxiety."70 Much of this unrest centered on the fear of continuing totalitarianism and of the seeming inability of Western civilization to develop, despite its emphasis on the inviolability of the individual human being, the necessary social and political instruments to safeguard adequately that inviolability.

For a variety of reasons it would seem that this period was more fraught with anxiety and unrest for Bell than it was for other intellectuals. Bell, in recalling this period, has indicated that several things following his departure from the _New Leader,_ in addition to his experience with the monopoly state book, shook his confidence and put him into a "real tailspin."71 There was, first, the persistence of a set of lingering doubts that were triggered when, in 1942, he was called upon to write New York State's platform for the American Labor party. There were doubts about the direction of socialism in America. At the time, Bell recalls that he thought "if I'm writing the state platform for the American Labor Party something's wrong with this whole situation."72   There was also the failure of his first marriage, an event that as Bell recalls had an incalculable but traumatic effect on his life.

Deepening his feelings of doubt and insecurity was the discovery of anti-Semitism in the American labor movement: a discovery that Bell helped to make when, working as a consultant for the Jewish Labor Committee, he participated in a joint study on anti-Semitism with Leo Lowenthal and Paul Massing. The findings of this study were never fully made public because as Bell recalls "they were too frightening."73

During this same period, Bell also participated in a series of discussions that were sponsored by the American Jewish Committee. The purpose of these discussions was to provide a forum for Jewish writers to define the role of the Jewish writer in American society. Out of these discussions came the idea for Commentary, a monthly publication whose success played, according to Bell, an important part in the theme of the end of ideology.74 In recalling these discussions, Bell stresses that they served to touch off in him "a fear of mass actions, a fear of passions let loose."75 Bell shared these fears with others who participated in those discussions, especially with the historian Richard Hofstadter. Bell recalls:

> I remember having long discussions with Dick Hofstadter during this time. What arose in our conversations has, I think, shaped a lot of subsequent work. I mean a fear of mass action, a fear of passions let loose. A lot of this goes back in many ways to a particularly Jewish fear. In traditional Jewish life, going back particularly to the Assyrian and Babylonian episodes, the first creativity, there's a fear of what happens when man is let loose. When man doesn't have halacha, the law, he becomes chia, an animal.76

For Bell these discussions also served to spark a deep-seated sense of camaraderie with a group that has sometimes been called the "family" or the "New York Jewish intellectuals." Over the years this camaraderie continued to grow. Its effects would, as we shall see, be registered in his writings and in his political activities, that is, in his participation in the 1955 Milan Congress for Cultural Freedom meetings. Some of the members of this group were Eliott Cohen, the founding force and dominant spirit behind Commentary, and Delmore Schwartz and Isaac Rosenfeld, two leading Chicago-based literary figures. Other members included Richard Hofstadter, who collaborated with Bell on the Radical Right; Irving Kristol, who was to become his coeditor of Public Interest; and Seymour Martin Lipset.

Another contribution to Bell's feelings of insecurity and uncertainty during this period was his appointment to the University of Chicago, where he taught from 1945 through 1948. Teaching, Bell found, was a scary experience. Having been away from the academic world since 1939 when he finished work toward a Masters degree in sociology at Columbia University, Bell found himself thrust into a high-powered intellectual world.

While at the University of Chicago, Bell was forced to come to terms with a variety of overlapping issues. Those issues crystallized around a debate that was central to many disillusioned Jewish intellectuals of his generation: a debate between Sidney Hook and Reinhold Niebuhr. During the 1930s both had been outspoken intellectual defenders of Marxism. By the early 1940s both became very outspoken and articulated supporters of liberalism.

The Hook-Niebuhr debate centered on the issue of Stalinism and the nature of its origins. The issue was whether Stalinism was a function of a particular set of historical accidents, as Hook had insisted it was, or a function, as Niebuhr had insisted, of something much deeper and more fundamental: man and the will to power that cuts across all political movements.[77] The issue was whether what had happened in the Soviet Union was a "function of a series of accidents in which a minority group taking power in a backward country faced with external enemies and having to mobilize a society against the intervention of its enemies created a dictatorial regime as a response to external events or was what happened in the Soviet Union a function of power when it is unchecked by inner restraints."[78]

What made the Hook-Niebuhr debate a really important one for Bell and for many other ex-radical Jewish intellectuals and writers of his generation was the deeper issue that it raised: how, in the light of such devastating events as Stalinism, the Second World War, and the Holocaust, could one retain a utopian, progressive, or even optimistic view of human nature and of society.

In reviewing Bell's writings during the three years that he was at the University of Chicago, Job Leonard Dittberner stressed that they registered the effect of Bell's disillusionment with Marxism. While this is an accurate characterization up to a point, it is inadequate when it is projected as a final assessment of Bell's work. As we shall see in the next chapter, Bell's writings during this period register the effects of his efforts to develop a new approach; an approach that rests on the idea that a critical acceptance of Welfare State liberalism need not, either in principle or in practice, result in the suspension of criticism and utopianism. This framework, with its ultimate emphasis on the virtues of interest group liberalism as a system of checks and balances, seems to have been fashioned as a response to the issues that the Hook-Niebuhr debates were instrumental in defining for a whole generation of intellectuals.[79]

This point needs to be kept in mind. The fact of the matter is that a comprehension of the Hook-Niebuhr debates serves to identify an essential dimension of Bell's writings after 1944-1945, one that is registered in his essay on the end of ideology through the statement "the end of ideology need not mean the end of utopia as well." Registered is the tension that one finds in much of his post-New Leader writings; tension that results from balancing the faith common to Dewey and Hook that man can effect through reason rational solutions to fundamental social problems with Niebuhr's view that, given the irrational nature of man, some problems have no ultimately rational solutions, they only have proximate and shifting solutions.

Notes

1.   Webster's New World Dictionary of the American Language, college ed. (1966), s.v. "epilogue."
2.   Daniel Bell, "The Mood of Three Generations" in The End of Ideology, p. 300.
3.   Ibid.
4.   This is Bell's estimate. See "The Mood of Three Generations" in The End of Ideology, p. 302.
5.   The closest glimpse we ever get from Bell

about his personal involvement in the 1930s is a nostalgic piece that he wrote for the New Leader, "The Moral Vision of The New Leader," New Leader, 24 December 1973, p. 283.

6. For Mannheim's discussion about Thomas Munzer and the Anabaptists see Ideology and Utopia, pp. 211-229.

7. For Weber's discussion see his essay "Politics as a Vocation," in From Max Weber, ed. Hans H. Gerth and C. Wright Mills (New York: Oxford University Press, 1946), pp. 120-23.

8. Karl Mannheim, Essays on Sociology and Social Psychology, ed. Paul Kecskemeti (New York: Oxford University Press, 1953), p. 77.

9. By the time that he joined the New Leader, 1938, he was using the name Bell.

10. For an interesting discussion of this phenomenon see Betty Yorburg, Utopia and Reality (New York: Columbia University Press, 1969). This book draws on a number of interviews with former members of the Young People's Socialist League.

11. Daniel, Bell, "The Moral Vision of The New Leader," New Leader, 24 December 1973, p. 10.

12. Ibid.

13. Ibid.

14. Ibid., pp. 10-11.

15. Ibid., p. 11.

16. Ibid.

17. The old guard was drawn largely from veteran New York Jewish socialists and veteran members of successful local organizations from Milwaukee, Wisconsin, Reading, Pennsylvania, and Bridgeport, Connecticut. The leaders of the old guard were Louis Waldman, Algernon Lee, and James Oneal. The old guard's opposition to the "centralist" group headed by Norman Thomas stemmed in large part from its opposition to the inclusion of Trotskyites and Lovestonites at the national convention of the Socialist party in Cleveland. It also stemmed from the tactics of leftist factions who gained control of the Socialist party organization in New York. The origins of the split can be traced back to 1932 when an attempt was made to remove old guard Morris Hillquit from the party chairmanship. While accounts of the campaign to force Hillquit from his post vary, there is no doubt that anti-Semitism was a factor. As Martin Diamond puts it, "some who sought Hillquit's ouster wanted a native American to represent

the party and their language sometimes seemed to verge on anti-Semitism." Martin Diamond, "The Problems of the Socialist Party," in _Failure of a Dream?_ ed. John H. M. Laslett and Seymour Martin Lipset (Garden City, N.Y.: Anchor Press/Doubleday and Company, 1974), p. 378. For a more sharply worded account see Algernon Lee, "On the Split of 1936," _New Leader_, 10 May 1947, p. 3.

    18.   "Social Democratic Federation: Statement of Principles," _New Leader_, 30 May 1936, p. 1.

    19.   Interview with Daniel Bell, Harvard University, Cambridge, Mass., 23 February 1978.

    20.   Ibid.

    21.   Irving Kristol, "Memoirs of a Trotskyist," _New York Times Magazine_, 23 January 1977, p. 51.

    22.   Daniel Bell, "Clippings and Comment," _New Leader_, 19 September 1942, p. 2.

    23.   Bell took his role as a commentator on the student movement very seriously. At times he brought to that role a crusading zeal. Nowhere was that zeal more in evidence than in the article that he did on the American Youth Congress, "Memo to Mrs. Roosevelt: A.Y.C. Destroys Changes for a Progressive Youth Organization," _New Leader_, 6 July 1940, p. 4. In this article Bell charges that the American Youth Congress was a Communist party front whose leadership was dominated by communists and "fellow travelers." He charges the president's wife with being duped. He argues that Mrs. Roosevelt should have done her homework. He further charges that her support of the AYC contributed to the splintering of the "progressive youth movement."

    24.   For some general comments on the subject see John P. Diggins, _The American Left in the Twentieth Century_ (New York: Harcourt Brace Jovanovich, 1973), pp. 34-38.

    25.   For an extensive discussion of this point see Samuel H. Beer, _British Politics in the Collectivist Age_ (New York: Alfred A. Knopf, 1965), pp. 69-102. One of the chief peculiarities of the British political system is that in England the old often blends with the new. The Toryism of the Conservative party is, argues Beer, a case in point. Beer's point is that not only did this precapitalist, preindividualist, and preliberal creed survive in the era of the Welfare State and the managed economy but "it can also claim credit for having helped to create them" (p. 69).

    26.   The debate is over whether socialism should

be modified to attract the working class or whether it should remain faithful to Marxist principles. For a penetrating study of revisionism see Peter Gay, The Dilemma of Democratic Socialism (1952; reprint ed., New York: Collier Books, 1962).

27. The clearest statement of this revisionist position is made by C. R. Attlee in The Labor Party in Perspective and Twelve Years Later (London: Victor Gollancz Ltd., 1949). In this highly programmatic work, the British socialist leader declared that the Labour party as a working class movement is "not the creation of a theorist. It is seeking to show the people of Great Britain that the Socialism which it preaches is what the country requires" (p. 34). It is a socialism that is tailored to the exigencies of the English people.

28. William English Walling, The Larger Aspects of Socialism (New York: Macmillan and Co., 1913), p. 373.

29. Ibid.

30. For a further discussion of the role of Walter Lippman and Max Eastman in establishing a line of continuity in the United States between pragmatism and Marxism see Diggins, The American Left in the Twentieth Century.

31. Sidney Hook, Reason, Social Myths, and Democracy (New York: John Day Co., 1940), p. 132.

32. Sidney Hook, John Dewey: An Intellectual Portrait (1939; reprint ed., Westport, Conn.: Greenwood Press, 1971), p. 174.

33. Hook, Reason, Social Myths, and Democracy, p. 131.

34. Dewey's position was quite clear. Lockean liberalism's lack of historical sense and interest served an immediate pragmatic value in that it enabled liberals to undercut the appeal to origin, precedent, and past history by which their opponents, the defenders of a decaying feudal social order, gave sacrosanct quality to existing inequalities and abuses. But that same lack of historical sense and interest also served to retard the progressive development of liberalism in the nineteenth century.

35. John Dewey, Liberalism and Social Action (New York: G. P. Putnam 1935), p. 34.

36. Ibid., p. 32.

37. Ibid., p. 34.

38. Ibid., p. 54.

39.   Ibid., p. 54-55.

40.   Ibid., p. 55.

41.   In addition to Karl Mannheim's _Ideology and Utopia_ one can turn to Judith Shklar's "The Political Theory of Utopia: From Melancholy to Nostalgia," _Daedalus_ 94 (Spring 1965): 367-81.   Another important work is Adam Ulam's "Socialism and Utopia," _Daedalus_ 94 (Spring 1965): 382-400.

42.   For an elaboration of this point and an analysis of instrumentalism in general, see Hook, _John Dewey: An Intellectual Portrait_, pp. 88-105.   For a critical treatment of this point, one that highlights the limits of instrumentalism, see Henry David Aiken, "Sidney Hook as Philosopher," _Commentary_, February 1962, pp. 143-151, and his essay "American Pragmatism Reconsidered: John Dewey," _Commentary_, October 1962, pp. 334-344.

43.   Richard Hofstadter, _Anti-intellectualism in American Life_ (New York: Vintage Books, 1963), p. 388.

44.   For Matthew Arnold, the Hellenistic and the Hebraic represented two different orientations to life. As he explained in his critique of English social life, _Culture and Anarchy_ (New York: Macmillan and Co., 1883), the Hellenistic represented a predisposition toward spontaneity while the Hebraic represented a habit of mind based on conscience and restraint.   We shall have more to say about Arnold as this study progresses.

45.   The change in the _New Leader_'s masthead occurred in the 30 May, 1936 issue.

46.   "Editorial," _New Leader_, 30 May 1936, p. 8.

47.   "The Real Issue," _New Leader_, 18 January 1936, p. 3.

48.   Bell identified some 86 corporations that pursued such policies, with Standard Oil of New Jersey, Sterling Products, Dow Chemical Company, and DuPont being very high on the list.

49.   Daniel Bell, review of _Patents for Hitler_, by Guenter Reimann, in _New Leader_, 7 November 1942, p. 3.   In elaborating on this point Bell states that "In its coming a long way from the individual industrial entrepreneurs of sixty years ago corporate wealth has become anonymous and institutionalized.   Morgan and Rockefeller, hollow names of their forebearers, are merely convenient fictions for American capitalism." This is a statement that Bell would return to in the mid-1950s.   It would be the basis of "The Breakup of

Family Capitalism," which was an essay in which Bell developed his critique of managerial capitalism. The essay will be examined in greater detail later in this study.

50. See Stuart Chase, "Socialist-Liberalism Is Out of Date," Common Sense, December 1942, pp. 418-19.

51. Daniel Bell, review of "Dated Socialist-Liberalism" by Stuart Chase, New Leader, 5 December 1942, p. 2.

52. Ibid.

53. Ibid.

54. Bell feared that the mixed economy would serve as the mechanism through which business and government would become one unit. Behind Bell's fear was his concern over the compatibility of collectivism with democracy and the compatibility of a mixed economy with full efficiency. These issues were the focal points of a debate between Charles Dreher and John Chamberlain. In the November 1942 issue of Common Sense, each wrote articles that attacked the other's position. For Dreher, Chamberlain's views on planning and collectivism represented the "middle way" and were thus reactionary. In calling for collectivism Dreher argues that democracy and socialism are not incompatible. He also argues that a collectivist industrial scheme could be developed that contains checks and balances and that would accommodate America's technological drives for national defense and welfare without jeopardizing America's basic democratic traditions. Chamberlain's response to Dreher's views is brief but to the point. In arguing that there are certain things that belong to the individual and that sharp distinctions must be made between each sphere, Chamberlain accuses Dreher of not absorbing the lessons of the 1930s, the lessons provided by the Soviet Union. Convinced of the irreconcilability of democracy and socialism, Chamberlain accuses Dreher of an "ignorance of history." With a December 1942 New Leader article called "Collectivism and Freedom," C. Wright Mills joined the debate. His position is that there was no reason why the aims of socialism need not be the aims of classical democracy. In a call for socialism Mills argues that, given the power of big business in the United States, a mixed economy "would not be a mixed economy for very long, nor would it lead to a mixed and competitive political regime." Mills also argues that business and government were becoming one. He warns that unless Congress steps in business

may well become government. After calling Chamberlain
the spokesman of Fortune magazine, Mills goes on to
argue that Fortune in its December 1942 issue on the
mixed economy had accepted a "bastard version of the
Marxian theory of the state." This is a version, Mills
argues, that legitimates Fortune's efforts to become
the political committee for the ruling stratum of big
business. C. Wright Mills, "Collectivism and Freedom,"
New Leader, pp. 5-6. Fortune's views on the mixed
economy will be discussed in some detail later in this
study. Other New Leader articles related to the
Chamberland-Dreher debate are "Collectivism and
Freedom" by Abba P. Lerner, New Leader, 29 November
1942, p. 2; and "Blueprints, but Not in a Vacuum," by
Alfred Braunthal, New Leader, 26 December 1942, p. 2.
        55. Daniel Bell, "Two Steps toward Monopoly
State," New Leader, 26 February 1944, p. 5.
        56. Daniel Bell, "Washington '44--Prelude to the
Monopoly State," New Leader, 29 January 1944, p. 4.
        57. Ibid.
        58. Ibid.
        59. Daniel Bell, "The Balance Sheet of the War,"
New Leader, 21 October 1944, p. 8.
        60. Alarmed by the proposed pipeline, Bell warns
that the United States is "walking into a new political
cockpit which may wind up as World War III." Daniel
Bell, "Pipeline to Imperialism," Common Sense, April
1944, pp. 130-33.
        61. The term conversion experience was first
used by Bell in The Reforming of General Education. He
uses this phrase to describe the impact of contemporary
civilization and humanities courses at Columbia College. "For many students, these courses were a conversion experience, a shock of ideas that gave them a new
appreciation of the dimensions of thought and feeling--
a conversion, so to speak, to culture." Daniel Bell,
The Reforming of General Education (New York: Doubleday
and Co., 1966), p. 210. The same phrase was later used
by Norman Podhoretz to describe his own experience at
Columbia. Norman Podhoretz, Making It (New York: Random House, 1967), pp. 42-43. Bell would later come to
use the phrase conversion experience in his polemic
against the Columbia University administration's handling of 1968 student protests. We shall discuss that
polemic in greater detail later in this study.
        62. Interview with Daniel Bell by Dittberner,

"The End of Ideology and American Social Thought,"
p. 443.

63.   Peter Gay, The Dilemma of Democratic Socialism (1952; reprint ed., New York: Collier Books, 1962),
pp. 309-310. Gay's argument is that "despair can be
just as modish, just as unpolitical, as certain forms
of Utopianism" (p. 309). He further argues that "it
may be that we must free ourselves from the social
worker's cant; but the anti-social worker's cant, based
on a misreading of Reinhold Niebuhr coupled with self-
hatred for one's radical past, is far more dreary and
far less constructive" (p. 310). In defense of socialism Gay argues that, while "the programs needed to
improve at once the standard of living and the quality
of life" may be undertaken by a society committed to
the preservation of private property and a mixed economy the task would not be pursued without some assis-
tance from socialists (p. 310). His argument is that
"such programs will become realities only if existing
governments are continuously and intelligently pushed
from the left" (p. 310). Gay concludes his argument
with the following set of observations; "it may the
fate of socialists to invent programs that non-social-
ists will carry out. It may be that democratic socialists will make their mark in history by thinking and
criticizing rather than by governing. But even if that
should be so, socialist thinking will become more rather than less necessary as the welfare state continues
on its blithe, unideological path. The Bernsteins of
this world may be so many Moseses, pointing to the
promised land they cannot enter. But without their
direction, the promised land would lie forever in ob-
scurity. And it is not a bad fate to be a Moses" (p.
310). It seems safe to say that this sentiment was
derived as much from Gay's study of Eduard Bernstein as
his own experience. Like Bell and Kristol, Gay's experience was that of an American Socialist who lived
through the disappointments of the 1930s.

64. William James, in discussing both religious
and nonreligious conversions, refers to conversion as a
unifying process. Conversion is described by him as a
process that enables a troubled individual to overcome
a sense of discord and incompleteness that he or she
feels. According to James, the nonreligious conversion
may either come gradually or suddenly. There is no
general rule. But conversions in general, he noted,
always follow some period of crisis, some disruption of

the way one looks at the world. For James's analysis
of the conversion process see William James, The Varieties of Religious Experience (1902; reprint ed., New
York: Modern Library, 1920) pp. 163-253.
    65. This does not preclude the possibility that
Bell may have experienced a counterconversion. But
counterconversions are generally rare. According to
James, they are rare because converts in having committed themselves to the life they have chosen tend to
identify with that life no matter how much their enthusiasm for it declines. For an elaboration of this
point see William James, The Varieties of Religious Experience, pp. 173, 253.
    66. Daniel Bell, "Adjusting Men to Machines,"
Commentary, January 1947, p. 80.
    67. Ibid., p. 87.
    68. Daniel Bell, review of Business as a System
of Power by Robert Brady, in Partisan Review, July-
August 1943, p. 377.
    69. Interview with Daniel Bell, Harvard Univer-
sity, Cambridge, Mass., 23 February 1978.
    70. Arthur Schlesinger, Jr., The Vital Center
(Boston: Houghton Mifflin Company, 1949), p. 1.
    71. Interview with Daniel Bell, Harvard Univer-
sity, Cambridge, Mass., 23 February 1978.
    72. Ibid. The American Labor party was formed
in the summer of 1936. Primarily a New York State
political party, its intention was to permit labor to
support President Roosevelt, Governor Lehman, and Mayor
LaGuardia. It came to an end as an active political
party soon after the 1944 primaries. For more detail
see Will Herberg, "The Stillborn Labor Party," Common
Sense, May 1944, pp. 160-63.
    73. Interview with Daniel Bell, Harvard Univer-
sity, Cambridge, Mass., 23 February 1978.
    74. Ibid.
    75. Ibid.
    76. Ibid.
    77. The debate was touched off by Reinhold Nie-
buhr's critique of Marxism in The Nature and Destiny of
Man (New York: Charles Scribner's Sons, 1941). The
thrust of Niebuhr's critique is that Stalinism was no
historical accident. It was the product of a "restless
vanity" and was very much an extension of enlightenment
rationalism. The restless vanity, a phrase used by
Bell as the title of his introduction to The End of
Ideology, is in Niebuhr's view endemic to humanity. It

is in his view a product of humans being creatures who do not and cannot, a priori, know their limits. We shall discuss Niebuhr's thought in greater detail in the next chapter. Hook's contribution to the debate is an essay titled "The New Failure of Nerve," Partisan Review, January-February 1943, pp. 2-23. This essay is part of a symposium called "The New Failure of Nerve" conducted by Partisan Review. Other participants in this symposium include John Dewey and Ernest Nagel. Hook continues his rebuttal of Niebuhr in "The Failure of the Left," Partisan Review, July-August 1943, pp. 165-77. The debate was scarcely limited to the pages of Partisan Review. In the early 1940s the New Leader also featured a number of articles that figure in this debate. One important article is Max Eastman's "Socialism and Human Nature," New Leader, 24 January 1942, pp. 5-6. The tone of this article is even more pessimistic than the tone established in Niebuhr's post-1930s writings. Other relevant New Leader articles are Reinhold Niebuhr, "Despite Flaws Marxism Provides Realistic Insight into Society," 7 February 1942, p. 5; Reinhold Niebuhr, "Ideologies: Mental Corruption Is No 'Capitalist' Monopoly, Special Interests Pervert Thinking on the Left," 16 August 1941, p. 4; and Sidney Hook, "Social Change and Original Sin: Answer to Niebuhr," 8 November 1941, pp. 5, 7. The Hook-Niebuhr debate is also the focal point of several articles that appeared in Commentary. One of the most significant of these articles from the standpoint of Bell's development of the end of ideology thesis is Will Herberg's "From Marxism to Judaism," Commentary, January 1947, pp. 25-32. In this article Herberg relates the failure of Marxism to meet the challenge of totalitarianism to its "being infected with the same disease" (p. 26), to its rejection of an ethic that would transcend "the relativities of power and class interest" (p. 26). In short, Herberg relates Marxism's failure to its being a false religion guided by a set of false claims and a corrupted image of history. This, he explains, is an image of history that obscures the paradox that humans find themselves the center of: humans are at the same time both free and bound. They are free to examine, to criticize, to know, and to create. Yet they are subject to "the restless forces that control [their] outer life" (p. 27).

   78.   Interview with Daniel Bell, Harvard University, Cambridge, Mass., 23 February 1978.

79. If there were ever a study written about the origins of the "politics of limits" so prevalent during the late 1970s and 1980s it would have to start with Reinhold Niebuhr. Niebuhr's influence is best gauged through the works of other anti-communist liberal pragmatists. The most notable of these, as James Young suggests, is Arthur Schlesinger, Jr. What makes Schlesinger so important is his position as a presidential adviser and respected intellectual whose influence has extended beyond the Kennedy-Johnson Administrations that he served in the 1960s. In The Politics of Affluence, Young details the Niebuhrian elements of Schlesinger's The Vital Center, a work that served as a manifesto for the Americans for Democratic Action in the late 1940s and early 1950s and which, in its strong anti-communist and anti-utopian emphasis, contains one of the earliest statements of the end of ideology thesis. This is a statement that can be understood to constitute the intellectual foundations of neoconservatism. Like Niebuhr, Schlesinger locates the failure of liberalism to its "excessive faith in logic and in the perfectability of man. The solution to this [reasoned Schlesinger] is a more mature and therefore somewhat more pessimistic (or realistic) view of the nature of man." Arthur Schlesinger, The Vital Center (Boston: Houghton Mifflin Company, 1949), p. 170. Schlesinger's defense of democracy is straight out of Niebuhr. "The people as a whole are not perfect; but no specific group of people is more perfect: that is the moral and rationale of democracy. Consistent pessimism about man, far from promoting authoritarianism, alone can innoculate the democratic faith against it" (p. 170). As Young quite correctly notes this statement is shaped by Niebuhr's view that "man's capacity for justice makes democracy possible; but man's inclination to injustice makes democracy necessary." Reinhold Niebuhr, Children of Light and the Children of Darkness (New York: Charles Scribner's Sons), p. xi. Young is quite right when he argues that it is this view that shaped Schlesinger's indictment of liberalism. "Liberalism, Schlesinger contends, must give up its optimism about the nature of man and the possibility of progress. It must 'accept the limitations and possibilities' of the real world, and return to a 'tradition of a reasonable responsibility about politics and a modern pessimism about man.' Only then can there be a politically and intellectually sound noncommunist left."

James P. Young, The Politics of Affluence, pp. 31-32.
Schlesinger himself offers perhaps the best characterization of the nature of Niebuhr's influence in shaping
American political thought in the post-World War II
period. "The penetrating critic of the Social Gospel
and of pragmatism, he ended up, in a sense, the powerful reinterpreter and champion of both. It was the
triumph of his own remarkable analysis that it took
what was valuable in each, rescued each by defining for
each the limits of validity, and, in the end, gave the
essential purposes of both new power and new vitality."
Arthur Schlesinger, Jr., "Reinhold Niebuhr's Role in
American Political Thought and Life," in Reinhold Niebuhr: His Religious, Social, and Political Thought, ed.
Charles W. Kegley and Robert W. Bretall (New York:
Macmillan Co., 1956), p. 149. Ultimately, Schlesinger
argues that it was Niebuhr's genius to show that the
"refutation by history of democratic illusions need not
turn into a refutation of democracy; that the appalled
realization that man was not wholly good and reasonable
need not turn into a repudiation of man as wholly evil
and impotent; that men and women could act more effectively for decency and justice under the banner of a
genuine humility than they had under the banner of an
illusory perfectibility." Ibid., p. 150. Related to
Niebuhr's influence on political thought is his impact
on Jewish theology. In a 1958 Commentary article, "A
Critique of the New Jewish Theology," Judd L. Teller
details Niebuhr's influence on American Jewish thought.
Teller wrote of both Niebuhr's influence on American
Jews who "progressed from Marxism to Judaism" and of
his influence on modern Jewish theology. "The American
Jews who have progressed from Marxism to Judaism in
recent years may be divided into two general categories. There are the 'vulgar' but not necessarily anti-
secularist ba-alei t'shuvah (returners), the Samuel
Ornitzes and Michael Blankforts who produced lachrymose
fictional atonements for having broken with parental
piety in their youth. And then there those penitents
who required a complete refurbishing of their psyches a
new 'system' to replace the one that collapsed. These
latter are the 'wrathful' prophets, anti-seculists to
the hilt. Their mentor on the way to t'shuvah and
Judaism has been, perhaps to his own surprise, a Christian theologian, Reinhold Niebuhr, the chief exponent
of American Christian existentialism. But Dr. Niebuhr
has influenced more Jews than just those who were once

Marxists.   The rabbis seem the most addicted.   Today
nearly all American rabbinical periodicals in English
manifest some kind of preoccupation with Niebuhr."
Teller, "A Critique of a New Jewish Theology," _Commen-_
tary, March 1958, p. 243.

3

The Road to the End of Ideology

The University of Chicago Years

If teaching at the University of Chicago was an intimidating experience, it was also an exciting and rewarding experience for Bell, one that was crucial to his intellectual development. For the first time he got, as he puts it, "a real education."[1]

That education included the opportunity to reread Marx, and study, for the first time, neoclassical economic theory. It also included an active involvement with study groups both on and off the University of Chicago campus. These groups were devoted to discussions of philosophical issues and to the works of scholars that were related to various historical and theological aspects of Judaism. One such study group was devoted to the Talmud and to the works of Maimonides. And finally, Bell's education was fashioned by his participation in the University's social science program.

Largely coordinated by Edward Shils, the social sciences were not divided into specialized courses, as is generally the case in most colleges, but were, instead, organized on the basis of a specific problem area. The first year of the three-year program was devoted to an analysis of American democracy, its philosophical presuppositions, and issues related to American society. The second year was organized around the theme of society and culture, with a heavy concentration on the impact of industrial society on the individual. The third year was devoted to considering the problem of freedom and control and to generating questions concerning economic freedom and its relationship to politics and bureaucracy. In all, the program was tied together by what Bell later recalled was "an explicit effort to indicate the relationship of social science inquiry to philosophical issues."[2]

The social science program placed a great deal of emphasis on cooperation. All courses were interdisciplinary and staff taught. Weekly staff meetings were held to review materials, to present coaching materials for staff members insufficiently acquainted with a topic, and to discuss questions that should be raised in class. There were a number of highly respected scholars connected with the social science program. The staff included Nathan Glazer, Barrington Moore, Sylvia Thrupp, Philip Rieff, David Reisman, Philip Selznick, and Benjamin Nelson. But Shil's opinions on books and writers carried special weight.

> I suppose that in so far as the education I got taught--perhaps a little too much--a respect for the idea of the book, for learning, there was always some secret notion [among us] about the man who knows. You can write a book and everyone will praise it, but there's always someone who knows, not God, but some smart guy. Edward Shils used to always play this role. That was Shils' power. If he said yes, fine. But if he said swish swish, that was the end of it.[3]

There is no question that by virtue of Shils's influence, the quality of staff that it attracted, and the sense of intellectual camaraderie that it fostered the University of Chicago had a lasting effect on Bell's intellectual development. But the salient question is, what was the nature of that effect? How did his experiences at the University of Chicago affect his post-New Leader writings and ultimately contribute to his formulation of the end of ideology thesis?

One answer would be that Chicago brought him under the direct influence of Edward Shils, who of course was one of the principal architects of that thesis. But that answer obscures more than it reveals. Obscured are the tensions and contradictions that punctuate and qualify Bell's movement toward the end of ideology. If those tensions and contradictions--the tensions and contradictions that arise when one seeks to reconcile certain parochial identities such as Hebraism with the universal aspirations embodied in Hellenism as refracted through the prism of John Dewey's writings--existed for Shils, they are never reflected in his writings. Shil's writings are hardly those of a man in quest of certainty. The certainty, however tenuously based on fact, is always in evidence.

Together with the study groups on Judaism, the University of Chicago provided Bell with an intellectual environment that enabled him to broaden his thinking on the Holocaust and the problems that it touched off for him and other American Jewish intellectuals. But even more importantly, Chicago helped him discover the intellectual sources against which he would elaborate much of his thinking on alienation, ideological politics, and the limits of planning, subjects that elicited in him a fundamentally pessimistic response. These sources were Max Weber and Reinhold Niebuhr.

Bell was not alone in his appreciation of Weber's and Niebuhr's respective works. During the 1940s, the writings of both came to be widely known and read. Prompted by deep-seated fears about totalitarianism, many intellectuals raised questions that led them to turn to seminal thinkers like Weber and Niebuhr for answers. These questions called out for perspectives that would enable them to develop some understanding of the deeper causes of the Holocaust and of the origins of totalitarianism. In this regard it is not without historical significance that Commentary, a publication with deep roots in the American Jewish intellectual community, chose a paper by Niebuhr to initiate their series on the "Crisis of the Individual."[4]

Even though many of his writings had not been translated by the mid-1940s, Weber's standing in American intellectual circles had by then been firmly established. Talcott Parsons effectively summarizes the range of Weber's influence during that period. "More than any other single writer in the background of our generation, Weber gave us the primary reference points for analyzing the broad common patterns of modern social political and economic development."[5]

One of the principal factors that accounted for the popularity of Weber's work during this period was that even more than Karl Marx he, to paraphrase Dennis Wrong, appeared then to be the prophet of the past who had most fully drawn the face of the contemporary enemy, bureaucracy.6 It was Weber who placed the emergence of bureaucracy into a distinct socio-historical framework. That framework was one that traced the source of modern man's malaise to an irreversible social process: the general trend in the West toward rationality. And finally, it was Weber who located in bureaucracy the characteristic institution of modern society.

Reinhold Niebuhr and His Critique of Liberalism

Just as Weber's popularity in American intellectual thought grew in the 1940s, so too, for the same basic reason, did Niebuhr's. Like Weber, Niebuhr had developed an intellectual framework that was widely referred to as a way of understanding the deeper underlying conditions that had given rise to totalitarianism in the twentieth century. But Niebuhr went even further than Weber in his emphasis on the significance of the general trend toward rationality in the West as a source of totalitarianism. He addressed himself to the very nature of man.

The intellectual framework that Niebuhr developed in his writings during the early 1940s located the sources of totalitarianism in man's failure to come to terms with his own limits as a creature who yearns for absolutes but who is bound by his own finiteness. It projects an image of man as a permanently restless creature who, propelled by his desire for absolutes, his desire for control, cannot balance his aspirations and his limitations. Driven by his restlessness, it is a balance he always transgresses.

Niebuhr locates the failure of Western society to develop the necessary social and political instruments to check man's "will to power," his need to dominate others, in its adherence to a set of utopian illusions that obscured the real meaning of the original sin; man lives in a state of permanent anxiety because he does not fully know the limits of his possibilities.

In no place is this theme as systematically developed than in his book The Nature and Destiny of Man. There are two books that seem truly instrumental in shaping Bell's total thought. One of those books is Dewey's Liberalism and Social Action; the other is Niebuhr's The Nature and Destiny of Man. What makes

Niebuhr's books so instrumental is that it contains a Pauline or Augustinian image of humanity that Bell uses as a paradigm.   Though sometimes tempered by Dewey's optimism, his faith in humanity and reason, the paradigm always remains intact.   Though sometimes left behind, it is always the luggage that Bell takes with him on his travels.

The paradigm is one of humanity caught between two worlds: the world of its aspirations and the world of its limitations.   It embodies the image of man as both Adam and Sisyphus.   It is a paradigm that Bell uses when, in the mid-1940s, he writes about alienation.   It is also the same paradigm that Bell uses when, in the mid-1970s, he writes about the necessity for a philosophy of the public household, for a philosophy of modern liberalism.

The Nature and Destiny of Man   is, therefore, a book that warrants considerable attention.   It is a book that offers both a theological and political analysis of the moral and spiritual degeneration of modern society.   In it, Niebuhr traced the inability of liberalism to provide modern man with an integrating political philosophy to its failure to understand the true nature of man and the ambiguity that defines the human situation.

For Niebuhr the nature of that ambiguity can only be grasped by understanding the relationship between freedom and sin as it was revealed through original sin.   Charging that seventeenth-century rationalists failed to understand that relationship--the relationship that makes man an ultimately tragic figure--Niebuhr stressed that man is a unique creature.   He is "both strong and weak, both free and bound, both blind and far seeing."[7]   In short, he is a creature of nature.

What makes man a creature of nature is the fact that he is bound to a particular time and place and to particular environmental features that shape his destiny.   But he is also, explains Niebuhr, a creature of spirit because he has the mental ability to stand outside of himself and thus see and understand his situation.   Similarly, he can see, articulate, and try to avoid nature's contingencies.   But while man's awareness of the limits within which he lives allows him, in some sense, to transcend those limits, he can never fully transcend them, for he can never fully escape his finiteness.   Because of this ambiguous situation humanity is made permanently anxious.

Man's anxiety, asserts Niebuhr, is inevitable
because of the paradox that underlies and defines his
situation. The paradox has its starting point in man's
freedom. As an infinite creature who has the capacity
to stand outside of himself because of his unique
mental abilities, "man knows more than the immediate
natural situation in which he stands."8 Similarly, as
a creature of spirit he has the necessary freedom to
try to understand his immediate situation in terms of a
total situation. This freedom is made use of because
he "constantly seeks to understand his immediate situation in terms of a total situation."9 But there is a
problem here: the nub of the paradox.

Because he is also a creature of nature, a creature whose capacity for knowing is fixed by time and
space, "he is unable to define the total human situation without colouring his definition with finite perspectives drawn from his immediate situation."10 This
failing leaves man in a vulnerable position, one that
leads to the existence of temptation as a permanent and
inevitable condition. Driven by the realization of the
relativity of his knowledge, he is ultimately made
vulnerable to self-deception.

> The realization of the relativity of his
> [man's] knowledge subjects him to the
> peril of skepticism. The abyss of mean-
> inglessness yawns on the brink of all his
> mighty spiritual endeavors. Therefore
> man is tempted to deny the limited char-
> acter of his knowledge which is beyond
> the limit of finite life. This is the
> "ideological taint" in which all human
> knowledge is involved and which is always
> something more than mere human ignorance.
> It is always partly an effort to hide
> that ignorance by pretension.11

The key to man's vulnerabilities, the immutable
dynamic that makes him reach beyond his grasp and test
the limits that bound him, is anxiety. To be at the
same time both free and bound, both limited and limit-
less, is to be anxious. Thus it is no surprise that
Niebuhr concludes that "anxiety is the inevitable concomitant of the paradox of the freedom and finiteness
in which man is involved."12

Granted, humanity can make the proper response to its situation and accept its insecurities by trusting that they will ultimately be overcome. That course offers some relief. But it offers only a temporary solution, a fleeting moment. The anxiety is fixed in the human condition. It is pervasive. The reality is that anxiety is simultaneously the cause of humanity's achievements and the precondition of its sins.[13]

What makes man an ultimately tragic figure is that because he has some sense of the total situation of which he is a part, he knows something of the imitations that bound him. But he can never fully know where the limits are. Thus, "man may, in the same moment, be anxious because he has not become what he ought to be; and also anxious lest he cease to be at all."[14] The tragedy, then, is that no achievement can represent perfection, and there can be no place for man to rest in his struggle to escape his finiteness. Anxiety is inevitable and, given man's nature, necessary.

But anxiety is not sin. It is only the basis of temptation. The line between temptation and sin is crossed when the human situation is misinterpreted. It is only then that anxiety produces a rebellion by humanity against the limits that have been set for it by God. But, unlike anxiety, rebellion is not inevitable.

Given the possibility of trust in a redeemer God, one can overcome the insecurities of history, the abyss of meaninglessness and death. Man's anxiety need not, in theory, lead to pride or sensuality. And it need not lead to rebellion. Because he is essentially free, man can choose whether to place his trust in God. That choice is his and his alone. This, argued Niebuhr, is what liberalism in its optimism about man has failed to grasp adequately. There is no one contract, no one covenant, fixed by reason and perpetuated by eternal truths. The tragedy is that that failure gives rise to a certain naivete; it gives rise to a political innocence that feeds upon romanticism and utopian illusions.

The basic thrust of Niebuhr's criticism of liberalism is that liberals make the mistake of not knowing when to temper their hopes with reality. They fail to realize that good plans--plans that on paper should work given their rational design and their humanitarian ends--are in themselves not enough. Such plans are in

fact futile unless they are administered by men wise
enough to understand the depth of man's lack of wisdom
and unless they are formulated with a moral enlightenment that enables them to be responsive to the strength
and pervasiveness of human sinfulness. This viewpoint
is best summarized in the following quotations taken
from The Nature and the Destiny of Man, and another
early work, Christianity and Power Politics:

> The utopian illusions and sentimental
> aberrations of modern culture are really
> all derived from the basic error of nega-
> ting the fact of original sin. This
> error . . . continually betrays modern
> man to equate the goodness of men with
> the virtue of their various schemes for
> social justice and international peace. .
> . . Obviously there are various degrees
> of sin and guilt and some men and nations
> are more guilty than others of disobedi-
> ence to the heavenly. Also there are
> specific evils in history, arising from
> the specific maladjustments in social and
> political organization. But these evils
> can be dealt with most adequately if men
> do not give themselves to the illusion
> that some particular organization of
> society might be found in which men would
> no longer stand in contradiction to the
> law of their being.15

> The assumption of rationalists in the
> past centuries has been that either edu-
> cation or the equalization of economic
> interests would finally fashion the mind
> into a perfect instrument of universal
> and absolute knowledge, and would ulti-
> mately destroy social friction by elimi-
> nating the partial perspectives which
> prompt men to assess social issues in
> conflicting terms. But this assumption
> fails to recognize that the most intelli-
> gent and disinterested person can never
> escape his fate as a child of nature and
> finitude. . . . Thus even the most re-
> fined spiritual achievements of humans
> can never result in an unqualified syn-

> thesis of human hopes and aspirations.
> At some point they will always accentuate
> social conflict by making men more stub-
> born in the defense of their interests,
> under the illusion that their interests
> represent universal values.[16]

These quotations attest to the strength of Niebuhr's belief that the moral and spiritual degeneration
of modern society along with the failure of liberalism
to develop a realistic political philosophy that could
address itself to that condition is the product of
modern culture's inability to come to terms with what
makes man an ultimately tragic figure: man's inability
to accept his own limits.

If there is one constant that marks Bell's efforts
to develop a theory of the public household--an effort
that is implicit in all his work from 1949 to the mid-
1970s--it is the strength of Niebuhr's indictment of
modern culture. That indictment is one that Bell fully
shared with Niebuhr; it is an indictment that Bell
would elaborate upon with growing conviction in the
1960s and 1970s. In Bell's work it is an indictment
shaped by a certain perceived sense of alienation; an
alienation that is grounded in Bell's sense of Jewish
identity, his sense of being a member of the "twice
born" generation.

The Discovery of Doubt: Jewish Alienation

Both the nature of Bell's approach to the problem
of alienation and Jewish identity and the influence of
Weber and Niebuhr in helping to fashion it are in
evidence in an article that Bell wrote in 1946 for
Jewish Frontier called "Parable of Alienation." The
importance of the article is that it is a sign-post of
Bell's intellectual development. It provides us with a
sense of the intellectual mood that later permeates his
writings on the end of ideology, a mood grounded in a
particular attitude toward alienation, which comes out
of his experience of being a part of a "homeless radical generation." It is also a mood that stresses the
"permanent tension" that humans live in, and the sense
of tragedy that dominates their lives as creatures
whose homelessness is bred by not being able to know
the limits of possibilities in a world that their

restlessness--their need to know--compels them to explore.

Bell begins "A Parable of Alienation" by depicting the life of contemporary man as being marked by tension, strain, and anomie. He attributes these conditions to the divorce in the modern world of moral and secular conceptions of life and work. He views the alienation of modern humanity as a given and attributed that alienation to the progressive institutionalization of a state of otherhood in modern life. He defines this state of otherhood as a state of estrangement in which humans were made to live in a state of permanent tension between the universal need for community and the failure of Western capitalism to replace the traditionalistic ethic that it destroyed as a precondition of its growth.

In "A Parable of Alienation" Bell combines strains of Weber's thought on bureaucracy, rationalization, and the progressive disenchantment of the world with a set of implied references to Niebuhr's notion that no embodiment of community can ever, given human nature, be final. Using these ideas as a starting point, Bell interprets the homelessness of the modern Jew as a symbol of the estrangement of modern humanity and of the sense of permanent psychological crisis that it experiences in a world marked by contradictions.

Epitomizing the crisis was the Jewish intellectual. Bell uses as his model the novelist Isaac Rosenfeld. Rosenfeld's novel Passage from Home details the life of a prodigal son. It details the life of a Jewish adolescent who, caught between the world of his immigrant parents and the secular world of urban American, abandons the former for the latter.

Why Rosenfeld? The answer is that he fit all the requirements. While a student at the University of Chicago he has been a member of the Socialist party. In the late 1930s Rosenfeld had joined the Trotskyites. He left that faction only when the general futility, rigidity, and the deadly Bolshevik direction of the party was revealed. Now, without the Trotskyites, he was left homeless. Yet he remains a radical.

> Today, he stands, as many, a homeless,
> independent radical. For unlike some
> captious radicals, who, in their fear of
> Stalinism have identified democracy with
> capitalism, Rosenfeld still retains a

> deep critical sense regarding the inequa-
> lities, injustice, mechanistic, oppres-
> sive nature of an exploitative society.
> At this junction he, with many like him,
> are in mid-passage.17

But what does it mean to be a homeless radical in "mid-passage"? Presuming not only to speak for Rosen-feld but for a whole generation--the "twice born" gen-eration--Bell made it very clear that if that gener-ation did not know what it would accept from the world it, at least, knew what it would reject.

> We reject the basic values of American
> society as they stand. The increasing
> centralization of decisions, the narrow-
> ing of the area of moral choice, the
> extension into all domains, particularly
> the cultural, of the rationalized, stilt-
> ed forms of mass organization and bureau-
> cracy, the rising sense of nationalism as
> a product of the war, all of these
> heighten the awareness that the way of
> life resulting from these pressures--the
> rawness, vulgarity, mass sadism and
> senseless sybaritism, the money lust and
> barbaric extravagances--can only stifle
> creativity and free living.18

The quotation is very clear. There is no question that Bell views the modern world as repressive. The only unanswered question that remained was "what mean-ingful role can the young Jewish intellectual play in such a world?"19 But Bell is cautiously optimistic: the problem was not unsolvable.

The answer rests in the intellectual's awareness of the underlying dimensions of the problem. The prob-lem, Bell declares, "inheres in the very nature of being a Jew and an intellectual."20 It is resolved when the young Jewish intellectual is able to under-stand both the creative potentialities and the limits that enrich and constrain his activities. These poten-tialities and limits are grounded in being an intellec-tual and a Jew.

As an intellectual he or she knows that the very effort to understand serves to inhibit action. He or she therefore knows that if the principal aim is to understand then he or she "cannot surrender . . . wholly to any movement," for the Jewish intellectual knows all too well "the ambiguities of motives and interests which dictate individual and institutional action."21 The Jewish intellectual also knows that he or she cannot "make those completely invidious utopian judgments regarding the nature and needs of man which the cynic and romantic make."22 It is know, then, that he or she can "only live without dogma and without hope."23 For as an intellectual, he or she can only "realize his [or her] destiny--and by consciously accepting it, rework it--through seeing the world . . . as disenchanted."24

As a Jew who has roots in a Yiddish immigrant world, the Jewish intellectual knows too that he or she can never return home. The intellectual knows too that he or she must accept the alienation that restlessness, the need to know and explore, has made inevitable: for all that has been left from the world that he or she has left is "the hardness of alienation, the sense of otherness."25 The intellectual also knows that a sense of otherness has produced a special critical faculty. That faculty is "an unwillingness to submerge our values completely into any 'cause' because of the germ cells of corruption which are in the seeds of organization."26 The intellectual knows that this faculty is one that cannot exist within a territorial demarcation so that Zionism, with its emotional appeal of a Jewish homeland, may be a solution for many but cannot be for him or her. The intellectual knows that the "otherness" that makes him or her a part of a homeless radical generation can only exist "as the attitude of an eternal stranger in a foreign land."27

Thus, the young Jewish intellectual, argues Bell, stands in a unique and precarious position. He or she has a special quality that would disappear in a Zionist world. That quality is something that goes even beyond the unwillingness to submerge his or her values into a cause or movement, for the assumption of alienation does not mean withdrawal or nihilism. Rather, it means assuming a role that requires him or her to live without dogma and without any hope of finding personal salvation. This is the assumption of the role of the prophet, of the one who, through an ethical conscience, speaks the truth freely, indicting the baseness of the world and pointing to the need for brotherhood. But this role of the permanent skeptic, of the prophet, is a lonely one. It is, Bell warns, a role that having been fused out of inheritance and experience creates both a life and destiny of its own.28

No less lonely was the fate of the alienated Jewish intellectual. With a sense of resignation that rings principally of Niebuhr, Bell located his fate in tension and tragedy.

> The plight--and glory--of the alienated Jewish intellectual is that his role is to point to the need of brotherhood, but as he has been bred, he cannot today accept any embodiment of community as final. He can live only in permanent tension and as a permanent critic. The Zionist message is extremely strong. Like migratory terns we need to make our way back and the Zionists offer a haven for prodigal sons. But the whole world is our world, we were born in the ghettoes and have a special place. Each man has his own journey to make and the land we have to travel is barren. Out of this fact emerges the tragic sense of life, that we are destined to waste it.29

How commonly Bell's attitude of and toward alienation was shared by other Jewish intellectuals of the "twice born" generation is a moot point.30 Whether the attitude was prevalent among Bell's contemporaries has little bearing on the ultimate value of Bell's article. For us, its value is that we find that by 1946 Bell was approaching some of the basic themes that permeated his essay on the end of ideology. The sense of permanent tension between action and understanding that grows out of the kind of experience of alienation described by Bell, the need for permanent doubt in the face of movements that promise total solutions where experience has indicated that no total solutions can exist are themes that Bell returns to in the title essay of The End of Ideology.

"A Parable of Alienation" also enables us to see Bell as he saw himself in 1946; as a young Jewish intellectual in transition. Then 27 and in "mid-passage," Bell saw himself sharing a common cultural heritage and a common intellectual attitude toward the

world with other sons of immigrant Jews who had sought
to find during the 1930s a sense of personal meaning
and community in politics. Their cultural heritage was
one of homelessness. Their attitude was one of permanent doubt, of skepticism and detachment rather than of
withdrawal. It was an attitude that called upon its
holder to point out the need for brotherhood, to, in
effect, remind humanity that it still has the spontaneity to change the conditions that have led it to feel
estranged and helpless. Thus, Bell saw himself as a
skeptic, to whom both doubt and radicalism are a permanent and necessary part of life.

Radicalism and Permanent Doubt:
The Making of a Social Critic

The nature of Bell's radicalism was derived from
the belief common to Marx and Dewey that modern humanity need not accept the pattern of authority relations
in existing capitalist institutions as final and inevitable. Ultimately, the significance of his 1947
Commentary article "Adjusting Men to Machines," is his
forceful expression of this radical thesis.

The primary thrust of Bell's articulation of that
thesis will be recalled from our earlier discussion of
that article. By accepting the existing system of work
in the factory as a given, sociologists and industrial
psychologists serve only to reinforce the notion that
those relations are historically necessary and inevitable. It is also argued in that article that the problem of modern humanity's malaise, its alienation, can
only be met when its creative potentialities are re-
leased through a radical reform in the existing structure of organizational life.

While "Adjusting Men to Machines" was the most
radical of his writings during the late 1940s, it was
by no means the only place where Bell expressed his
radicalism.

In an article published in 1948 by Commentary,
"Screening Leaders in a Democracy," Bell again took
industrial sociologists and psychologists to task for
not realizing the implications of their work. He also
took them to task for not raising the kinds of questions that would permit them to assess critically their
role as social scientists. Undeniably, the efforts of
some human relations experts to promote greater group

participation in the making of decisions in the factory were well motivated. But those efforts reflected a marked naivete. Could they not recognize that "the tendency of much present day social science, which is to fit people into a niche in a previously determined bureaucratic and hierarchical structure, violates the values of both free scientific inquiry and democracy"?[31]

The reality is that "participation as a goal in its own terms in meaningless."[32] That fact was equally demonstrated under fascism and communism. If the human relations experts really wanted to humanize factory work they would turn their energies to developing a thoroughgoing analysis of the problem of democratic leadership. That analysis would force them to recognize that the problem of humanizing factory work is not resolvable through the promotion of better communications between workers and management. Ultimately, it would force them to recognize that the problem of participation in the factory "is shaped by the fact that while we live in a political democracy, almost all basic social patterns are authoritarian and tend to instill feelings of helplessness and dependence."[33]

The failure, Bell warns, of well-intentioned analysts concerned with the problem of humanizing bureaucracies to take this fact into account will not stand them in good stead in the scientific community. Their continued neglect of this fact will result in making their stress on participation within the factory system become just another form of ideological support for precisely those authoritarian economic and industrial structures that many of them wish to eliminate. To this warning Bell adds another warning, one that while even sterner than the other was tempered by a provocative but, nonetheless, encouraging observation.

> The overwhelming difficulties that confront the democratically minded researchers working in this field cannot serve as an excuse or pretext for ignoring the basic contradiction between their democratic goals and the authoritarian purposes which their experiments are most often made to serve. Possibly the forthright recognition of this contradiction will enable them to formulate a different and broader framework for their

future work.34

The fact that in both "Screening Leaders in a Democracy" and "Adjusting Men to Machines" Bell's radicalism and skepticism were virtually inseparable should not be taken for granted or minimized. Ultimately, it serves to refute Job Leonard Dittberner's conversion argument. But, when measured against the panorama of Bell's complete work, the significance of this fact should not be overestimated either. The real question is, does Bell ever really develop the kind of framework that he asks of the human relations experts; does he ever develop a framework that would enable him to resolve his own contradictions? That question cannot be answered here. It can be fully answered only at the end of this study when all the "facts" are in and carefully weighed. The question that can be answered in this chapter is whether the inseparable radicalism and skepticism of Bell's two Commentary articles are in evidence in his other late-1940s writings, the core of which are concerned with the nature of American society and politics in the postwar period.

From 1946 to 1949 Bell wrote several reviews of books that generally offered either liberal or Marxist interpretations of American society, its problems, and its potentialities. Generally, these reviews were highly critical. They in most instances reflected a growing impatience with those who, despite the political and economic lessons of the 1930s, continued to frame their analysis of postwar American society in terms of traditional Marxist categories. Similarly, most of these reviews reflected a disdain for writers who "lapsed into the old radical jargon."35 They reflected a disdain for writers who offered Marxist or liberal panaceas in place of realistic social analysis, that is, in place of analysis that seeks to specify "the range of activities through which people can genuinely share in the decisions that affect them."36

Writers like Saul Alinsky and Fritz Sternberg, one an activist liberal and the other a Marxist, came under heavy fire. The former came under fire for his naive faith in the "power of the people," the latter for his "utopian" faith in the power of economic crisis to produce a radical transformation in the consciousness of the American masses. While Alinsky neglects to focus on questions concerning the limits of individual activity in a technologically organized and power-oriented society, Sternberg obscures, in favor of an outdated and unproved theory of economic crisis, the real political problems confronting the postwar American economy.

Directed almost exclusively to the repudiation of the political and economic formulations of the left, these book reviews rested on a coherent image of American society, its complexities, and its strengths. It was also an image of American society that gave evidence of Bell's belief that business could no longer be viewed as the natural and irreconcilable enemy of a free society. Similarly, Bell locates the strength of American society in the tremendous range and diversity of its people and their interests. In turn, these book reviews reflect a growing emphasis on the need to discuss economic problems and policies within the framework of interest group politics and government spending priorities within the framework of "political economy." Finally, in anticipation of the public household, they reflect a growing sensitivity for the need of a free society to develop a democratic philosophy that could effectively harmonize ideals and material interests.

Bell's image of American society, his assessment of the major problems confronting postwar American liberalism, his impatience with Marxist and liberal panaceas, and the reasons for his impatience with them are particularly evident in his 1949 review of Irwin Ross's book Strategy for Liberals: The Politics of the Mixed Economy.

Didactic in nature, the review titled "Has America a Ruling Class?" served Bell well. It served as a platform from which to retract the "vulgar Marxism" of his New Leader days and in the process to delineate the grounds upon which he would structure his efforts to develop a coherent image of American society.

There was no doubt that Bell was impressed with Ross's work. Toughminded, realistic, and far reaching were some of the superlatives Bell uses to describe the strategy for liberal economic and social reform elaborated by Ross. Ross's proposals would require the nationalization of industry. But nationalization would be limited to only those corporations whose monopolistic practices serve to restrict production. The rest of the private sector would remain untouched. Yet Ross's work was flawed.

The book's weakness rests with its being grounded

less in the American than in the European experience.
This led Ross to misread the American capitalists when
he argues that they would turn fascist if the corporations were nationalized. Built into his reading of the
American capitalists is the assumption that American
society must recapitulate the European experience, that
American capitalism must follow European patterns.
That assumption had no basis and was wholly unwar-
ranted.

America is a unique country. Distinguished by the
tremendous diversity of its people and their interests,
it had produced a political system in which the politician stood at center stage, not the ideologue. This is
a system that had always been based on "the shifting
sands of coalition in which interests are rarely explicitly defined."37 This was the central fact that Ross
had missed. It was a fact that allowed Bell to argue
(in contradistinction to both Ross and his New Leader
writings of less than five years past) that the possibility of a demagogue like Hitler welding together the
diverse forces in American society and imposing upon
them an arbitrary system of rule was remote. No less
plausible was Ross's efforts to build a theory of the
ruling class.

In developing his argument Bell stresses that Ross
had misread the drift of American toward becoming a
technological and managerial society. Implicit in
Ross's suggestion was the notion that business was
defined by a single set of interests; that it was a
cohesive community of groups joined together into a
ruling class. Granted, business groups exercise tremendous influence in the United States, but it is still
impossible to talk about business as a single class.

The term class implied both a community and continuity of interest. Business in the United States, Bell
argues, lacks these qualities. It lacks them because
there are no family, status, or legal property ties
that serve to bind business groups together. There are
always temporary and partial coalitions of power among
business groups but one could hardly derive from this a
theory of the ruling class. The fact of the matter was
that the sources of authority in the United States were
so diverse that it was increasingly difficult to maintain a uniform pattern of action. How then, asks Bell,
could Ross seek to apply the idea of the ruling class
to the United States?

The answer was relatively simple: it sprang from

what David Reisman has observed was the "almost animistic feeling that since things run, somebody runs them."[38] Granted, in the immediate sense somebody does run things. But so what? It is obvious, argues Bell, that this somebody is a part of a larger system of action. The vulgar Marxism that Ross sometimes slipped into provided no answer. Indeed, if "it was one of the major contributions of Marx to demonstrate how a social system operates independently of the will of individuals, and in some sense molds them," then it is "the contribution of his vulgarizers to created bogeymen."[39]

Who, then, if not the "ruling class" is the real enemy of American society and of liberals especially? This is a complex question with no ready-made, sure-fire, answer. The best that could be done was to look at American society in such a way that the major problems affecting it could be more readily discerned. Needed, then, was a new paradigm.

In anticipation of The Coming of Post-Industrial Society, Bell proposed that American society could for analytical purposes be divided into three institutional spheres: the economy, the polity, and the cultural. With the tentative grounds of the paradigm defined, Bell went on to indicate what he thought were the major problems facing the United States in 1949. "The problem of the American economy is the power of monopolistic enterprises to create drags on economic development. The problem of American culture is the standardization of mind and taste induced by mass consumption markets. The problem of American politics is (metaphorically) the small-town mentality."[40]

While the paradigm he was suggesting was incomplete, his criticism of Ross was not. Appalled by Ross's neglect of the small-town mentality, Bell expresses his concerns about the danger it posed. Much in anticipation of his 1950s writings on American right-wing politics and anti-intellectualism, Bell argues that unless combatted the small-town mentality threatened to exploit America's lack of an integrative moral philosophy. The threat was large and the dangers imminent.

Ever the prognosticator, Bell predicts that if the pressures for conforming evident in postwar American society were to squeeze harder on the lower middle class then, en masse, they would be driven to embrace the small-town mentality. The greatest danger, however, is that if American society continues to grow

more amorphous and undifferentiated, then the sense of
panic of the small-town mind when confronted by social
changes would rise, leading to unrest and violence.
Grievous would be liberalism's neglect of the facts:
narrowness, anti-intellectualism, and prejudice find
their greatest expression in the small-town mind.

Bell's review of Ross's book is thus more than a
book review. It is not merely limited to a critique of
Ross's Strategy for Liberals. Rather, as we have seen,
it is a stage from which Bell could elaborate on the
central theme that runs through his other book reviews
during this period of his career: the inadequacy of
"straight-jacketed" theorists on the left to grasp the
complex and changing realities of American life. If
there is one constant in Bell's work from the late
1940s to the 1970s it is the centrality of that theme.
It both inundates and frames his work. Ultimately, it
is also the catalyst for that work right up to The
Coming of Post-Industrial Society and including The End
of Ideology.

If his review of Ross's book has any enduring
significance it is that it echoes Bell's 1949 Commentary article "American's Un-Marxist Revolution." It is
in this article that Bell would supplement his discussion of the changing structure of American society with
his first call for a new public philosophy; a philosophy of the public household. It was also in this
article that Bell would present his image of postwar
America as a "broker state." That image and the call
for a new public philosophy that was derived from it
would become the cornerstones for much of his subsequent work.

The Broker State and the Initial Call for a Philosophy of the Public Household

Bell begins "America's Un-Marxist Revolution" in
his customary fashion. He begins the article, which
was subtitled "Mr. Truman Embarks on a Politically
Managed Economy," with an assessment of the state of
political analysis in the United States.

The deficiencies were striking. The prevailing
ideologies of the left and the political right were
still "unconsciously obedient to the Marxist notion
that only a bald class struggle reveals the realities
of politics."41 Thus, the importance of Truman's Fair

Deal program could not be seriously appreciated by political writers on either the left or the right.

For Bell the Fair Deal represented America's movement into political economy. It served as an assertion that no privileged interest group, including business, could run a modern industrial society. The Fair Deal was a "square assertion" that the federal government must manage the economy. The only question that remained was, "managed for whom?" This was the same question Bell raises in his New Leader articles. His approach to it now, however, is somewhat different.42

Bell, in general, is optimistic. Truman's budget message with its emphasis on establishing a full employment economy was acknowledging several developments that ultimately would serve to make the United States more a broker state than it had been under the New Deal. In its call for business to plan for full industrial capacity and its request for the president to be given the authority to develop, in the absence of the private sector, measures to guarantee that result, Truman's budget message was acknowledging the necessity of the American government establishing more than a housekeeping and economic budget. It was acknowledging that the American government must establish a budget that directs the nation's resources to fulfilling human needs. And finally, Truman's budget message acknowledged that the free market system no longer worked; that it works against the general welfare of the nation.

The only problem that remained was building on the realities of the socialized economy that under the New Deal had become accelerated, not the least of which was the reciprocal interdependence of business, agriculture, and labor. The Depression made the managed economy created under the New Deal inevitable. The measures that each of these collectivities would predictably resort to for protection against the risks of the free market in time of depression dictated the inevitable. It dictated that the federal government intervene in the economy in order to prevent the entire economy from being overturned.

These were not temporary changes nor could they be. The demands of postwar reconstruction and the national debt incurred by America's war economy made it impossible for the government to withdraw from the management of the economy. Truman's "housekeeping budget" was a recognition of this fact. Yet not all was right.

The Fair Deal, like the New Deal before it, was a limited response to the dictates of a managed economy. On the economic front, the Fair Deal had to move beyond classical economics and substitute in its place a picture of the overall economy that would permit it to develop an economic budget that states the major magnitudes of economic interaction for American society as a whole. Because it saw the economy in terms of infinite numbers of single units instead of small numbers of basic aggregates, classical economics proved an outdated model.

On the political front, the managed economy required leaders who recognized the shift in relations between economic and political power. No longer was economics the key to power and politics. Acknowledgment needed to be given to the place of politics in the broker state.

A symbolic expression, the broker state embodied a system of reciprocal relations between the federal government and the major interest groups dependent on it. Under the New Deal business, agriculture, and labor were brought into partnership with the federal government. The consequences were obvious: the broker state required the different interest groups to compete with each other for greater rewards from the government. It required them to become more political. It required them to seek a competitive edge in government with the result that the ability to influence government policy through the exercise of politics served as the definitive means of registering social and economic decisions. The trade-off, of course, is that these interest groups became the vital organs of the body politic.

Serious attention would also have to be given to the place of ideology in planning. The broker state serves to sharpen more than pressure group identifications. It also forces business, agriculture, and labor to adopt an ideology that can justify its claims on the government, "and which can square with some concept of national interest."[43]

The broker state is based both on competition and accommodation. Should certain conflicts become more visible, namely clashes between industry and government on capital expansion and clashes between sectional interests seeking to expand their share in industrial expansion, then the basic weakness of New Deal liberalism will be exposed. That weakness is its lack of some overall mechanism responsible for the crucial decisions regarding the balancing of the economy.

In giving this problem the kind of attention it warrants, the Truman administration would have to recognize that government planning presupposes that no one is ever fully free to follow his own self-interests. The inescapable reality is that there is "an overriding social decision, established before action, which tends to shape each man's actions. And this social decision is necessarily ideological."44

The ideological nature of planning requires that serious attention on the political front be given to the distinction between the public and the private. Ultimately, one of the major problems the broker state has to face is to preserve a balance between the two. That could be an awesome task if ideological arguments continued increasingly to influence political outcomes and Welfare State liberalism remained without a general theory as to how the satisfaction of varied group interests may be harmonized with the general welfare of the nation. Thus, what was ultimately required by the broker state was a convincing theory of social justice.

Doubting that "transient majority coalitions" can ever offer a convincing theory of social justice, Bell concludes "America's Un-Marxist Revolution" with some critical reflections on America's lack of an integrative moral philosophy; reflections that imply that American was in the midst of a deep-seated moral crisis.

> We are floundering, both in practice and in analysis, because we no longer know what holds a society together. The political strength of the American founding fathers . . . was the fact that their thinking was rooted both in tradition and in a coherent moral order that assigned men a certain place both in nature and vis-à-vis one another. Their moral conceptions were rooted either in Locke's theory of natural rights or in Hobbes' theory of the need of law and authority to keep the passions of men in check; out of these arose conflicting descriptions of the rights and privileges of men. But we have little basis today for accepting either of these political myths.45

If a democratic society is to survive, warns Bell, then "some new sense of civil obligation must arise that will be strong enough to command the allegiance of all groups and provide a principle of equality in the distribution of rewards and privileges of society."[46] Thus, concludes Bell, the central task that lies ahead for the Truman administration and eventually the American body politic to work out is "the relationship between government and people in a way that permits this civil sense to emerge and sustain itself."[47] Whether or not this can be done was problematic. It would not be until 25 years later, 1974, that Bell would seek to develop the framework for a philosophy of the public household that would accomplish that goal.

By far, "America's Un-Marxist Revolution" stands as the most definitive single piece that Bell wrote during the immediate postwar period. One of the principal reasons that this is so is that, in identifying and making explicit his interpretation of American society, it makes explicit the basis of his criticism of Marxist and liberal writers. This, of course, is their failure to understand the complexities of American society. Another major reason why this article stands out is that it identifies a set of concerns that, as we shall see in the next chapter, serves to define the character and direction of his writings in the 1950s up to and including "The End of Ideology in the West: An Epilogue." These, again, are his concerns about the nature of American liberalism and about its need to develop a new integrative moral philosophy; concerns that became the focal point of his participation in his 1955 Congress for Cultural Freedom in Milan.

Earlier, the question was raised of the status of the radicalism of Bell's "Adjusting Men to Machines" article. The issue was whether the radicalism evidenced in that article would also be found in his other late 1940s writings. The answer is yes.

The radicalism of Bell's "Adjusting Men to Machines" article is evidenced in "America's Un-Marxist Revolution." It is manifested in Bell's attack against business spokespersons who decried government interference in business. He lashes out at these "ideologues" for failing to learn that economics follows no "natural laws."[48] His argument is just as radical as the arguments of Marx, Dewey, and Georg Lukacs concerning the

reification of man through the deification of economics. Bell holds that if economics did follow a set of
natural laws then the ability of humanity to transform
its social environment by conscious intelligence would
be denied. But the reality is that "economics is not a
science of discovering a set of hidden supra-human
absolutes and obeying them, but an assertion that if
certain human goals are desired then certain means must
be fashioned to attain them."[49]

But it should be noted that the skepticism that
Bell claims as a virtual birthright is significantly
tempered and compromised by his acceptance of the legitimacy of the broker state. Inferred in Bell's acceptance of the broker state is the normative assumption
that the equilibrium effected by the federal government
between major interest groups through its adoption of a
managed economy constitutes an optimal condition. It
may very well be true that that equilibrium is optimal,
however, but where does this leave Bell? Recalled is
Bell's assessment of the twice-born critics fate: no
embodiment of community can be considered final.
"America's Un-Marxist Revolution" gives evidence of his
willingness to help bolster and perpetuate the foundations upon which the broker state rests.

We can only conclude that his fear of the small-
town mentality was just as pervasive as his contempt of
the human relations school and the system of management
it served to reinforce. Yet his acceptance of the
broker state suggests a willingness to tolerate the
conditions that would permit the perpetuation of that
system.

Ultimately, "America's Un-Marxist Revolution" is
not the work of a skeptic. Rather, it is the work of a
social critic whose fear of the mob and distrust of
Marxist panaceas led him to sacrifice his skepticism
and embrace, with all its flaws, Welfare State liberalism. "America's Un-Marxist Revolution" is the work of
a man who, while somewhat distrustful of the crooked
roulette wheel he is playing on, knows that it is the
only wheel in town.

That much is made clear in the animus that one
finds in Bell's assault on left-wing political analysts. Ultimately, all Bell's arguments in favor of
the broker state rest upon the need for a moral order
that could integrate and unify American society and
that would provide a moral framework within which American society as a whole and its respective interest

groups could calculate their shares of rewards and
efforts. The moral standards, social standards, perhaps an ideology, did not exist in the present. Bell
calls for their creation, but does not know from whence
they would come. They were, for Bell, an unfinished
task. Perhaps, he would finish the task, or perhaps he
was a John the Baptist, continually demanding that
ideology, that definition of a moral community, that
would end the end of ideology.

The end of ideology is thus more than a detailed
resume of the failure of Marxism, itself an ideology of
the "end of ideology." The end of ideology is a demand
for a new pragmatic ideology. Perhaps this is a contradiction in terms, but the moral community that could
make planning, pragmatism, and the calculation of responsibility possible (the moral community that Bell
could find a possible home in) would be a consensually
held ideology. It is not the end of ideology that Bell
calls for, but the replacement of a particular ideology, Marxism.

This fact is confirmed by both Marxian Socialism
in the United States and his articles for Fortune.
Ultimately, it is in these and other 1950s writings
that Bell completed the paradigm for the end of ideology that he initiated in the late 1940s, the paradigm
that calls for the emergence of a new pragmatic ideology to replace Marxism.

Notes

1. Interview with Daniel Bell, Harvard University, Cambridge, Mass., 23 February 1978.
2. Bell, The Reforming of General Education,
p. 32.
3. Interview with Daniel Bell, Harvard University, Cambridge, Mass., 23 February 1978.
4. The paper chosen was titled "Will Civilization Survive Technics?" This paper appeared in the
December 1945 issue of Commentary.
5. Talcott Parsons, introduction to The Sociology of Religion by Max Weber, (1922; reprint ed.,
trans. Ephraim Fischoff, Boston: Beacon Press, 1956)
pp. lix-lx.
6. Dennis Wrong, Max Weber (Englewood Cliffs,
N.J.: Prentice-Hall, 1970), p. 71.
7. Reinhold Niebuhr, The Nature and Destiny of

Man, 2 vols. (New York: Charles Scribner's Sons, 1941), p. 181.

8.   Ibid., p. 182.
9.   Ibid.
10.   Ibid.
11.   Ibid.
12.   Ibid.
13.   Niebuhr drew upon Martin Heidegger's Being and Time to elaborate this point. The connective link rests in Heidegger's idea of transcendence. That idea summarizes the Christian analysis of human nature in modern times. It locates man as "something which reaches beyond itself." It is an idea that views man as "more than a rational creature." Martin Heidegger, Being and Time, trans. John Marquarrie and Edward Robinson (New York: Harper, 1962), p. 49.
14.   Niebuhr, The Nature and Destiny of Man, p. 184.
15.   Ibid., pp. 273-74.
16.   Reinhold Niebuhr, Christianity and Power Politics (New York: Charles Scribner's Sons, 1940), p. 156.
17.   Daniel Bell, "A Parable of Alienation," Jewish Frontier, November 1946, p. 18.
18.   Ibid.
19.   Ibid.
20.   Ibid.
21.   Ibid., pp. 18-19.
22.   Ibid., p. 19.
23.   Ibid.
24.   Ibid.
25.   Ibid.
26.   Ibid.
27.   Ibid.
28.   Ibid. In elaborating on this point Bell quotes the Hebrew essayist Akhad Ha-am, who describes the prophet in the following terms: ". . . he is a man of truth. He sees life as it is with a view unwarped by subjective feelings; and he tells you what he sees just as he sees it, unaffected by irrelevant considerations. He tells the truth not because he wishes to tell the truth, not because he has convinced himself, after inquiry, that such is his duty, but because he needs to, because truth telling is a special characteristic of his genius--a characteristic of which he cannot rid himself, even if he would. . . ."
29.   Bell, "A Parable of Alienation," p. 19.

30. This concept of double alienation was first elaborated by Delmore Schwartz in a symposium sponsored by the Contemporary Jewish Record called "Under Forty: A Symposium on American Literature and the Younger Generation of American Jews," Contemporary Jewish Record, February 1944, pp. 12-14. It was later the subject of a series of reviews by Irving Howe of Isaac Rosenfeld's Passage from Home: "Review of Passage from Home," Commentary, August 1946, pp. 190-92; and "The Lost Young Intellectual," Commentary, October 1946, pp. 361-67. Howe offers his own opinion about the problem of the Jewish intellectual's double alienation. "My personal opinion is that any conclusion which affirms the necessity of returning home to one's people is-- like it or not--unrealistic and unlikely to be effected; the Jewish intellectual cannot, even if he wished to, return to a world no longer his. Possibly he can find some alleviation in individual psychotherapy, but even that can only ease individual problems without touching the cause. Ultimately the problem can only be solved if an American society appears in which both the Jewish intellectual and his people, along with everyone else, can find integration, security and acceptance. At the moment he must live in a society providing none of these; he must continue at what he is: the rootless son of a rootless people. He can find consolation and dignity, however, in the consciousness of his vision, in the awareness of his complexity, and in the rejection of self-pity. To each age its own burdens." Howe, "The Lost Young Intellectual," p. 367.

31. Daniel Bell, "Screening Leaders in a Democracy," Commentary, April 1948, p. 374.

32. Ibid.

33. Ibid. In elaborating this thesis Bell argues that this repressive pattern of authority was equally reflected in the family, the school, and the factories. "We live as dependent beings, in the family situation. The nature of middle-class morality drives parents to impose the basic patterns of conformity which will subsequently be demanded elsewhere. Our schools also, despite the long years of effort toward progressive education, still operate largely on authoritarian models. Our factories, hierarchical in structure, are, for all the talk of human relations programs, still places where certain men exercise arbitrary authority over others." Daniel Bell, "Screening Leaders in a Democracy," Commentary, April 1948, p.

375.

34.   Ibid.

35.   Daniel Bell, review of The Coming Crisis by
Fritz Sternberg, Commentary, May 1947, p. 494.

36.   Daniel Bell, review of Reveille for Radicals, by Saul Alinsky, Commentary, March 1946,
p. 94.

37.   Daniel Bell, review of Strategy for Liberals: The Politics of the Mixed Economy, by Irwin Ross,
Commentary, December 1949, p. 606.

38.   Ibid.

39.   Ibid.

40.   Ibid.

41.   Daniel Bell, "America's Un-Marxist Revolution," Commentary, March 1949, p. 208.

42.   Absent were Bell's earlier suspicions about
business being able to get its way by coopting the
planning process.

43.   Bell, "America's Un-Marxist Revolution,"
p. 212.

44.   Ibid., p. 213.

45.   Ibid., p. 215.

46.   Ibid.

47.   Ibid.

48.   Ibid., p. 213.

49.   Ibid.

4

The Road Toward Pragmatism: The *Fortune* Years

Bell's Rejection of Marxian Socialism

Bell did not come to make his call for the re-placement of Marxist socialism with a more pragmatic ideology as a stranger to socialism. The years spent as a member of the Social Democratic Federation were complemented by his brief tenure as coeditor with the Russian emigre and once high-ranking Menshivik Raphael Abramovitch of a quarterly publication called Modern Review. He joined that publication when he returned to New York upon his departure from the University of Chicago in 1948. For a brief time his tenure with Modern Review was concurrent with his employment at Fortune magazine, a publication that was hardly associated with socialism.

Put out by the American Labor Conference on International Affairs, Modern Review sought to "bring together leading figures of the international labor and socialist movements to re-think the problems of Socialist theory in the post-war period."1

At the same time that Modern Review proved unsuccessful as a journalistic venture, Bell achieved literary success with the publication in 1952 of The Failure of Marxian Socialism. Initially, the product of research begun in the mid-1940s, the book treats the failure of socialism to become an effective political movement in the United States as the product of the Socialist party's own failings.

Pervasive was the Socialist party's inability to determine whether it was to function as a political party or an ethical movement. Ultimately, it was the shuttling back and forth between these two positions that produced the series of schisms and ambiguous positions that left the Socialist party impotent.

But the failure of the Socialist party to resolve this continuous dilemma was symptomatic of its failure to accept certain harsh realities of modern political life. Blinded by self-righteousness, it could never accept the gulf that modern societies demanded between politics and ethics. Arrested in images of what the world ought to be rather than accepting the world as it is, the Socialist party minimized the consequences produced by the separation between politics and ethics.

As a result of this separation, the distribution of tangible rewards and privileges in modern societies has no fixed ethical basis. No theory of justice dictates how these rewards and privileges ought to be distributed. Lacking such a standard, politics in modern society often becomes a struggle for power by groups who promote their claims to reward and privilege through ideologies.

If the goal of a group is to seek a redivision of the rewards and privileges allocated by a society, then the group must translate its recognition of these realities into more than unmasking the self-serving myths of other groups who seek to preserve the legitimacy of their claims on society: it must accept the fact that "it is only on the field of politics that such a struggle can take place."[2] The separation between politics and ethics makes no other alternative possible. Moreover, if a group is genuinely committed to pursuing through politics its vision of a better society it must "accept the hazards of evil that are implicit in politics and shun utopianism."[3] It must, in other words, accept the distinction between the ethics of responsibility and the ethics of conscience. But this acceptance presupposes that the group recognize that success in politics means the acceptance of relevant alternatives, and the system one must operate in to secure its ends.

Singled out by Bell are the messianistic and utopian elements that made the Socialist party a movement that was "in but not of the real world." Drawn to Marx but equally to the utopianism of Edward Bellamy and Laurence Gronlund and the agrarian insurgency of the Greenbacks and the Populists, the Socialist party had placed itself in a position that made its dilemma inevitable. Ultimately, it was under the weight of its

messianistic and utopian impulses that it rejected the
institutional framework of American society. The party's rejection of that framework remained constant even
during those periods when it sought to operate within
that framework.

In characterizing the twists and turns in history
of the Socialist party as the product of this incongruity, The Failure of Marxian Socialism highlights the
events and controversies that led the Socialist party
to become removed from the American worker and from the
trade-unionist movement. Among them were the failure
of the Socialist party to adopt a pro-American policy
toward World War I, the debates on revolution and party
orthodoxy that from 1919 to 1936 remained unresolved,
and the failure of the Socialist party to accept Roosevelt's New Deal labor policies. Ultimately, its inability to do no more than adopt a moral stance against
fascism in the 1930s was its final failure.

Just as he did not make his call for the replacement of Marxist socialism with a more pragmatic ideology as a stranger to socialism, Bell did not approach
his study of socialism as a nonpartisan. Reflected in
The Failure of Marxian Socialism are Bell's loyalties
to the Social Democratic Federation and the Eduard
Bernstein revisionist worldview it embodied. That
worldview favored pragmatism over abstract theory and
doctrinaire politics. It was that worldview that led
the British socialist leader C. R. Attlee to assert
that if socialism were to be successful in a particular
country, then socialist leaders must be prepared to
modify their programs to satisfy the conditions as well
as the national character unique to that country.[4] And
it was that worldview that led Bell to offer the American Federation of Labor as the model upon which the
socialist movement could have patterned itself in its
drive to win support from the American worker and
establish itself as a mass movement. The problem was
that the socialist movement lacked at the helm a leader
like Samuel Gompers.

Ultimately, it was the genius of Gompers, the
guiding spirit behind the American Federation of Labor
and a product of the socialist movement, to recognize
that progressive labor movements cannot neglect the
needs of the worker for immediate reforms. It cannot
neglect the need of the workers for higher wages and
safer working conditions by substituting the pursuit of
ultimate, absolute ends for the satisfaction of those

needs without alienating him.

If Gompers was not the perfect socialist he at least approximated Bell's and the Social Democratic Federation's image of a socialist who was both in and of the real world. Self-taught and hardbitten, he molded the American labor movement "in his own stubborn and pragmatic image."[5] An economic determinist who was often given to Marxist rhetoric, Gompers nonetheless stood out in sharp contrast to Daniel DeLeon the staunch uncompromising purist whose adherence to Marxist dogma led the socialists consistently to misread the American working class. It was Gompers, not DeLeon, the leader and guiding force of the Socialist Labor Party who recognized the wisdom of Frederick Engels's warning to the socialist community: the isolation of the Socialist Labor party "proves how useless is a platform--for the most part theoretically correct --if it is unable to get into contact with the actual needs of the people."[6]

Adapting himself and the American Federation of Labor to the realities of American politics and the immediate needs of the worker, Gompers was able to fashion a political movement that was relatively free of the factionalism and discord that marked the development of the Socialist party. Limiting its aims to the immediate problem of wages and hours, the AFL under Gompers's leadership could and did reject all the alliances that had proved the undoing of its forerunners, the National Labor Union and the Knights of Labor.

By limiting its demands to the immediate problem of wages and hours, the AFL could also openly accept the concentration of economic power as an inevitable fact of industrial capitalism. The fact that it did accept the power of the new rising capitalist class and its role as a permanent class within American society enabled the AFL "to create an institutional framework for its continued existence."[7]

In Gompers, then, the labor movement found a man who, after having participated in the interminable theoretical wranglings that marked the socialist movement, developed a skepticism of Marxian politics as applied to the American scene. He could develop a strategy that the Socialist party could not follow, for Gompers's approach required a minimal acceptance of capitalist society. His strategy was simply one of seeking a secure place within capitalist society and "when powerful enough slowly transforming it by demanding a share of the power."8

Ultimately, then, it was Gompers's success in molding the trade-unionist movement that underscored the inherent weaknesses of Marxian socialism: its inability to rise above Marxist dogma. Fixed on its thinking, Marxian socialism failed to understand the logic of business unionism. It failed to understand that the AFL was protecting itself through the trade agreement from the realities of the marketplace: that unless barred from doing so by mutual agreement capitalists could take advantage of the large reservoir of unskilled workers available to it to depress wages and break strikes.

Marxian socialism would have required that the AFL abandon its "collaborative" association with capitalism in favor of militant, uncompromising leadership of the masses aimed at the elimination of capitalism and the promotion in its place of socialism. Trade agreements and lower wages provided no solution to the capitalist crisis. If anything, they led to self-deception and, hence, had to be guarded against. The socialist position, thus, was that "some ultimate goal had to be fixed lest the workers gain illusions that the trade union was a sufficient instrument for melioration."9

Ultimately, what role the union would serve in the postwar period remained an open question. For Bell the socialist position served only to raise the question in terms of the problem that it was grounded in: the problem of trade unionism versus social movement unionism. Was it enough that the unions should follow Gompers's strategy of focusing on immediate, day-to-day, bread-and-butter issues or should they uncompromisingly align themselves with their natural allies in the struggle against capitalism and poverty. This was a problem that Bell would focus on in Fortune, a publication that has a strange place in American journalism. Like the irrelevance of Marxian socialism, that problem would be a part of the paradigm for the end of ideology.

Fortune Magazine

Conceived by Henry R. Luce before the 1929 Depression and run by him from 1930 until well after Bell's 1958 departure, Fortune's policy of "unbridled curiosity" and commitment to journalistic independence went side by side with an unremitting optimism over the capacity of business to provide intellectual and moral leadership in a free society. These features led Luce to employ a number of writers on its staff who were by reputation liberals. Prominent among them were John Kenneth Galbraith, who was on the staff when Bell was hired, and Dwight MacDonald, who was affiliated with Fortune from 1930 to 1936, before he became a Trotsky-ite.

MacDonald wrote some sharply critical pieces for Fortune; articles that dealt with monopoly capitalism and the inevitability of socialism. Those articles suggest the kind of publication that it was during the 1930s and 1940s: eclectic and pragmatic. MacDonald's reflections on his involvement with Fortune would even suggest that, in spite of Luce, it was a rather liberal publication.

> The New Deal was inspiring to me, as to my fellow writers on Fortune. To Luce's dismay, we became increasingly liberal; we wanted to write about . . . the C.I.O., the Wagner Act, unemployment, social security, anything but business. Luce was divided between his pro-business convictions and his journalistic instinct, which told him the C.I.O. was news and that the wonders of American Cyanamid Co. weren't; his typically American pragmatic fascination with Power and Success told him the same thing. He compromised (as did we) and for a few years Fortune was a pastiche of mildly liberal articles on social themes and reluctantly written "corporation pieces" dealing with enterprises that somehow managed to make a profit.10

Luce's tolerance was reflected by Fortune's 1942 national economy report, the thrust of which was that American business had failed to understand Keynesian economics and the potential that it can have in creating a political economy that could provide Americans with security and freedom. The report charged Keynesian economists, who called for the elimination of private enterprise in favor of total government control of investment and fiscal management, with underestimating the creative potentialities of the "risk-taking enter-priser." For the editors of _Fortune_ this represented a striking failure: the failure of these economists to think through the problem that Keynes raised.

The report further charged that no theory of em-ployment can be complete without a theory of business enterprise. In the absence of such a theory _Fortune_ proposed a program that represented "a genuine recon-ciliation of the profound but perplexing American de-sire for both security and freedom."[11] _Fortune_ called for a program that would constitute a synthesis of conflicting economic elements, one that would promote full employment, vigilant federal policing of the free market, and active government encouragement of the risk-taking individual. It called for a "new democra-tic capitalism."[12]

The immediate goal of the editors of _Fortune_ in drafting the domestic economy report was to encourage the business community to deepen its understanding of the implications of America's emergence as a broker state. This was a goal that Bell shared.

In his writings for _Fortune_ Bell sought to satisfy that goal by explaining to the business community the ways in which labor too was affected by America's transformation to a broker state. In the process he focused on the conflict between trade unionism and social movement unionism as the background around which the rumblings of labor in the postwar period could better be put into perspective. Ultimately, it was to explicate the dimensions of that conflict and the im-pact of labor's uncertainty in the broker state that "The Language of Labor" and "Labor's Coming of Middle Age" were written. Because of their emphasis on the "exhaustion of the left" they are probably the earliest statements by Bell on the end of ideology. Both these articles were written in 1951.

In "The Language of Labor" Bell was trying to account for the resurgence of labor militantism as embodied in the growing popularity of John L. Lewis; a phenomenon that business could not understand since labor had achieved respectability. Like their business counterparts labor leaders were constantly being asked to serve on civil boards, community chests, and in patriotic organizations; like business leaders they too were the recipients of honorary degrees and other awards that connoted respectability and legitimacy.

Bell's explanation is swift and to the point.

What business had to realize is that despite the relative success of the labor movement labor was anxious and uncertain about its future.   But then how could it not be?   Labor's uncertainty was a response to the United States being a broker state that was undergoing a swift transformation.   So swift had the changes been that the coalitions established under the New Deal were giving way with the result that power could not be permanently located in any one generally recognized group.   This is a situation which inevitably produces in everyone anxieties about the future.   After all, people like to know who is in charge because it is only then that they know where they "fit--and whom to fight."13   Thus, it is the absence of stabilized power in the contemporary situation that becomes one of the major sources of labor's anxieties and ultimately of its need, when threatened by hard-line conservative business leaders, to revert back to a language that masks its insecurities.

Bell pursues this theme still further in "Labor's Coming of Middle Age."   In that article he traces labor's insecurity to the actions of the postwar Republican Congress, particularly its passage of the restrictive Taft-Hartley Act.   That legislation signaled that the government and labor alliance fostered under the New Deal was at an end.   The fact that they had to "strongarm" Truman into giving them some of the recognition they sought during the war further reinforced labor's perception that the alliance between them and the federal government was finished: they were now once again outsiders.   This would not be an anxiety-provoking situation for labor if, Bell argues, its leadership were certain of which way to turn.

The uncertainty of labor's leadership about the political course labor should take was the result of the absence of a defined trade union ideology.   No politically viable alternative to leaning on President Truman for concessions was being offered.   The only alternative being proposed was the one that was being loudly suggested by John L. Lewis, the outspoken maverick president of the United Mine Workers.   Lewis believed in militant trade unionism.   While doubting that labor would ever accept Lewis's "egoistic" leadership, there was, cautions Bell, no doubt that his militant trade unionism would continue to appeal to other labor leaders for the same reasons that left labor without a defined ideology.

Bell cites two reasons why Lewis's brand of trade unionism, with its emphasis on labor relying on its own economic strength instead of on coalitions between it and the government, was growing in appeal among many labor leaders.   Each highlighted the conflict between trade unionism and labor as a social movement, and underlying them was an "exhaustion of the left."[14]   The first concerned the decline in influence of Walter Reuther, then president of the United Auto Workers and the principal spokesman in American for trade unionism as a force for large-scale social planning and change. The second concerned the fact that many labor leaders were tired of the "mantle of social leadership" that liberal and New Deal intellectuals had cast upon them during the 1930s.[15] This fact was underlined by the obvious reluctance in 1949 of the labor leaders to participate with left-wing intellectuals in the Americans for Democratic Action. But these, implies Bell, were only surface factors.

One of the underlying factors that prompted labor leaders to move back under Lewis' prodding, to the traditional Gompers business union attitude with its focus on the market situation and collective bargaining was the threat of losing their base of political support.   The office of union president made them focus their concerns on the particular unions they represented rather then on larger social interests. But the overriding factor was "the exhaustion of the left." By this Bell meant the failure of the political left to provide union leaders interested in social planning with a new set of philosophical legitimations.

Lest there be any confusion about the phrase "the exhaustion of the left," Bell is quite specific about the conditions that justified his use of it to describe where labor stood in 1951.

> . . . In the last five years the social impulses that had agitated the minds of labor intellectuals and radicals have been almost completely exhausted. The enthusiasm for planning is probably at its nadir. Attempts to articulate a philosophy of labor have practically ceased. The organizational and ideological influence of the once-powerful left-wing groups, notably the sociologists, have disappeared.[16]

Perhaps the greatest symbol of the exhaustion of
the left was David Dubinsky, the ex-socialist leader of
the Ladies Garment Workers Union. For Bell, Dubinsky's
reflections on the nature of his rejection in 1944 of
socialism dramatized the shift in the labor movement
away from "ideology" to trade unionism. Bell shares
those reflections with his readers.

> When I resigned from the Socialist Party
> in 1936 it was for purely political rea-
> sons. We . . . wanted Roosevelt re-
> elected. But since that time I have come
> to the conclusion that socialism certain-
> ly the orthodox variety will never work.
> Trade unionism needs capitalism like a
> fish needs water. Democracy is possible
> only in a society of free enterprise, and
> trade unionism can only live in a demo-
> cracy. . . . But capitalism . . . must be
> made responsible. Nobody but a lunatic
> could believe in a system--or rather a
> lack of system--that produces violent
> business cycles, mass unemployment, and
> misery for millions of people. . . .
> Where do we draw the line in a society as
> infinitely complicated as the modern
> industrial world? . . . I'm for the New
> Deal, with all its faults, because it's
> an American attempt to make capitalism
> work in terms of industrial democracy.
> . . . I don't think that we in America
> are in danger of a European kind of stat-
> ism.[17]

Business should not make any mistake about the trends.
The exhaustion of the left was not a passing phenomenon. Rather, with the reversion back to trade unionism
the possibilities of labor assuming, in the fashion of
the 1930s, a strong ideological role in American politics were virtually nonexistent. The reasons for
Bell's assessment had less to do with external factors
then with the underlying nature of trade unionism.
    Bell's central thesis is that it is fundamentally
business union-oriented trade unions who promote conditions that create constraints against them becoming
part of a social movement. Business unionism commits
labor to work within the limits of a specific indus-

trial environment. It commits each union to protect
the health of the particular industry that its survival
is dependent upon. The "market role," because it
stresses immediate economic problems, tends to divide
unions along the economic lines of the industries in
which they operate. Trade unionism thus serves to
restrict the chances for cohesion among the different
unions. Operating as a conservative force within the
labor movement, trade unionism predisposes each union
to develop vested interests that it works to protect.
The result is that politics is seen as a means of
winning specific and narrowly defined union ends rather
than broadly based social ends.

The exhaustion of the left and the reversion of
the unions to business unionism thus makes the politics
of labor very predictable. In discouraging a trade-
union social movement, business unionism prevents labor
from anything more than a reactive movement. In lacking any positive drive of its own, labor reacts to
other groups in the social order; it seeks to at least
maintain parity with them.

It is very possible that the intent of "Labor's
Coming of Middle Age" may have been to soften management. After all, Bell went to great lengths to assure
management that labor's militant language was not a
language of nihilism or revolution but, rather, one of
protest against exclusion. That language "challenged
the right to rule, but not the nature of the rule."18
In general, the intent of this article may have been to
soften _Fortune_'s readers' view of labor and to produce
in them more tolerance and understanding for labor.
Yet the article serves to accomplish more than these
ends.

Presented in "Labor's Coming of Middle Age" are
both the concept of the exhaustion of the left and the
end of ideology thesis. The left, in failing to provide labor with a planning ideology, is deficient. But
implied in his argument is the necessity of such an
ideology, a planning ideology that would give labor a
place in a larger moral community. Again Bell is
arguing that the end of a particular ideology requires
a new, pragmatic planning ideology; in his terminology
a "philosophical legitimacy," within which planning is
acceptable and can be made to work.

While most of his writings for _Fortune_ after 1951
are largely devoted to reports on scandals and corruption in the unions, Bell continued to elaborate his

argument concerning the "anti-ideological" effect of trade unionism and social movement or planning unionism. Ultimately, this was the significance of his 1953 _Fortune_ article "Labor's New Men of Power," an article that sees Bell compare Walter Reuther with George Meany and other top labor leaders.

In a reworking of the "in but not of the real world" framework that he uses to explain the demise of the Socialist party, Bell pictures Reuther as a labor leader who was now approaching the proverbial fork in the road. Having "shrewdly" seized the issue of the guaranteed annual wage as his own, Reuther, who was then the president of the CIO, now had to decide whether he wanted to be a political leader with broad appeal and thus seek to organize a broad-based social movement around this issue or be a more narrowly focused trade unionist. Reuther was in Bell's view a man caught in the middle of a real dilemma.19 It is very conceivable that the "End of Ideology" may have been written for Reuther's benefit.

Outside of his writings for _Fortune_ Bell continued to write about many of the same issues that were related to his interested in the anti-ideological effect of trade unionism and the tension between business unionism and social planning. The exhaustion of the left, the existence of status anxieties as a result of both prosperity and the absence of defined ideologies, and the political exigencies of the broker state were all issues that Bell continued to write about during the 1950s. Indeed, the ultimate value of his introductory essay to _The Radical Right_, "Interpretations of American Politics," was that in it Bell seeks to establish a theoretical framework for understanding the underlying sources of tension in American society of the 1950s largely on the basis of his reflections on these issues.

Bell continues these reflections in the two papers that he gave at the 1955 Milan Congress for Cultural Freedom meetings. Like his writings on American socialism and trade unionism, these papers helped shaped Bell's efforts to develop his end of ideology thesis.

The New York Jewish Intellectuals

Throughout the 10 years that he was employed at
Fortune, Bell became increasingly drawn through his
intellectual, social, and political activities to the
overlapping informal circles that made up the group
life of the New York Jewish Intellectuals.

The New York Jewish Intellectuals, or the "family"
as Norman Podhoretz referred to them in his book Making
It, were a group that joined together three generations
of writers and intellectuals drawn largely from the
literary and journalistic world.   Generally acknowledged to evolve around the New York City world of
publishing, many of its members were contributors to
Commentary, Partisan Review, and the New Leader.

In his reflections about it, Bell concedes that if
there is any "story" behind the "End of Ideology" it is
of the success of Commentary; it is the story of the
growth of Commentary as a social phenomenon.20 It is
the story of the New York Jewish Intellectuals and the
acceptance of their writings into mainstream American
social thought.   And finally, it is the story of the
ability of its editor and guiding force, Elliot Cohen,
to mold that publication into an expression of the
impatience of the "twice born" generation with Marxist
panaceas.

Well into the 1950s Commentary continued to mirror
the fears and aspirations of that generation.   It also
continued to serve as a forum for the discussion of
issues central to the New York Jewish Intellectuals;
issues concerning the Holocaust, Jewish identity in the
diaspora, the political and moral bankruptcy of communism, and the role of the intellectual in contemporary
society.   Featured were articles that served to elaborate the Hook-Niebuhr debates of the early 1940s; articles by Reinhold Niebuhr, Sidney Hook, and John Dewey.

Outside of Podhoretz's account of the New York
Jewish Intellectuals and some relatively brief and
highly personalized accounts written by Irving Howe and
by Bell, there has been little written about this
highly informal group.   Bell's delineation of its members on the basis of their "coming of age" (a reference
to both their disillusionment with communism and left-
wing panaceas and their animosity toward Stalin) thus
serves a useful function.

New York Jewish Intellectuals[21]
c. 1935-c. 1965

1. The Elders: coming of age in the late 1920s and early 1930s

Elliot Cohen	Lionel Trilling	Hannah Arendt
Sidney Hook	Meyer Shapiro	Diana Trilling
Philip Rahv	William Phillips	

Gentile
Cousins: Max Eastman   Fred Dupee
Edmund Wilson   Dwight MacDonald
Reinhold Niebuhr   James T. Farrell

The "Other Synagogue": Michael Gold   Joseph Freeman

Magazines: <u>Menorah Journal</u>   <u>The New Masses</u>
<u>Partisan Review</u>

1.A. The Younger Brothers: coming of age in the mid and late 1930s

Alfred Kazin	Harold Rosenberg
Richard Hofstadter	Clement Greenberg
Saul Bellow	Lionel Abel
Delmore Schwartz	Paul Goodman
Bernard Malamud	Isaac Rosenfeld

European Relatives: Nicola Chiaramonte
George Lichtheim

Gentile
Cousins: Mary McCarthy   William Barrett
Elizabeth Hardwick   Richard Chase
James Baldwin   Ralph Ellison
Arthur Schlesinger, Jr.

Magazines: <u>The Nation</u>   <u>The New Republic</u>
<u>Partisan Review</u> <u>Commentary</u>
<u>Politics</u>

2. The Second Generation: coming of age in the late 1930s and early 1940s

Daniel Bell	Irving Kristol	David Bazelon
Irving Howe	Melvin Lasky	Nathan Glazer

        Leslie Fiedler   Gertrude Himmelfarb
        Robert Warshow   S. M. Lipset

    Gentile Cousins: Murray Kempton   C. Wright Mills

    Magazines: Commentary   Partisan Review
                Encounter   New Leader
                Dissent   The Public Interest

2.A. The Younger Brothers: coming of age in the late
     1940s and early 1950s.

        Norman Podhoretz   Jason Epstein   Norman Mailer
        Steven Marcus   Robert Silvers   Phillip Roth
        Robert Brustein   Susan Sontag
        Midge Decter   Theo. Solotaroff

    Gentile Cousins: Michael Harrington

    Magazines: Commentary   Partisan Review
                New York Review of Books
                The Paris Review

    Institutional Attachments: Columbia University
                                Congress for Cultural
                                   Freedom

    Influentials--at a Distance:

        T. S. Eliot   Robert Lowell   Edward Shils
        W. H. Auden   James Agee

The distrust of Marxist panaceas and Stalinism
common to the New York Jewish Intellectuals was borne
largely from the "Popular Front" crusades of the 1930s
when the American Communist party joined forces with
the socialists and liberals to foster a united progressive front only to reverse themselves with the signing
of the Nazi-Soviet Nonaggression Pact. It is thus not
surprising given the resurgence of popular front activities in the late 1940s and early 1950s that many of
the New York Jewish Intellectuals came to be involved
with the activities of the Congress for Cultural Freedom.

Bell and the Congress for Cultural Freedom

The Congress for Cultural Freedom was an organization of well-known figures in the worlds of art, science, and social thought drawn from America, England, Germany, and Western Europe. It originated at the Berlin Congress for Freedom meetings in June of 1950 to serve as a permanent political and educational organization. Its aim was to realize the pledges made at these meetings. These pledges included encouraging those behind the Iron Curtain, particularly intellectuals, to resist communist tyranny. The 125 members in attendance at these meetings also pledged to prevent Western intellectuals from making compromises with Stalinist oppression. Other pledges made at the Berlin meeting included the provision of scholarships for East European students and inexpensively priced books for German citizens.

The history of the Congress for Cultural Freedom, like the history of its American affiliate, the American Committee for Cultural Freedom, has been shrouded in controversy. From its very beginnings suspicions were voiced about its claim to being an independent organization. These suspicions were reinforced when in May of 1967 it was disclosed by no less an authoritative source than the New York Times that the Congress for Cultural Freedom had been receiving funds from the American Central Intelligence Agency.[22] Since this disclosure it has come under sharp attack by both the old and the new left.

Despite this controversy there has been remarkably little unbiased reporting on the Congress for Cultural Freedom and its American affiliate, an organization created largely through the efforts of Sidney Hook.[23] What is known about the Congress for Cultural Freedom is that it openly functioned as a political organization whose principal task was to provide a response to the communist-dominated 1948 Wroclaw peace conference and the 1949 Paris peace conference. The latter conference ended with "third force intellectuals" winning control and declaring "a plague" on both the communists and the anti-communists.[24]

Bell's involvement with the Congress for Cultural Freedom extends back to the early 1950s when with Hook, Irving Kristol, and Melvin Lasky he helped organize meetings for the American Committee for Cultural Freedom. He continued that involvement in the mid-1950s by

participating in the Milan Congress for Cultural Freedom meetings where he presented two papers: "The Ambiguities of the Mass Society and the Complexities of
American Life," and "The Breakup of Family Capitalism."
Later retitled "America as a Mass Society: A Critique,"
the "Mass Society" essay and "the Breakup of Family
Capitalism" were published in different "family" magazines: Commentary and Partisan Review. They were also
included in The End of Ideology. For a year, 1956-
1957, Bell also served while on leave from Fortune as
director of international seminars for the Congress and
was stationed in Paris.
     Bell's "Mass Society" paper was written in order
to elaborate on what he believed were the theoretical
and substantive limitations of the theory of the mass
society as applied to mid-century American society. In
focusing on the United States, Bell develops an analysis of the complexities of American life that led
Edward Shils to speak of Bell's paper as a "gratified
contemplation of American life" and an "exculpation" of
the masses.25
     Projected in Bell's analysis is an image of the
United States as a country where the rising levels of
education and the steadily increasing amounts of money
spent on cultural items all indicated the "growth of a
vast middlebrow society."26 Also represented is an
image of the United States as a country that was ideologically opposed to conformity; a country where conformity was in decline, where crime was decreasing, and
where the increasing divorce rate might, instead of
indicating the disruption of the family, be a reflection of a new, more individual approach to marriage.
Projected in Bell's analysis, then, is an image of the
United States as a country that was ideologically committed to social change; a country that, in lacking a
feudal tradition and in possessing a pragmatic ethos,
had adopted change and innovation into its culture. In
short, the United States was a country that was "providing one answer to the great challenge posed to Western
--and now world--society over the last two hundred
years: how within the framework of freedom, to increase
the living standards of the majority of people and at
the same time maintain or raise cultural levels."27
     Bell supplements his critique with a call for an
alternative social theory. His arguments is that aside
from its decidedly conservative implications and its
skewed image of the world, the mass society theory

failed to provide a useful framework for locating the
sources of social change in modern societies in general, and the United States in particular. There may
not, Bell remarks, be enough data on which to construct
such an alternative theory but there were certainly
recent developments in the United States that warranted
closer analysis than the mass society theory, in all
its variations, could freely allow.[28] These developments included

> America's change from a society that was
> once geared to frugal saving but was not
> impelled to spend dizzily; the breakup of
> family capitalism, with the consequent
> impact on corporate structure and politi-
> cal power; the centralization of deci-
> sion-making, politically, in the state
> and, economically, in a group of large
> corporate bodies; the rise of status and
> symbol groups replacing specific interest
> groups.[29]

While Bell's "Mass Society" paper was presented
for the purpose of detailing the shortcomings of the
mass society theory, his "Capitalism" paper was presented in order to detail the deficiencies of accepted
economic theory for comprehending the changing structure of postwar capitalism. The thrust of "The Breakup
of Family Capitalism" is that American capitalism was
undergoing a series of changes, the importance of which
could not be fully comprehended by the friends and
critics of capitalism unless each were prepared to give
up the elaborate myths they held about modern capitalism. One of those changes was the increased separation between property and authority. That change had
produced a managerial class who, lacking an ideology of
their own, had long been searching for both an intellectual spokesperson and an ideology.
   Bell's central thesis is that the drive of the
corporate managers in the United States to "find an
ideology to justify their power and prestige" reflected
both the uniqueness and the dynamic nature of modern
American capitalism.[30] "In no other capitalist order,
as in the American, has this drive for an ideology been
pressed so compulsively."[31] This was because "in other
orders it was less needed."[32] In European capitalist
societies "private property was always linked, philoso-

phically, to a system of natural rights; thus property itself provided a moral justification. But private productive property, especially in the United States, is largely a fiction, and rarely does one hear it invoked any longer as the moral source of the corporate executive power."33

The fact that private property could no longer serve as the moral source of the corporate managers' power meant that the managers had to find a new ideological basis of legitimacy for their position in the corporate world. Bell leaves no doubt that a clear understanding of the changing structure of capitalism would reveal the direction they would follow to satisfy that end.

> As we have had in the corporation the classic shift from ownership to managerial control, so, on the symbolic level we have the shift from "private property" to "enterprise" as the justification of power. And, as with any ideology, "performance" for its own sake has become a driving motive to the American corporate head.34

Though perceptive, Bell's analysis of managerial capitalism is hardly comprehensive. "The Breakup of Family Capitalism" leaves unanswered a crucial set of questions. Could managerial capitalism in the absence of a defined ideology continue to claim legitimacy for itself? Would productivity and performance be enough to sustain managerial capitalism in the event of double-digit inflation? Or, under the weight of runway inflation would managerial capitalism have to turn elsewhere to justify its relative autonomy and the righteousness of its claims? It would not be until the early 1970s that Bell would address these questions.

The tenor of "The Breakup of Family Capitalism" is at the same time both optimistic and cautious. It clearly elaborates the irrelevance of private property as a basis of legitimacy in the United States. The paper clearly, then, heralds the "end of ideology." It heralds the end of traditional ideology. The paper revels in the failure of Marxist theorists to perceive the irrelevance of Marxism. Consequently, it goes into great detail about the limits of their ruling-class model as an inappropriate paradigm for comprehending the changed structure of American capitalism. Yet the paper bears the stamp of Bell's basic pessimism about the inability of political and economic theorists to come to terms with the shortcomings of contemporary economic theory to respond to the Welfare State's absence of a defined public philosophy. That pessimism was originally reflected in an earlier essay: "The Prospects of American Capitalism."[35]

Like "The Breakup of Family Capitalism," "The Prospects of American Capitalism" seeks to detail the deficiencies of postwar economic theory. It also details the shortcomings of the Marxist ruling-class model, as well as managerial capitalism's search for a new ideology. But it actually goes farther than "The Breakup of Family Capitalism."

"The Prospect of American Capitalism" takes economist John Kenneth Galbraith to task for his failure to answer the question that his 1952 book __American Capitalism__, with its emphasis on American society being a broker state held in equilibrium through the ability of business, labor, and agriculture to use countervailing power, had raised. That question was why both the business community and the left were "captives of a description of reality that no longer exists."[36] It takes Galbraith to task for never coming to terms with why businessmen and liberals found the myths of free enterprise and the fear of bigness more compelling than the reality of countervailing power. What Galbraith does is to provide a truer picture of that reality. But in the process he commits the same mistake that one makes in "telling a neurotic that his fears are groundless: they may be, but the answer cannot convince the neurotic of the fact until the sources of the fear are laid bare."[37]

In attacking Galbraith for this omission explanations are given to account for both the left's and the right's denial of the existence of countervailing power as the new American reality. Those explanations center on "the breakup of family capitalism," the amorphousness of American society, and the increasingly technical nature of decision-making that served to make the liberal an outsider. Ultimately, it was easier for the liberal to hunt for some sinister power source behind technical decisions concerning the distribution of government contracts than it was for him or her to accept the new reality of countervailing power. But those explanations were secondary.

The primary thrust of "The Prospects of American Capitalism" is its push for a political and moral calculus to replace or supplement the purely economic calculuses of John Maynard Keynes, Joseph A. Schumpeter, and John Kenneth Galbraith. It raises the demand for a new theory of Western political economy. The demand for such a theory is of course implicit in "The Breakup of Family Capitalism."

One of the hallmarks of Bell's writings in the 1950s is that there was the same repeated call for a new theory of Western political economy. In the 1970s that call would be articulated as the call for a new philosophy of the public household. But the essentials remained the same.

The new theory would have to provide the basis for making allocations of costs and benefits on moral and political grounds. It would also have to make new societal institutions clear to the left and the right; to the liberals, the intellectuals, and to the corporate managers. Ultimately, the theory would have to reconcile them with their emerging reality.

But those repeated calls were marked by the same pattern. The program for its construction is always presented but it is always presented on the basis of some momentary vision of an emerging society. Never does Bell present the actual theory. It is always in the process of construction. Frameworks are laid and conceptual prisms elaborated but the issues that evoke the demand for the new theory are never resolved. This same pattern is repeated in The Radical Right, a book that is the culmination of a series of Columbia University seminars on McCarthyism.[38]

The Radical Right

The central theme elaborated by The Radical Right is the inadequacy of standard explanations of American political behavior in comprehending both the origins and appeal of McCarthyism. Closely related to this theme is the book's emphasis on the need to understand the emergence of McCarthyism in terms of status politics and status anxiety.

Collectively, these themes were represented in what Bell in his introductory essay "Interpretations of American Political" refers to as the new framework established by the radical right for comprehending the sources of social strain and anxieties in American society. This new framework, with its emphasis on "the deeper running social currents of a turbulent mid-century America," was "derived from an analysis of the exhaustion of liberal and left-wing political ideology."39 It was also derived from "an examination of the new, prosperity-created 'status groups' which in their drive for recognition and respectability, have sought to impose older conformities on the American body politic."40

In the course of defining the nature and function of The Radical Right as a "thesis book" that added a "new and necessary dimension to the analysis of American society," Bell explores the limits of "conventional political analysis" in comprehending the "deeper social undercurrents that had produced McCarthyism."41 Thus, "Interpretations of American Politics" is much more than a restatement of views developed in other essays in The Radical Right.

Though no doubt shaped by the views of some of the contributors to the book and by others whose views were absorbed into several of the essays, namely, Theodore W. Adorno and Edward Shils, Bell's "Interpretations of American Politics" stands on its own. It stands as an essay that not only fuses together many of the strands of his earlier writings but also as an essay that reflects a strong interest in providing a supplement to conventional interest group explanations of American politics.

This interest stemmed from Bell's belief that while the role of interest groups in shaping and modifying legislative policy provided a useful framework for understanding "traditional political problems" it, like other traditional approaches to the analysis of American politics, left the modern day analyst ill-equipped to understand the issues that have dominated political disputes since the end of World War II.

Bell's argument is that, like the anti-ideological effect of the American electoral structure and of the democratic tradition of American politics, the emphasis on interest group politics did not help the modern day analyst to understand McCarthy's exploitation of the communist issue or the growth of McCarthyism in general. Needed, then, was a new framework; a framework that could allow the analyst to comprehend McCarthyism in relation to the groups behind Senator McCarthy "and the changed political temper which these groups have brought."42   For Bell the role of status groups as a major entity in American life and status resentments as a real force in politics provided such a framework principally because it enabled political analysts to raise some new and important questions about the political theory and political temper of American democracy.

For all his emphasis on new frameworks, Bell's principal focus is on encouraging political analysts to broaden their perspective on McCarthyism in particular and extremism in general.   Bell calls upon them to recognize that McCarthy's ability to transform the issue of communist infiltration into an ideological issue reflected a significant shift in the moral temper of the United States.   He calls upon them to recognize that the tendency to convert politics into "moral" issues was being reinforced through the political rhetoric of both the right and the left, with equally dangerous consequences.   The strong anti-communist rhetoric of the McCarthyite intellectuals, James Burnham, William Schlamm, Max Eastman, and their "minor epigoni," were serving to create a political environment where "traditional conservative issues no longer count in dividing liberals from anti-communists."43 The only issue that remained was whether one was to be "hard" or "soft" in opposing communism.   But the left was no better.   Largely under the influence of "vulgar Marxist thinking," the political left was helping to convert in the public mind interest groups into "symbolic groups" (labor, business, the farmers) being invested with a greater coherence and sense of purpose than, given the reality, could reasonably be accorded them.

Finally, Bell calls upon political analysts to recognize that "the tendency to convert issues into ideologies, to invest them with moral color and high emotional charge, invites conflicts which can only damage a society."44   In calling upon them to recognize the allegedly inherent dangers of ideology, he calls upon them to appreciate the political virtues of American pragmatism.   As he puts it, "the saving glory of the United States [is that] the politics has always been a pragmatic give-and-take rather than a series of wars-to-the-death."45

All of these observations indicate that, apart from its value in setting the tone for The Radical Right, "Interpretations of American Politics" conveys much of Bell's own thinking about the nature of American politics in a changing society. Part of his thinking was apparently grounded in the belief that, in the face of the "ideologizing" of American politics by the extreme left and right, efforts must be made to preserve the boundaries of the civility that sometime earlier Edward Shils had located in Western political tradition. This belief resonates in Bell's evaluation of Theodore Roosevelt as the model of the political pragmatist.

> One ultimately comes to admire the "practical politics" of a Theodore Roosevelt and his scorn for the intransigents, like Godkin and Villard, who, refusing to yield to expediency, could never put through their reforms. Politics, as Edmund Wilson has described T. R.'s attitude, "is a matter of adapting oneself to all sorts of people and situations, a game in which one may score but only by accepting the rules and recognizing one's opponents, rather than a moral crusade in which one's stainless standard must mow the enemy down."[46]

It seems equally apparent that much of Bell's thinking about American politics and the disruptive potential of ideological politics in a democratic society was grounded in a worldview that equated liberalism with civility. This observation is borne out by Bell when, in extolling the virtues of American democracy, he speaks of democratic politics as a process that necessarily involves both bargaining and consensus within the framework of the "rules of the game."

> Democratic politics is bargaining and consensus because the historic contribution of liberalism was to separate law from morality. The thought that the two should be separate often comes as a shock. Yet, in the older Catholic societies, ruled by the doctrine of "two swords," the state was the secular arm of the Church, and enforced in civil life the moral decrees of the Church. This was possible, in political theory, if not

in practice, because the society was homogeneous and everyone accepted the same religious values. But the religious wars that followed the Reformation proved that a plural society could only survive if it respected the principles of toleration. No group, be it Catholic or Protestant, could use the state to impose its moral conceptions on all the people. As the party of the Politiques put it, the "civil society must not perish for conscience's sake."

These theoretical foundations of modern liberal society were completed by Kant, who, separating legality and morality, defined the former as the "rules of the game" so to speak; law dealt with procedural, not substantive issues. The latter were private matters of conscience with which the state could not interfere.47

Ultimately, Bell's worldview is that of a New Deal liberal who was committed to establishing through The Radical Right in general, and "The Interpretations of American Politics," in particular, the groundwork for serious reflection on the underlying threat of extremism and ideology in American politics. It is the thesis of this book that "Interpretations of American Politics" constitutes both a reformulation of liberal political theory and a defense of American liberalism that, like Bell's distrust of Marxist panaceas, his fear of the extreme right, and his recognition of managerial capitalism's need for a new ideology, became absorbed into his essay on the end of ideology.

Collectively, each of these features of Bell's 1950s writings became absorbed into the end of ideology paradigm. That paradigm calls less for a new theory of Western political economy than for a new pragmatic planning ideology that, in replacing Marxism, would again provide the philosophical legitimacy necessary for the acceptance of comprehensive social planning, as well as the conditions upon which such planning can be made to work within the framework of a liberal democratic society.

Notes

1. Daniel Bell, "Modern Review, New York, 1947–1950," in The American Radical Press 1880-1960 vol. 2, ed. Joseph R. Conlin (Westport, Conn.: Greenwood Press, 1974), p. 644.

2. Daniel Bell, "American Socialist: What Now?" Modern Review, January 1949, p. 347.

3. Ibid.

4. C. R. Attlee, The Labour Party in Perspective and Twelve Years Later (London: Victor Gollancz Ltd., 1949).

5. Daniel Bell, Marxian Socialism in the United States (Princeton, N.J.: Princeton University Press, 1952), p. 37.

6. Ibid., p. 36.

7. Ibid., p. 37.

8. Ibid.

9. Ibid., p. 44.

10. Dwight MacDonald, Memoirs of a Revolutionist (New York: Farrar, Straus and Cudahy, 1957), pp. 8-9.

11. "The United States in a New World: The Domestic Economy," Supplement to Fortune, December 1942, pp. 1-17.

12. Ibid.

13. Daniel Bell, "The Language of Labor," Fortune, September 1951, p. 211.

14. Daniel Bell, "Labor's Coming of Middle Age," Fortune, October 1951, p. 114.

15. Ibid.

16. Ibid.

17. Ibid., p. 137.

18. Ibid., p. 150.

19. Daniel Bell, "Labor's New Men of Power," Fortune, June 1953, p. 151. In this article Bell also characterizes Reuther as a "new Machiavellian." The new Machiavellian, as Bell puts it in quoting H. G. Wells, is one who sees "an organized state as confident and powerful as modern science, as balanced and beautiful as a body." Bell, "Labor's New Men of Power," p. 149. He is a person who holds that "the organized state should end muddle forever." Bell, "Labor's New Men of Power," p. 149. Bell's justification for his characterization of Reuther as a new Machiavellian is that "while many people once attracted to such a vision have now recoiled from it, Reuther has not. Intellec-

tually he knows the possibilities of evil that arise from concentrated power. But his emotional drive is still toward the social engineering of the ordered society. These emotions have been bred into his character. The sources are the old Lutheran duty to work, instilled by his father; the German sobriety of purpose; a nineteenth-century Protestant ethic fused with an immigrant family's desire for self-improvement. Temperamentally Reuther is no rebel. His tastes, cultural ideas, manners, morals, and habits are conventional. Nor is he an intellectual; he is not concerned with ideas as steps in a critical theory of knowledge. He is primarily, in Veblen's sense, an engineer. His emphasis is always on efficiency. His criticisms of capitalism turn on the 'tragedy of waste' that a loose society entails. In that sense he is a radical; he is the cold idealist who wishes to create the functional society." Bell, "Labor's New Men of Power," p. 149.

20. Interview with Daniel Bell, Harvard University, Cambridge, Mass. 12 February 1978.

21. Daniel Bell, "The Intelligentsia in American Society," in Tomorrow's American, ed. Samuel Sandmel (New York: Oxford University Press, 1977), pp. 34-36.

22. The disclosure was first made by Thomas W. Braden, a former official of the Central Intelligence Agency, who asserted in the 20 May 1967 issue of the Saturday Evening Post that the Agency had placed an "agent" in the Congress of Cultural Freedom. On 14 May 1967 Michael Josselson, in submitting his resignation as its executive director, acknowledged that for 16 years the Congress for Cultural Freedom had received funds from the CIA. His resignation was not accepted. Daniel Bell was among the 16 members of the Congress who voted on Josselson's resignation. After stating that it had been a "grievous burden" for him to conceal the source of the funds received by the Congress, Josselson went on to add in a New York Times interview that "he regretted having accepted the funds 'because the ends do not justify the means.'" "Cultural Group to Keep Director," New York Times, 15 May 1967, p. 19.

23. Christopher Lasch's The Agony of the American Left (New York: Alfred A. Knopf, 1969) offers an analysis of the Congress for Cultural Freedom. But his analysis reads more like a polemic than anything else. Lasch highlights the CIA infiltration of the Congress and the fact that many of its members were duped. Yet

one hears little from the supporters of the Congress in Lasch's analysis. On the other side of the ledger one can find various apologies for the Congress by its supporters in "Liberal Anti-communism Revisited: A Symposium," Commentary, September 1967, pp. 31-79.

24. Francois Bondy, "Berlin Congress for Freedom," Commentary, September 1950, p. 246.

25. Edward Shils, "The End of Ideology?" in The End of Ideology Debate, p. 58.

26. Daniel Bell, "America as a Mass Society: A Critique," in The End of Ideology, p. 33. This essay first appeared in the July 1956 issue of Commentary.

27. Ibid., p. 38.

28. In "American as a Mass Society" Bell cites a number of variations. Distinctions between aristocratic, Catholic, and existentialist theories of mass society are elaborated. Reviewed by Bell are the works of Ortega y Gasset, Gabriel Marcel, Emil Lederer, Hannah Arendt, George Simmel, and Karl Mannheim.

29. Bell, "America as a Mass Society," p. 38.

30. Bell, "The Breakup of Family Capitalism," in The End of Ideology, p. 44.

31. Ibid.

32. Ibid.

33. Ibid.

34. Ibid.

35. "The Prospect of American Capitalism" initially appeared in the December 1952 issue of Commentary. Like "American as a Mass Society" and "The Breakup of Family Capitalism," it was later reprinted in The End of Ideology.

36. Bell, "The Prospects of American Capitalism," in The End of Ideology, p. 89.

37. Ibid.

38. From the standpoint of defining its focus, the chief contributors to The Radical Right are Richard Hofstadter and Seymour Martin Lipset. Other contributors include Bell, Peter Viereck, Talcott Parsons, David Reisman, and Nathan Glazer. The idea for the book, according to Bell, first arose in 1954.

39. Daniel Bell, "Interpretations of American Politics," in The Radical Right, p. 47.

40. Ibid.

41. Ibid., p. 48.

42. Ibid., p. 61.

43. Ibid., p. 68.

44.   Ibid., p. 71.
45.   Ibid.
46.   Ibid.
47.   Ibid.

5

The Function of the End of Ideology in the West

A Profile in Conflicting Moods

The End of Ideology was published after Bell left Fortune, but, with two very notable exceptions, the essays that make up that book were written during the 10-year period that he worked for that publication.

"Work and Its Discontents," is an essay that was completed in 1956, but it includes a key section from Bell's 1947 Commentary article, "Adjusting Men to Machines." "The End of Ideology in the West: An Epilogue" was a new essay. It was written in 1959 when Bell, as a fellow at the Center for Advanced Study in the Behavioral Sciences, was allowed by Columbia University to revise the other 15 essays in The End of Ideology so that he could receive a Ph.D. in sociology from that institution.

Accepted as a doctoral dissertation in 1959, The End of Ideology is a peculiar book. Despite the claim made by Bell in the book's introduction, "The Restless Vanity," the essays that make up The End of Ideology are not united by any one problem nor by any one mood. Instead there are 16 essays embodying a set of overlapping problems, issues, and themes. Not one but two underlying moods frame The End of Ideology. The most pervasive mood, a distinctly pessimistic one, was derived from Reinhold Niebuhr; the other was derived from John Dewey.

In fairness to both Bell and his critics (particularly C. Wright Mills and Irving Howe) the simultaneous presence of these divergently different moods ultimately serves to temper the results of any comprehensive evaluation of "The End of Ideology in the West: An Epilogue." It makes difficult the assessment of that essay in any other way than as an essay that is seeking to provide a balance between these two moods when in it Bell proclaims that the end of ideology "is not--and should not be the end of utopia as well."

In "The End of Ideology in the West: An Epilogue" Bell seeks to balance the fundamentally pessimistic mood that runs throughout the overwhelming majority of the essays in The End of Ideology with Dewey's optimism; an optimism that embodies an almost utopian faith in science and man. This interpretation of the "Epilogue," of course, only makes sense if we grant two largely untestable assumptions. The first is that, when Bell said that the end of ideology need not mean the end of utopia, he was not engaging in some exercise in rhetoric but making a statement that reflected deeper sentiments. The other assumption is that Bell knew enough about Karl Mannheim's distinction between ideology and utopia to know that utopias as "situationally transcendental ideas" are not ideas or plans whose costs can always be specified. If we grant that these are plausible assumptions (certainly in the case of the second of the two there is more than enough evidence of its plausibility, judging from Bell's use of Mannheim's analysis of Thomas Munzer and the Anabaptists to frame his study of American socialism), then it is legitimate for us to discuss "The End of Ideology in the West: An Epilogue" in these terms.

The Essays in The End of Ideology

It is one of the glaring weaknesses of "The End of Ideology in the West: An Epilogue" that one derives no immediate sense of its culminating quality when one reads it as an epilogue to the other essays in The End of Ideology. This is because the book as a whole does not present any uniform image of Bell, the intellectual, engaging in the intellectual, political, and emotional struggles that clearly defined his path to the idea of the "end of ideology." And yet when we read back through the prism of Bell's life, some of the essays not only register the effect of those struggles but also focus upon the central issues that sparked those struggles.

This is not to say that The End of Ideology stands

as some systematic exposition of Bell's life or, for that matter, of the times in which he developed his thought.   Nothing could be further from the truth. The End of Ideology has an internal coherence but that coherence is not one of revealing so much the line of development underlying Bell's struggles as it is of bolstering the conclusions he elaborated in the "Epilogue."   The initial chapters thus serve to make those conclusions sound inevitable and evidential.   In this sense The End of Ideology is very much a "thesis book." Its thesis contains a polemic.   The development of this polemic represents the book's primary purpose; the demonstration that some problems, especially the problems of planning, work, and management, have no final, total, and absolute solution but only partial and relative ones.

The starting point in reading Bell's life back through The End of Ideology is "The Mood of Three Generations."   What resonates in that essay is the strong distrust of communism that was one of the preeminent features of Bell's early New Leader writings.   As the words "ours is a generation that finds its wisdom in pessimism, evil, tragedy, and despair," would suggest, there is also in this essay a sense of the tragic.   It is the sense of no longer wanting to take chances or of making investments in political enterprises that do not specify, in advance, their costs.   Hardbitten, the essay recounts the frustrations and the anguish of a 1930s generation that has not forgotten the communist popular front tactics, the Moscow trials, and the Nazi-Soviet Nonaggression Pact.

There are two other essays that provide some glimpse into the experiences that were part of Bell's life in the 1930s.   One of the essays is "The Two Roads from Marx: The Themes of Alienation and Exploitation and Worker's Control in Socialist Thought."   The other is "The Failure of American Socialism," which is an abridged version of Marxian Socialism in the United States.

While the "Two Roads" essay provides liberal references to the Kronstadt rebellion and Trotsky's role in putting it down, the "Marxian Socialism" essay conveys the attitude of the socialist right wing or the "old guard" faction Bell supported after the 1936 split in the American Socialist party.   The attitude of the right-wing faction was that under Norman Thomas the Socialist party was becoming an irrelevant force in

American life. This attitude gave expression to the
belief that if socialism were to be made into an effective force some compromises with American labor leaders
were required even if this meant socialist support of
Franklin Delano Roosevelt and other liberal candidates.
This was a belief that Bell editorialized in the pages
of the New Leader.

Just as "The Failure of American Socialism"
touches upon Bell's New Leader period so too does his
critique of C. Wright Mills's The Power Elite in "Is
There a Ruling Class: The Power Elite Reconsidered."
It is one of the ironies of this essay that there is in
it no explicit reference to that period in the early
1940s when both Bell and Mills were writing articles
for the New Leader about the threat of monopoly capitalism resulting from the institutionalization of a
then emergent military-industrial complex. This is to
say that while Bell makes no specific reference at all
to the fact that, like Mills, he too at that time had
expressed the same basic concerns, fears, doubts, and
warnings about corporate capitalism that one finds in
The Power Elite.

Their once common approach provides a backdrop to
the drama that is played out by Bell's 1956 critique of
Mills's analysis of political power in postwar American
society. Bell rather condescendingly dismisses that
analysis as a "romantic protest" against the bureaucratization of American life. The drama centers on the
relationship between two intellectuals who went in
different intellectual directions during the 1950s.
Reunited at Columbia University, where they both taught
during the 1950s, their relationship, as we shall soon
see, personifies two sets of conflicts that resonate
through much of the end of ideology debate: the conflict between proponents of the elite and pluralistic
theories of American democracy and the conflict over
the relevance and future of socialism in the United
States.

While Bell's critique of Mills's The Power Elite
evokes memories of his New Leader writings and his
efforts, in general, to develop a theory of state
monopoly capitalism, his essay "Status Politics and New
Anxieties: On the Radical Right" touches upon another
period of his life in the 1940s when Bell became absorbed by the issue of anti-Semitism in the American
labor movement. In addition to containing large segments of his essay "Interpretations of American Poli-

tics," this essay also contains segments from a 1944 _Jewish Frontier_ article, "The Face of Tomorrow," that drew critical attention to this issue. Highlighted in these segments is Eugene Debs's mourning of the death of Tom Watson, a southern populist who succeeded in being elected to the United States Senate largely on the basis of the appeal of his attacks on Jews. The attacks portrayed the Jews as "the active agents of a closed conspiracy for world control."[1]

Touching upon this same 1940s period is the introduction to _The End of Ideology_, "The Restless Vanity." In this brief set of introductory remarks is a reaffirmation of the same Niebuhrian concept of alienation with its emphasis on alienation as "a positive role, a detachment, which guards one against being submerged in any cause, or accepting any particular embodiment of community as final," that one finds in Bell's 1946 essay "A Parable of Alienation."

While these essays touched upon one facet of Bell's writings during the 1940s, "Work and Its Discontents" touches upon another: the strong sense of indignation that characterizes his 1947 _Commentary_ article "Adjusting Men to Machines." The moral indignation centered on industrial psychologists and sociologists being concerned more with "what is" than with larger social issues and questions of moral values. "Work and Its Discontents" reaffirms Bell's attack on the human relations school. Large sections from Bell's _Commentary_ article were absorbed into it.

Bell's attack, it will be recalled, is upon technicians who seek to "adjust" the worker to his job so that the human equation will match the industrial equation. It is an attack against social scientists who work within a fixed ideological framework that serves to rationalize the claims and objectives of management rather than representing a genuine scientific effort to explore more human systems of work and management. Hence, it is an attack on a network of social scientists whose work ultimately serves to lend legitimacy and historical necessity to those claims.

But aside from constituting a reaffirmation of his 1947 polemic against the human relations school, "Work and Its Discontents" covers a lot of new ground. In it Bell elaborates his views on the problems of work satisfaction and planning in industrial societies. These views, however, register the effects of Bell's socialist training and, to varying degrees, the impact of John Dewey and Reinhold Niebuhr's work on his think-ing.

Evoked in "Work and Its Discontents" is a Marxian conception of work. It is evoked initially in order to refute the claims of David Reisman that the impersonal-ity of work in modern industrial societies should be viewed as a positive development that challenges the worker to live more creatively and find greater emo-tional fulfillment in leisure and play.2 Bell's Marx-ian conception of work treats work as an existential phenomenon. It locates humanity's potential for mean-ing in the work process itself and views play as having meaning only in relation to work.

Evoked too in Bell's repudiation of Reisman's claims are the normative conceptions of work elaborated by Sigmund Freud and A. D. Gordon, the theoretician of the Zionist cooperative communities. Both of these conceptions emphasized the therapeutic and regulatory benefits of work. Yet it was the Marxian conception of work that Bell appealed to most. Coupled with Dewey's philosophy of education (his philosophy of learning by doing) with its emphasis on the rejection of prefigured experiences in favor of the search for problems that called for new solutions, that conception helped set the stage for his critique of the "cult of efficiency" in the United States and the Soviet Union. It is in that critique that Bell elaborates his views on work satisfaction and planning and administration in indus-trial societies.

If there is any precedence for Bell's theory of the postindustrial society it is his critique of the cult of efficiency. Elaborated initially in "Work and Its Discontents" and later extended in the "Two Roads from Marx" essay, Bell's critique collapses capitalism and socialism into a single category. Distinctions are made between market and nonmarket economies but it is the concept of efficiency endemic to the United States and the Soviet Union that is highlighted as the common thread that makes the discussion of these countries in the same terms possible.

Highlighted in Bell's critique of the cult of efficiency is the inability of capitalism and socialism to substitute in the place of efficiency a more human standard of work performance and the failure of the unions in free societies to challenge the efficiency standard. Highlighted also is the moral bankruptcy of Lenin and the Soviet leadership in propagating that standard in the Soviet Union.

Far from being a negative critique in the sense of tearing at the foundations of popular conceptions of work and leaving nothing in their place Bell's critique of the cult of efficiency offers alternatives.   Struck by Charles Walker and Robert Guest's study of The Man on the Assembly Line, Bell advocates steps toward making factory work less wearisome.[3] In anticipation of Peter Drucker's work, Bell advocates job rotation and job enlargement as solutions to what management textbooks now refer to as "burnout." But Bell was pessimistic about those measures being adopted in the United States and the Soviet Union.

Ultimately, Bell's pessimism was fed by several wells.   There was no doubt in his mind that the determination of whether industrial societies would choose to adopt these kibbutzim-like measures on a wide scale, particularly at the cost of productivity, constituted a value problem that tested the limits of planning and rationality as specified by utilitarianism. "Should work be organized so as to increase output and decrease costs and--assuming these benefits are passed on--so that there is a larger product for society? Or should work be organized so as to benefit the individuals on the job? Some relative costs are the variable around which our utilitarian calculi revolve, who shall bear the costs, the consumer or the worker?"[4]

There was equally no doubt which way capitalist America would resolve that problem if it had preferences.   Historically, market societies have always resolved the problem of relative costs in the consumers' favor.   The reality is that under a competitive economy it is the only answer possible since no single company can be expected to take on the burden of increased costs unless all its competitors were to do likewise. Ultimately, the rejection of efficiency in favor of increased worker satisfaction could not be expected from individual companies in any market society to come. It could only come from the society as a whole; from the political process as it was made subject to the demands of the unions.

Bell's pessimism was also fed by the failure of the British and American unions to challenge the norms of efficiency dictated by the market society.   His pessimism was further fed by the success of Lenin and Trotsky in usurping the workers' councils and within a year of the Bolshevik revolution adopting efficiency measures that surpassed in harshness those employed in the West.

But if there was one central well that fed Bell's pessimism it was the relative absence of thought in socialism to the problems of planning and administration. It disturbed Bell greatly that socialist leaders "from Marx down sought to win millions of people for the idea of a new society without the slightest thought about the shape of that future society and its problems."[5]

If there is any one statement that conveys the pragmatic mood of Bell's "Epilogue" and the impatience with Marxist panaceas registered by that mood, it is the statement Bell makes in the "Two Roads from Marx" essay about the arrogance that conditioned the blind faith of the socialist theoreticians. Their arrogance is ultimately the same intellectual arrogance that Niebuhr located in Marxism and liberalism; it is an arrogance that can only serve to obscure the necessity for substituting utopian rhetoric with systems of planning calculated to facilitate solutions to basic administrative problems and tasks.

> In part, these men could do so, confidently, unthinkingly because of the apocalyptic belief that "the day after the revolution," rationality would make its heralded appearance on the historic scene and put all society aright. In a striking passage, Trotsky once described capitalism as an anarchic economic system "in which each man thinks for himself, and no one thinks for all." Under socialism, presumably, "one" would think for all. How the "one," the Universal Mind, would think for all was never elaborated. It was simply assumed that capitalism was basically irrational, and that the creation of a "social direction" would impose order on society.
>
> Although socialism today is largely identified with planning, there are few clues in the patristic writings as to what planning—the organization of production, the allocation of resources, the determination of wage payments, the supervision of work, the creation of new

products, the proportion of investment to
consumption--would mean.   The paucity is
extraordinary.[6]

It is one of the characteristic features of Bell's
writings, at least up to and including The End of Ideology, that where one essay ends another on frequently
begins.   This is certainly the case with "Work and Its
Discontents" and the "Two Roads from Marx."   There is a
firm line of continuity between these essays on the
subject of planning and administration.   The common
thread that Bell weaves through these two essays is his
attention to three themes that helped ultimately to
shape his perspective on the end of ideology.   The
first is the limits of reason and planning.   Integral
to Bell's elaboration of this theme was the realization
that what compounds and ultimately limits planning is
that men are not always rational, that they tend to
function and make choices in terms of their own particular and immediate self-interests, often without regard for the larger social good.   This realization
underlies Bell's analysis of Lenin's adoption and then
movement away from the utopian blueprint of the socialist society projected in his State and Revolution.   It
also gives impetus to the second theme that Bell elaborates in "Work and Its Discontents" and the "Two Roads
from Marx" essay: the necessity of "piecemeal" over
total planning as a condition for other industrial
societies avoiding the same fate that the "eschatologi-
cal visions" projected in State and Revolution had
brought to Russia.   The final theme was a familiar one:
the exhaustion of socialist and leftist thought in
general.   The absorption of the trade union into the
control system of the factory in both the West and in
the Soviet Union serves as the focus for Bell's elaboration of this theme.[7]

If there is one unifying theme to the great majority of the essays in The End of Ideology it is the
limits of planning at the substantive level.   Sometimes
explicitly, at other times implicitly, this is the
theme that resonates throughout the essays in this
book.   This is certainly one of the underlying themes
of "The Capitalism of the Proletariat: A theory of
American Trade-Unionism."   This essay sums up much of
what Bell had to say in his Fortune articles about the
political reality and constraints that, in his view,
defined the character of the American labor movement in

the postwar period. As in the _Fortune_ articles, Bell discusses the anti-ideological effects of trade union-ism on the labor movement. He concentrates much of that discussion on the tension between trade or market unionism and social planning unionism. Just as in those articles Bell's central point in the "Capitalism of the Proletariat" essay is that under trade unionism labor follows its own logic, its own rationality, one that is dictated by its own immediate economic inter-ests.

     "Crime as an American Way of Life: A Queer Ladder of Social Mobility" stands as the corollary to "The Capitalism of the Proletariat." Its basic point is that organized crime obeys its own rationality. "The Prospects of American Capitalism," "The Breakup of Family Capitalism," "Status Politics and New Anxie-ties," and "American as a Mass Society" also elaborate the limits of reason and planning theme. Each of these essay attempts to throw light on the irrational aspects of life that Reinhold Niebuhr emphasized in his cri-tique of Marxism and liberalism. Each of these essays, in other words, focuses on factors that mediate the success of total planning; factors that usurp the plan-ning process and render it subservient to grass-roots politics and ideological interests. Each focuses on such factors as fixed ideological thinking and status anxieties.

     One of the major problems in assessing the meaning of "The End of Ideology in the West: An Epilogue" as an epilogue to _The End of Ideology_'s 15 other essays is knowing where and to what extent each of the several themes elaborated by Bell in these and other writings from 1944 on, especially his article for _Jewish Frontier_, _Commentary_, and _Fortune_, enter into his con-struction of that essay. One of the distinguishing features of the final essay, the "Epilogue," is that much of it was written in a kind of intellectual short-hand, one that is hard to decipher without some aware-ness of both the social and historical background out of which Bell developed his views on the end of ideolo-gy and of the audiences to who he was writings.

The "Epilogue" as a Message to a
New Generation of Intellectuals

The reasons why much of "The End of Ideology in the West: An Epilogue" is expressed in an intellectual shorthand are varied. First of all, the essay is an epilogue to more than the 15 essays in The End of Ideology and Bell's personal experiences up to that time. It is also an epilogue to an era that spanned the 1930s, 1940s and 1950s. It expresses the different moods that shaped that era, especially for what Bell in his "The Mood of Three Generations" essay calls the "twice born" and the "after born" generations. The "after born" generation is the generation that Norman Podhoretz speaks of in a 1957 New Leader article, "The Young Generation of U.S. Intellectuals." Made up of intellectuals in their late twenties and early thirties, they were in his words the "non-generation."

A basic reason why much of the "End of Ideology" essay is written in intellectual shorthand is, in part, that it is a sermon written for an audience, namely Podhoretz and other intellectual spokesmen of the "after born" generation, who, presumably, know who they are and what the message of the end of ideology is. It is a commentary about them and the their feeling of having been "cheated" out of an "experience" and out of a "cause to believe in."[8]

Another reason for the shorthand character of the essay is that much of it is a polemic written for a relatively small audience who, having lived through the same experiences and debates that Bell participated in, presumably had a ready knowledge of the past intellectual controversies referred to in the "End of Ideology" essay. The most prominent controversy was the one that raged through the pages of Partisan Review and the New Leader in the early 1940s, the controversy between Sidney Hook and Reinhold Niebuhr over the extent to which Stalinism was the inevitable product of Enlightenment rationality in general and socialism in particular. It was a controversy in which Hook and his supporters rejected Niebuhr's anti-rationalist interpretation and substituted in its place the view that Stalinism was an historical aberration that had less to do with socialism than with the peculiarities of Russian history and culture. Finally, it was a controversy in which Hook accused Niebuhr and his supporters of abandoning the struggle to effect through science and planning a more rational and orderly world. In short, he accused them of a "failure of nerve."9 Bell's use of this phrase in the opening page of the "Epilogue" is a distinct reference to the Hook-Niebuhr controversy. The reference is not without significance since, as we shall shortly see, "The End of Ideology in the West: An Epilogue" can be understood as a reaffirmation of Hook's defense of liberalism and the scientific method against religious and ideological extremism.

A third reason for the cryptic character of the "Epilogue" is the fact that it contains a number of arguments that were fully developed in the other essays that appeared in The End of Ideology. Often these arguments are scarcely developed; they serve only as brief outlines and general reformulations of the arguments to which they refer. Thus, what emerges in "The End of Ideology in the West: An Epilogue" is that ideas and arguments are presented in a fashion that presumes that their context and content are already familiar to the reader.

A final reason why much of the "Epilogue" was expressed in intellectual shorthand relates to style. When Bell chooses, as in his analysis of the Marxian origins of ideology, he can be very thorough; but when he chooses to employ literary and journalistic flair he can be, and often is, elusive. As in much of his writing, there is a preference in the "Epilogue" for turning a phrase and for embellishing an idea so that it becomes invested with dramatic force and literary imagery. Sometimes this is done at the price of straightforward reasoning and clarity. The result is that we are presented with ideas that often have more force than precision.

As an intellectual sermon or message delivered by a member of one generation to another, "The End of Ideology in the West: An Epilogue" is addressed to two new generations, one an American, the other a European generation. The American generation was made up of intellectuals in their twenties and early thirties; they perceived themselves to have been cheated out of the "experience" of the thirties and out of a cause to believe in. They were the "after born" generation; the "restless generation" made restless by their "inability to define an enemy."10

The European generation was a new generation of intellectuals that Bell, in "The Mood of Three Generations," associates with "New Left" publications:

University and Left Review in England and Arguments in
France. The writers associated with these journals,
like those intellectuals associated with the American
publication Dissent are, in Bell's words, made up of
individuals "at odds with the doctrinaire interpretation of orthodox Marxism and at one with the search of
a new socialist humanism."11   However, there were
fundamental differences related to circumstance and
temperament between those intellectuals associated with
other publications.

Dissent was started by Irving Howe and Lewis
Coser. Both had been actively involved in non-Stalin-
ist communist movements and were, thus, "long schooled
in the doctrinal debates of Marxist exegetics."12
University, Left Review, and Arguments were all started
by younger men, who, because of their age, missed the
old ideological debates that Howe and Coser had been
active participants in. While Dissent was "a magazine
of the epigone, the after-born, jejune, and weary,"
these other publications "are intense, frenetic,
naive, bursting out with a new sense of autodidact
wonder about theoretical issues that have been wrangled
over by the Left twenty years before."13   In the case
of University and Left Review, these were intellectuals
whose search for a new socialist humanism was generated
by Khrushchev's admission that Stalin had thousands of
innocent communists put to death and the unrest that
admission generated in the communist world.   In the
case of Arguments, these were intellectuals whose
search was generated by the brutal suppression of workers in Poland and Hungary.14

In "The End of Ideology in the West: An Epilogue"
Bell lumps the American and European generations of new
intellectuals together. In doing so, he presents cryptic references to an assumed knowledge of the critical
events and debates of the past that may not have been
appropriate for these new audiences.

It is not without significance that Bell in the
"Epilogue" lumps these two generations together. Neither had a "meaningful memory" of the old ideological
debates that had consumed the passions of an older
generation in the 1930s and 1940s. Each of them was
made up of intellectuals, who, with no "secure tradition to build upon," were "seeking new purposes within
a framework of political society that has rejected,
intellectually speaking, the old apocalyptic and chiliastic visions."15   And if those descriptions were to

be believed, each of them needed an elder's patient counsel.

In offering the "Epilogue" as a message from the "twice born" to the "after born," Bell, on the basis of his own experience and authority, is providing both with a coda that was largely derived from his 1957 essay "The Mood of Three Generations." The coda is in part a reaffirmation of Reinhold Niebuhr's argument that life offers no final or total solutions. In greater part it is a reaffirmation of Sidney Hook's argument that the disavowal of liberalism and the scientific method in favor of religious and political extremism constitute a "failure of nerve" that would ultimately serve to undermine liberalism and the commitment toward rationalism and progress that it embodied.16 But the coda Bell offers the "after born" generation was also a response to Lewis Coser's 1956 Dissent article "What Shall We Do?" The article calls for veteran radical intellectuals to dedicate themselves to "maintaining, encouraging, and fostering the growth of the species radical."17

The coda that Bell offers to the restless generation is very simple: do not trust the communists. The desire for social change is a legitimate one but it must be tempered by a realistic sense of what can and cannot be done through science and planning. The communists will offer more than they can deliver. They will exploit your talents, your zeal, and your desire for "an experience" for their own political ends. Do not make the same mistakes that your elders made; learn from our mistakes. Build on our experiences, on our mistakes; don't suffer the same pain we suffered during the 1930s and 1940s. While liberal America is far from being the perfect society, it at least is pointed in the right direction; it at least offers you the basic freedoms that communism, in the name of expediency, will consistently deny you. Do not leave home; it is in liberal American that the utopian visions of Marxism and socialism can best be approximated. It is liberal America that has come the farthest in the realization of those visions.

The coda is filled with historical and political references. Included are references to the Moscow trials, the Nazi-Soviet Pact, the concentration camps, the suppression of the Hungarian workers, and the relative success of the Western democracies in promoting social reforms through the Welfare State. These ref-

erences document the sources for the descent of the
"old left" from the "faith ladder" that Marxism and
socialism had offered them in the 1930s. Ultimately,
it was the wisdom of the "old left" to realize that it
could no longer continue to climb a ladder "which in
its vision of the future cannot distinguish possibilities from probabilities, and converts the latter into
certainties."[18]

Bell's coda to the restless generation is tempered
by the sense that despite the words of warning, the
restless generation would pursue its own course. Ultimately, it would be their drive for passion that would
compel them, not history. His coda is also tempered by
the recognition that, while "social reform does not
have any unifying appeal, nor does it give a younger
generation the outlet for 'self-expression' and 'self-
definition' that it wants," in the absence of an "easy
left formulae for social change" and a utopia, it is
the only meaningful course open.[19]

In the face of these political lessons he offers
the restless generation, Bell argues that the pursuit
of social reform and the realization of the end of
ideology that served as its necessary precondition need
not mean the end of utopia, for while "the end of
ideology closes the book intellectually speaking, on an
era, the one of easy 'left' formulae for social change
. . . there is now, more than ever, some need for
utopia, in the sense that men need--as they have always
needed--some vision of their potential, some manner of
fusing passion with intelligence."[20]

If Bell's counsel is marked by the patience of an
uncle for an intemperate nephew it is also marked by a
father's sternness toward a son who has turned away
from the faith of his fathers: a faith that dictates
that the son not tear down what has come before him.
Thus, Bell's coda comes with a warning that at the same
time is both explicit and vague; a warning that implies
that the restless generation had a moral responsibility
that it could not, in the name of progress and expedience, turn its back upon.

> . . . If ideology by now, and with good
> reason, is an irretrievably fallen work,
> it is not necessary that utopia suffer
> the same fate. But it will if those who
> now call loudest for new utopias begin to
> justify degrading means in the name of

some utopian or revolutionary end, and
forget the simple lessons that if the old
debates are meaningless, some old verities are not--the verities of free
speech, free press, the right of opposition and of free inquiry.[21]

In a similar vein Bell warns that while it is true
that "there is now more than ever some need for a
utopia," the tragic events of the 1930s and 1940s have
dictated that "the ladder to the City of Heaven can no
longer be a 'faith ladder' but an empirical one: a
utopia has to specify where one wants to go, how to get
there, the costs of the enterprise, and some realization of, and justification for the determination of who
has to pay."[22]
    The coda that Bell offers his own generation, the
"twice born" generation, is less political than philosophical. Its terms are derived from his 1946 essay "A
Parable of Alienation" with its fundamentally Niebuhrian image of man as a creature that lives in a state of
anxiety brought on by his inability to know and, hence,
accept his limits. It is the Augustinian image of man
as a creature that must explore and test those limits
but who can only overcome his anxiety through faith.
While the specifics of this theme are developed in "The
Mood of Three Generations," it is reinvoked by Bell in
the "Epilogue" as a way for the "old left" to gain
perspective on the "New Left." That perspective
touches upon their own experience. They, like the
"after born" generation, had a deep-seated need for a
profound "experience," for the opportunity to explore
an exciting but unknown and untested world. Like the
"after born," they once had an impatience for social
reform; an impatience that was born out a need, untem-
pered by experience and wisdom, for radical social
change. The message that Bell offers his own generation is simply this: just as it is true that "no generation can be denied an experience, even a negative one"
it is equally true that

a radical is a prodigal son. For him,
the world is a strange place whose con-
tours have to be explored according to
one's destiny. He may eventually return
to the house of his elders, but the return is by choice, and not, as of those

who stayed behind, of unblinking filial
obedience. A resilient society, like a
wise parent, understands this ritual,
and, in meeting the challenge to tradition grows.23

That Bell's coda to the "twice born" generation
evokes much of the spirit and sadness of "A Parable of
Alienation" is indisputable. The reality is that that
1946 essay serves as a footnote to "The Mood of Three
Generations" and, in turn, the "Epilogue." But the
weaknesses of the "Epilogue" are more than the total of
the weaknesses of that earlier **Jewish Frontier** essay.
They are less the weaknesses of alienation than of
orthodoxy.

The weaknesses to which we refer are tied to the
weaknesses manifest in Bell's warning to the restless
generation. That warning was distinguished by Bell's
failure to mention who he is referring to when he
cautions those who would call loudest for new utopias
not to forget the painful lessons of the 1930s and
1940s. Those weaknesses are tied to Bell's failure to
specify anywhere in his "The End of Ideology" essay the
limits of his conception of utopia when measured
against Karl Mannheim's analysis of utopian thought.
Ultimately, Bell's weaknesses are the weaknesses of a
man given less to Hellenism than to Hebraism; a man
given less to the explicit use of language and concepts
than to the eclectic use of concepts that serve more to
convince than to illuminate.

In Mannheim's emphasis utopias were situationally
transcendental ideas, that is, ideas that by definition
cannot specify their costs in existing terms. Bell's
omission of this idea is somewhat ironic since much of
his analysis of ideology in the "Epilogue" explicitly
draws upon Mannheim's distinction between the particular and the total conceptions of ideology. The fact is
that throughout **The End of Ideology** book, he relies on
definitions of ideology and utopia that are either his
own creations or that lie outside the sociological
tradition. In Marx's sense of the term, an ideology
meant a political theory that justified the past, and a
utopia meant an "impossible dream." Mannheim, who gave
conventional meanings to both terms, defined an ideology substantively as a legitimating theory for the past,
and utopia as a legitimating theory based upon images
of the future. Bell's concept of ideology is his own

creation, referring to what in both Marx's and Mannheim's terms would be a utopia. Bell's notion of utopia refers directly to Marx's definition but only touches upon Mannheim's definition of a utopia.

The Marxian and Mannheimian notions of ideology (a justification of the past) do not exist in Bell's work nor does the notion of a utopia as a guide to short-range, piecemeal planning exist in either Marx's work or in Mannheim's sociology of knowledge. In giving these conventional terms new meaning, Bell undoubtedly confused a whole generation of critics who read conventional meanings into his intellectual creations. It is that confusion that gives some measure of the weaknesses of Bell's end of ideology thesis.

Weaknesses in Bell's End of Ideology Thesis

While his "The Mood of Three Generations" essay helps clear up some of the vagueness associated with his warning to the restless generation, the vagueness associated with Bell's use of the term utopia cannot be so readily overcome. It is one of the major weaknesses of the "Epilogue" that for all the attention that he gives to clarifying the different uses of the term ideology and to Mannheim's writings on the subject there is no attention given in this essay to the German sociologist's writings on utopian thought. Similarly, it is one of the major weaknesses of the "Epilogue" that Bell never explicitly defines his use of the term utopia.

There is a presumption on Bell's part that utopias are visions of the future that can specify their costs in existing terms. This leads us to suspect that it is a conception inspired by Dewey but expressed in Marx's and Mannheim's language. Yet it is one that owes more to Bell's interpretation of Dewey's philosophical and educational writings than it owes to Dewey himself. But the fact that Bell never deals with Mannheim's conception that utopias, by definition, cannot specify their limits and their costs cannot be underestimated. It serves to weaken the "Epilogue" immeasurably.

Instead of challenging Mannheim's conception, Bell in the "Epilogue" evokes, against the anti-rationalist stoicism and the tragic sense of life that permeates Reinhold Niebuhr's writings, a reaffirmation of Sidney Hook's arguments in favor of pragmatism and limited planning. Hook's argument, as elaborated in his "The New Failure of Nerve," is marked by its Deweyian faith in the capacity of man to effect change through a scientific or experimental philosophy of life. In this philosophy all values are tested by their causes and consequences. Rational solutions could thus be found to long-standing social problems like poverty and unemployment. If not in actual wording then certainly in spirit, this is also the argument that Bell, in his "Two Roads from Marx" essay, uses to justify his preference for piecemeal planning against the allure of total planning. This argument resonates through his proclamation that "one need not accept the fatalism of the machine process--or wait for new utopias in automation--to see that changes [in the nature of the work process] are possible."[24]

Yet forgotten in his restatement of Hook's argument is any serious reflection about utopias being situationally transcendental ideas that necessarily do not specify their costs in calculable terms. Moreover, there is no serious reflection in the "Epilogue" about what the absence of utopia as specified by Mannheim would mean. In this context, it is worth remembering that one of the principal dangers that Mannheim warns about in Ideology and Utopia as is noted in Chapter One, is that the disappearance of utopia would hinder humanity's social development, reducing it to "a thing," and making man a "creature of impulse." Ultimately, it would result in humanity forfeiting its ability to shape the future through the kind of rational control that comes with an understanding of the past. "Man would lose his will to shape history and therewith his ability to understand it."[25]

This observation is by no means incidental. Ultimately, what lends intellectual authority to the charges made by critics of the end of ideology like C. Wright Mills, Dennis Wrong, William Delaney, and Stephen W. Rousseas and James Farganis is that nowhere in "The End of Ideology in the West: An Epilogue" does Bell weigh the intellectual and political limits of his conception of utopia against the conceptions outlined by Mannheim in Ideology and Utopia. Nowhere in the essay does Bell weigh the effect of his conception of utopia in barring from consideration possible political approaches to problems that fall outside the range of short-term rational calculations based upon established paradigms of social analysis. Theologies, in the conventional meaning of that term, also serve functions, albeit short-term, specific ones, in providing a basis for the calculation of the costs of social action.

As discussed at the end of Chapter One, there is one central an overarching idea that underlies the charge made by Mills, Wrong, and these other critics of the end of ideology. This is the idea that the end of ideology thesis is far from being an independent assessment of a set of social and historical trends that culminated for the moment in the end of socialist political activity among Western intellectuals. The end of ideology thesis is itself an ideology; an ideology that serves to rationalize a set of unstated but distinctly political and ideologically conditioned functions. Within this context, it should be remembered that while Mills saw the end of ideology as an ideology of complacency, one that, in having made a "fetish of empiricism," provides both the "intellectual celebration of apathy" and the rationalization of the status quo, Wrong saw the "end of ideology" as an ideology of "moderation," one that serves to justify a retreat from politics. Similarly, it should be remembered that in expanding on these charges William Delaney viewed the end of ideology thesis as an argument that embodies a preference for utilizing administrative rather than political means to secure solutions to fundamentally political problems, while Rousseas and Farganis viewed the end of ideology as an expression of an "ideological positivism," one that amounts to nothing more than "an unthinking apologia for whatever is."26 Like Andrew Hacker, Rousseas and Farganis viewed the end of ideology thesis as an ideology that would justify the end of all utopian thought.

These are severe charges. So too are the charges of Peter Gay and Irving Howe that the end of ideology is a statement shaped by ex-radicals who expressed through it a self-hatred of their own radical past. But they are all charges that can justifiably be leveled at Bell, not only because they are necessarily true.

Given Bell's basically long-standing commitment to the mixed economy and to a two-party system based on the British model, the efficacy of Peter Gay's and Irving Howe's characterization is questionable. One cannot, as does Job Dittberner, imply a recent "conversion" by Bell to democratic planning. Bell's "conversion" from Marxism occurred before 1944. Since this is the case, the charge of overreaction certainly appears to be of marginal importance.

The charges made by Mills, Wrong, Delaney, and Rousseas and Farganis are each well deserved. Bell completely left himself open to these charges. He left himself open to them when he failed to weigh the intellectual and political limits of his conception of utopia in blocking from consideration possible political approaches to problems that fall outside the range of short-term rational calculation. Not only did he leave himself open to these charges, but partly for the reasons given and partly for reasons that shall be discussed later, he invited them.

Another aspect of Bell's work that contributes to the power of the charges leveled against his end of ideology thesis is that, in developing his thesis, Bell presents the basic speculative images subsumed in his argument as a set of facts. Nowhere in the "Epilogue" does Bell discuss the debates that surrounded these images when they were first presented in his earlier essays. In the ultimate essay, the "Epilogue," he presents what he originally defined as conjectures, speculations, and theories as facts. His definition of the "broker state" as the model for the legitimated plural Welfare State, the enthusiasm of intellectuals for the Welfare State and Bell's earlier reasons for the failure of socialism as a political movement were each subsumed as facts in his arguments for the end of ideology. The fact that each in their own way served to frame his construction of that argument with all that it means (namely, that aside from being a summary statement about a set of social and historical trends about a relatively brief period in Western history, Bell's end of ideology thesis is also a positive evaluation of those trends) is extraordinarily important. This collapsing of ideas of value and facts is extremely important because it allows us to define Bell's construction of the end of ideology argument as constituting, more than anything else, a two-sided polemic.

Bell's construction of the end of ideology argument as it is elaborated in the "Epilogue" is a polemic against the editors of **Dissent**, Irving Howe and Lewis Coser. It is also a polemic against intellectuals like Dwight MacDonald, the once radical polemicist who in the 1950s dropped out of political journalism to join the staff of **The New Yorker**. It is a polemic directed toward a representative figure of the "twice born" generation: one who, like many of his "twice born" fellow travelers had in frustration turned away from politics and embraced other, lighter, pursuits. Their fall, in Bell's words, "from innocence came in the horrifying realization that violence--and the drive for domination--was a craving in man, and, following Hannah Arendt, that modern society had become a bureaucratized apparatus for periodically, and necessarily, evoking and suppressing such violence."[27]

The polemic that Bell directs toward MacDonald is a simple and straightforward one. Its message is that even in a world filled with disillusionment and pessimism one must try to remain involved in politics despite its violence and betrayal. The political images evoked in the pessimistic theories of man and society described by Arendt "are conceptions that derive from heroic and ultimately romantic images of life and man's place in it."[28] In the final analysis the truth of such theories remains a difficult and perhaps unresolvable problem. Against these theories, to see "politics on the more mundane, and civil, level of reconciling diverse interests may be naive. But this has been the British experience and McCarthy apart, that of America, too."[29] If MacDonald could be excused his extremism and subsequent frustration with American politics it was because he was a "journalist-cum-intellectual" and not a social scientist. Ultimately, what separates the scientist from the intellectual is that while "the intellectual takes as his starting point his self and relates the world to his own sensibilities; the scientist accepts an existing field of knowledge and seeks to map out the unexplored terrain."[30]

Implicitly, Bell's polemic against MacDonald is as much a polemic against "twice born" generation social scientists who withdrew from politics as it is against MacDonald. In general, it is a polemic against apathy. That polemic has the same moral quality and the same faith in science and liberalism that framed Hook's polemic against Niebuhr as the former developed that polemic in "The New Failure of Nerve." Just as Hook's polemic was distinguished by its reaffirmation of Deweyian pragmatism and liberalism in the face of Niebuhr's negativism and his retreat from radicalism to theology, so too Bell's polemic against MacDonald is a reaffirmation of science and liberalism in the Deweyian mode. But Bell, in making these programmatic charges against MacDonald, fails to see, as he did in the case of his charges against the editors of <u>Dissent</u>, the substantive, political consequences of his purely programmatic position.

Bell's polemic against <u>Dissent</u> is somewhat more involved than his polemic against MacDonald. In part, the polemic against <u>Dissent</u> centers on that magazine's attacks on <u>Partisan Review</u> and <u>Commentary</u>. <u>Dissent</u>, charges Bell, attacked these publications "for not being radical enough."[31] But that is all that it did: "there was little in <u>Dissent</u> itself that was new; it never exemplified what it meant by radicalism; and it has not been able, especially in politics, to propose anything new."[32]

In greater part, Bell's polemic centers on what he considered <u>Dissent</u>'s misguided attacks against the quality of American life; attacks that were conditioned by its conception of American as a mass society. Bell's argument is that, while <u>Dissent</u>'s attacks on "advertising, the debaucheries of mass culture, and the like" smacked of radicalism because they were generally couched in the language of the early Marx with his emphasis on alienation, those attacks completely missed the mark. They made advertising and other problems of mass culture something they were not. Hence, in the final analysis they ended up obscuring the fundamental nature of those problems and of the contemporary task of radicalism in the United States. The point, explains Bell, "is that these problems are essentially cultural and not political, and the problem of radical thought today is to reconsider the relationship of culture to society."[33]

It might be argued that in giving himself so fully to polemics Bell neglected his role as a scientist. Ultimately, his failure to consider Mannheim's work on utopias might be thought of in that light.

Toward a Final Assessment

While we have been severe in criticizing Bell over the shortcomings of his presentation of the end of ideology argument, an argument that as Bell properly makes note of in his "The Mood of Three Generations" essay captures the mood and political stance of <u>Commentary</u>, <u>Partisan Review</u>, and the <u>New Leader</u>, our final estimate of Bell's efforts to bring new light to the argument must be tempered. In Bell's defense, it must be pointed out that in none of his writings up to and including "The End of Ideology in the West: An Epilogue" does he write as a theoretician, which is to say that nowhere in his writings up to and including 1960 does he write as a man who considers all the alternative arguments that would result from his failure to anticipate criticism.   Bell writes as an advocate and as a journalist, one who is pushing a position that he firmly believes in.   When he does write as a social scientist he writes as a scientist who seeks to invoke a paradigm, a scientific framework, that conveys what he thinks is problematic and therefore worth knowing. He is, hence, always the polemicist but sometimes the scientist.

As a social scientist Bell has tried to reconcile his inherent pessimism and caution about man with his faith in rationalism.   His belief that the end of ideology need not mean the end of utopia seems to be the product of his efforts to reconcile this seeming contradiction, a contradiction that ultimately derives from his efforts to reconcile the pessimism of Niebuhr with the optimism of Dewey and Hook.

Within this context, it is to Bell's credit that he could, within the framework of the end of ideology, intellectually reconcile for himself the seemingly contradictory positions that were at the heart of the Hook-Niebuhr debates on the Soviet Union.   In focusing on the combined failure of liberalism and socialism to temper their faith in the inevitability of progress with a realistic perception of human nature and its irrational dimensions, Niebuhr repeatedly emphasized the limits of planning.   The most salient aspect of Dewey's and Hook's thought was that while providing a pragmatic basis for planning, they each rejected overarching, utopian, total planning.   Their notions of pragmatism and science emphasized not total planning but a series of plans each geared to the specific context and specific knowledge of those contexts.   Both Niebuhr and the pragmatists rejected utopianism in planning and focused on the importance of particular plans, not overall planning.   In this rejection of total planning Bell could reconcile the positions of Dewey and Niebuhr in the 1960s while still claiming support for Dewey's utopianism of method.

For Bell the series of short-term specific plans that are an alternative to overarching "utopian" planning are, among other things, a means by which he could intellectually cope with the pessimism that he and others could find in Niebuhr's work. In focusing on pragmatic planning Bell, it seems, is able to answer to his own satisfaction the criticism of rationality and planning that is explicit in Niebuhr's work after 1940. The solution of pragmatic planning thus enables Bell not to reject the heritage of liberal humanitarianism in response to his horror at the inhumanity of totalitarian planning as he perceived it in the Soviet Union, especially under Stalin.

Yet in a basic sense, any final assessment of The End of Ideology must weigh the success of Bell's writings on the end of ideology against his efforts to call for, through Deweyian pragmatism, some way of measuring values, some way of developing a scientific approach to planning. This is because what emerges in the final analysis is less a picture of the end of ideologies in the West than the image of the end of socialism in the United States as refracted through the eyes of an ex-socialist who remains in principle a firm advocate of large-scale, centralized planning. Like the image of the United States as a broker state, as a society that, while lacking a clear-cut philosophy of planning has all the same embraced the necessity of planning, this image seems clearly to be subsumed into Bell's construction of the end of ideology thesis. A comparison between his "Epilogue" and his "The Breakup of Family Capitalism" essay with its emphasis on the corporate managers and their search for the new ideology necessary to justify their power and prestige helps to substantiate this point. In comparing these two essays it becomes very clear that in "The End of Ideology in the West: An Epilogue" Bell is using the term ideology in a limited way, one that has a far more restricted application than the way in which he uses that term in "The Breakup of Family Capitalism" and one that bears the imprint of his earlier writings on the failure of socialism in the United States.

The final assessment of The End of Ideology must also clearly distinguish what this book is from what it is not. This book of 16 largely journalistic essays is, on one level, the work of a man who is seeking in the "Epilogue" to reconcile his own pessimism, his own doubts about humanity and the inevitability to progress, with the faith in science and humanity that Dewey's and Hook's writings on instrumentalism evoked in him as an intellectual whose roots rested in the socialist tradition. That tradition, of course, is distinguished by an overriding faith in the inevitablity of progress through science and planning. Bell's doubts are the doubts that Reinhold Niebuhr's writings echoed for him and for a number of other Jewish intellectuals.34

On another level, The End of Ideology is the work of a social analyst who is describing a number of changes in American society during the 1940s and 1950s and who is critical of existing social and political theory because of its failure to grasp adequately and explain these changes. These changes, as indicated earlier, included the decline of socialism, the final shift away from socialism to business unionism in the American labor movement, the emergence of the broker state, the existence of status anxieties as a result of prosperity and the absence of ideology, and the amorphousness of power in contemporary America and its relationship to the breakup of family capitalism in the United States. At this level, The End of Ideology is the work of a social analyst who, in describing these changes and in commenting on the shortcomings of existing social and political theory in embracing them, is calling for a new theory of American society, a new ideology, that would replace the myths and ideologies of the left and of the right. He is reissuing through The End of Ideology the call that rings through his work in the mid-1950s: the call for a new theory of social change.

Bell's call for a new theory of social change, as discussed in the last chapter, is the call for a theory that would provide the basis for making allocations of costs and benefits on moral and political grounds and would make new societal institutions clear to liberals, intellectuals, corporate managers, and family business operators. It would reconcile them to their emerging reality. Hence, The End of Ideology is the work of a social analyst who in 1960 had still not constructed his new theory of social change, one whose need he originally specifies in 1955 in The Radical Right and "The Breakup of Family Capitalism."

When understood in this light we can speak of The End of Ideology as a book that represents the efforts of a social analyst who, while intellectually reconciling for himself the struggles of his generation (the struggles over the meaning and limits of ideology when viewed against the background of the Moscow trials, the popular fronts, the Nazi-Soviet Pact, and the struggles over the meaning of Stalinism as elaborated in the Niebuhr-Hook debates), was establishing an agenda of work that remained to be completed. Hence, The End of Ideology should not be thought of as a finished work but as the work of a man who was at a midpoint in his intellectual career. It should be regarded as the work of an intellectual whose working agenda called for both the development of a new theory of social change and a new system of legitimacy for Welfare State planning, as well as for a new way of looking at the problems discussed by the mass society theorists (especially Howe and Coser); one that would take into account the changing relationship between culture and politics. The fact that The End of Ideology serves as a platform from which Bell could document in his own terms the need for such measures can scarcely be minimized.

The End of Ideology, above all, should be understood as the work of a moralist, of a man who, against his perception of the excesses of the 1930s and the realities of the 1950s, was trying to establish a political and moral basis for modern liberalism as a philosophy of political pluralism and limited social planning. At this level, it is the work of a man deeply touched by the tragic events of the 1930s and 1940s and of an intellectual moved to seeking a format against which a new philosophy of planning could be developed, one that would continue to safeguard the principles of free speech, free press, the right of opposition, and of free inquiry. These were the principles that Bell saw Lenin and Trotsky, in their unremitting commitment to total planning, all too willing to sacrifice. These were the "old verities" he sought to protect against the ravages of ideology and the newer emerging left. In conclusion, then, The End of Ideology is less the work of a scholar writing a systematic exposition on the meaning of ideology than of an intellectual defining a range of problems that, as we shall see in the next two chapters, would continue in the 1960s and 1970s to frame and underlie his writings on the postindustrial society.

The Staggered March toward Postindustrialism

In profiling Bell through The End of Ideology and defining him as a moralist who was establishing through that work an agenda of what remained to be completed in subsequent works, we have established a context. That context serves as a necessary starting point for undertaking the problem of determining whether the concept of the postindustrial society is an ideologically derived construction and as a consequence whether Bell can be characterized as an ideologist.

The answer, as we shall explain shortly, has less to do with the values embodied in Bell's argument about the end of ideology than with his efforts to develop, in the course of his work in the 1960s and early 1970s, a scientific approach to planning and to the problem of legitimacy in a liberal society. These concerns were the basic value problems embodied in the end of ideology argument. They involve the methods of effecting the choice of science over ideology and anti-rational stoicism, the need to develop a system of comprehensive planning without sacrificing the principles of free speech, free press, the right of opposition and of free inquiry. These problems pose questions of value that were absorbed into Bell's construction of the end of ideology thesis, the principal one of which is whether the benefits derived from the realization of these preferences will outweigh their potential costs: the abandonment of socialism and the aspirations it embodies.

The values and assumptions implicit in the questions of value that were absorbed into Bell's construction of the end of ideology were in part the values and assumptions of a social scientist who, like John Kenneth Galbraith, viewed the "broker state" as a desired end. In greater part, they were the values and assumptions of a man whose first impulse was to move slowly.

Bell's preference for moving slowly, for exercising caution in responding to social problems, was a value that conditioned much of his perspective about the end of ideology. It was a value that permeated his writings on socialism and the labor movement. It was a value that led him to frame his analysis of the decline of American socialism in terms of the Weberian distinction between the ethic of responsibility and the ethic of conscience. Translated into the everyday world of ideas, Bell's preference for moving slowly was a preference for removing passion from politics.   In the final analysis, it was a preference, a value, that led him to embrace the principle of the "broker state," with its emphasis on order and consensus, and to defend against the socialism of his critics the politics of American pluralism, with its emphasis on politics as a game played between different interest groups each of whom keeps the other in check through a self-regulating system of countervailing power.

Heavily associated with Bell's endorsement of the broker state are the same set of normative assumptions that framed Galbraith's theory of countervailing power. Implicit in the notion of the broker state was the assumption that the equilibrium effected by government between major interest groups through the adoption of a managed economy constitutes an optimal state of functioning.   While Galbraith assumes countervailing power to be a special good, Bell's treatment of the broker state rests on the assumption that the maintenance of countervailing power is necessary if the United States is to remain a liberal society.   An underlying assumption that frames both Galbraith's theory of countervailing power and Bell's notion of postwar America as a broker state is that countervailing power is the only method by which a decentralized decision-making process that is harmonious with American political values can be developed and maintained.   This may or may not be so.   However, it is treated by both Galbraith and by Bell as a given, as an unquestioned truth, an axiom whose validity is for them firmly grounded in American historical experience and values.

The identification of these values and assumptions fosters two questions that we shall seek to answer over the next three chapters.   The first is: do these same sets of values and assumptions help to frame Bell's construction of the concept of postindustrial society and if so, how?   The second question is: how do we reconcile Bell's predisposition to move slowly within the framework of the duality that marks his work up to 1960?   This duality is between the activism of John Dewey, with its optimism about humanity and the inevitability of progress through science and planning, and the pessimism of Reinhold Niebuhr, with its emphasis on the limits of planning and reform.

The answer to the first question ultimately rests in defining the concept of the postindustrial society and how it emerges in his work.   That answer also

requires an examination of the contexts in which the
term <u>postindustrial society</u> is used by Bell to elaborate an emergent reality. Much of his work in the
1960s and early 1970s is devoted to describing that
reality. The answer to the second question is to be
found in another area. It is to be found, as we shall
argue in the concluding chapter of this study, in
Bell's efforts to reconcile Hebraism with Hellenism and
temper the radical idea with the conservative impulse.

Notes

1. Daniel Bell, "Status Politics and New Anxieties," in <u>The End of Ideology</u>, p. 117.
2. Reisman developed this thesis in <u>Lonely
Crowd</u>. Reisman's argument is that it was a "fallacy of
misplaced participation" for social scientists to
grieve about the impersonality of the contemporary work
process. If the impersonality of the productive and
distributive machinery within modern society permitted
the worker to find emotional fulfillment in play and
leisure it also provided social scientists with the
opportunity to reassess the meaning of work and leisure
in a changing American society. For a further elaboration of this argument see Reisman, <u>The Lonely Crowd</u>
(New Haven, Conn.: Yale University Press, 1950), p.
318.
3. What particularly struck Bell about Walker
and Guest's <u>The Man on the Assembly Line</u> (Cambridge,
Mass.: Harvard University Press, 1952) was their descriptions of the ways in which the factory workers
studied would "bulk the line" in order to introduce
variety and assert their own work rhythms. Considerable satisfaction is evidenced in Bell's summary of
Walker and Guest's work. Bell, "Work and Its Discontents," in <u>The End of Ideology</u>, p. 262.
4. Ibid., p. 263.
5. Bell, "Two Roads from Marx," in <u>The End of
Ideology</u>, p. 367.
6. Ibid., pp. 367-68.
7. For Bell the story of the exhaustion of the
left in the Soviet Union was a short but melancholy
one. It began with the Kronstadt rebellion and ended
with the Sixteenth Congress of the Communist Party in
1930 when Stalin called for an attack on equalitarianism in wages and for measures to assign workers perma-

nently to their factories. Stalin's actions prepared
the way for the establishment of laws that required the
worker to obtain the approval of the factory supervisor
to change jobs. His actions also led to sanctions
against workers in plants that failed to meet their
production quotas along with stiff fines for lateness.
For Bell the exhaustion of the left in the Soviet Union
was, in great part, the story of the failure of Marxist
theoreticians like Lenin and Trotksy to ever successfully resolve the issue that the little known Polish
revolutionary Waclaw Machajski warned about in 1899
through his book The Evolution of Social Democracy.
(While Machajski was never translated into English the
ideas developed in it were made known to Bell principally through an article by Max Nomad, "White Collars
and Horny Hands," Modern Quarterly, Vol. 6, no. 3,
Autumn 1932, pp. 68-76). The issue was the growth of
bureaucracy and the entrenchment in it of a new class
of professional leaders. It was also a story about the
discontinuity between Marx's early philosophical writings with their emphasis on the relationship between
work and alienation and his economic writings. It was
a story about how, unpublished and unknown in the years
when "orthodox" Marxism and Leninism were developing,
Marx's early philosophical writings (Karl Marx and
Frederick Engels, The German Ideology, New York: International Publishers, 1947; Karl Marx, Economic and Philosophic Manuscripts of 1844, ed. Dirk J. Struik, New
York: International Publishers, 1964) could not be
integrated by socialist leaders with his economic writings. These writings, thus, could not be made the
basis of a new and more humanistic conception of work.
In the final analysis, then, the exhaustion of the left
in the Soviet Union was the tragic story about how the
failure to understand this relationship led to Marxist
thought developing along "the narrow road of primiti-
vist economic conceptions of men, property and exploitation, while another road, which might have led to
new, humanistic conceptions of work and labor, was left
unexplored." Bell, "Two Roads from Marx," in The End
of Ideology, pp. 386-87.

    8. Bell, "The Mood of Three Generations" in
The End of Ideology, p. 300.

    9. Originally used by the historian Gilbert
Murray in his characterization of the Hellenistic period the phrase is evoked by Sidney Hook in a 1943 article that was written for a Partisan Review symposium.

The title of the article and the symposium is "The New
Failure of Nerve."

10. Bell, "The Mood of Three Generations" in
The End of Ideology, p. 301.

11. Ibid., p. 308.

12. Ibid., p. 309.

13. Ibid.

14. Ibid.

15. Bell, "The End of Ideology in the West: An
Epilogue" in The End of Ideology, p. 404.

16. "The bankruptcy of Western European civilization," argues Hook, is "the direct result of the
bankruptcy of the scientific and naturalistic spirit."
Sidney Hook, "The New Failure of Nerve," Partisan
Review, January–February 1943, p. 9.

17. Bell, "The Mood of Three Generations" in
The End of Ideology, p. 311.

18. Bell, "The End of Ideology in the West" in
The End of Ideology, p. 402.

19. Ibid., p. 405.

20. Ibid.

21. Ibid., p. 406.

22. Ibid., p. 405.

23. Bell, "The Mood of Three Generations" in
The End of Ideology, p. 302.

24. Bell, "Two Roads from Marx" in The End of
Ideology, p. 391.

25. Karl Mannheim, Ideology and Utopia, p. 263.

26. Rousseas and Farganis, "American Politics"
in The End of Ideology Debate, p. 215.

27. Bell, "The Mood of Three Generations" in
The End of Ideology, p. 308.

28. Ibid.

29. Ibid.

30. Ibid., p. 306.

31. Ibid., p. 311.

32. Ibid.

33. Ibid., p. 313.

34. For a further elaboration of this point see
Judd L. Teller, "A Critique of the New Jewish Theology," Commentary, March 1958, pp. 243-48. See also Will
Herberg's "From Marxism to Judaism," Commentary, January 1947, pp. 25-32. In this article Herberg credits
Niebuhr with providing him with the recognition that
"the worship of a holy God who transcends all relativities of nature and history . . . saves the soul from
taking satisfaction in any partial performance, curbs

self-righteousness, and instills a most wholesome humility which gives man no rest in any achievement, no matter how high, while a still higher level of achievement is possible" (Will Herberg, "From Marxism to Judaism," Commentary, January 1947, pp. 27-28). Herberg also credits Niebuhr with providing him with the recognition that "the worship of a holy and transcendent God who yet manifests himself in history saves us alike from the shallow positivism that leaves nature and history and life all without ultimate meaning, from a pantheism that in the end amounts to an idolatrous worship of the world, and from a sterile other-worldliness that breaks all connection between religion and life" (Will Herberg, "From Marxism to Judaism," Commentary, January 1947, p. 28). Ultimately, the gist of both Herberg's and Teller's articles is that Niebuhr provided the modern Jewish intellectual with a way back to Judaism, one based on his own neo-orthodoxy.

6

From the End of Ideology to the Postindustrial Society

Definitions of the Postindustrial Society

Written roughly over the same period, The Coming of Post-Industrial Society and The Cultural Contradictions of Capitalism are both books of essays, the majority of which were written between 1964 and 1972. Together, these books provide the outlines of a theory of social change that Bell calls for in The End of Ideology. At the core of this theory is the concept of the postindustrial society.

Bell comes to use that concept as both a methodological construct and as a major substantive theory. Bell repeats in The Cultural Contradictions of Capitalism the same pattern that he first establishes in The Coming of Post-Industrial Society; he uses that concept in both ways without making the distinction clear. Over the course of both works, Bell defines the postindustrial society in nine sometimes overlapping but at other times distinct ways. To complicate matters, while it is most often defined by Bell as a theoretical construct, it is also defined by him as an emergent reality, one that has been realized in the United States.

As a methodological or "theoretical" construct, the postindustrial society is defined by Bell as a "standpoint" from which models and theories of social change could be generated and as a conceptual scheme that "identifies a new axial principle of social organization and defines a common core of problems which societies that become more and more postindustrial have to confront."1 As a methodological construct Bell also defines it as an "ordering device" one that attempts "to describe and explain an axial change in the social structure of the society."2 By "social structure," Bell means the total of a society's economic and technological activity, as well as its stratification system.

Finally, as a methodological construct the post-industrial society is defined by Bell as both an "ideal type" and as a "social system," one that "does not succeed capitalism or socialism but, like bureaucratization, cuts across both."3 As an "ideal type" it serves as a "specification of new dimensions in the social structure which the polity has to manage."4

As an emergent reality the postindustrial society is defined concurrently by Bell in The Coming of Post-Industrial Society as a "knowledge society," a "service society," and a "communal society."5 As an emergent reality he also defines it as a society that "in its initial logic, is a meritocracy."6 As an emergent reality the postindustrial society is defined by Bell as a "crescive, unplanned change in the character of society, the working out of the logic of socio-economic organization, and a change in the character of know-ledge."7

A principal reason why there are so many different characterizations and definitions of the postindustrial society in The Coming of Post-Industrial Society is that, much like The Cultural Contradictions of Capitalism and The End of Ideology, it is basically a collection of essays that were written for separate purposes over an extended period. Hardly finished works, The Coming of Post-Industrial Society and The Cultural Contradictions of Capitalism represent the working out of a broad set of often discrete ideas and themes that coalesce in the concept of the postindustrial society. In the process the concept becomes stretched and enlarged to the point that it often takes on new and sometimes contradictory meanings even within the same chapter.

It has been said of Bell that he is a writer who does not write books but one who produces "large thoughts that fill books."8 In terms of both The Coming of Post-Industrial Society and The Cultural Contradictions of Capitalism this is both an accurate and far-reaching assessment of Bell's intellectual and literary style.

In each of these books the concept of the post-

industrial society embodies an image of American society torn by tensions resulting from historically contradictory impulses and tendencies within it. It is an
image that was based on a set of interlocking ideas and
themes that Bell developed largely between 1962 and the
early 1970s. These ideas and themes concerned mass
society and culture, the growth of advanced technological systems based on the codification of theoretical
knowledge, the growth of the university as the "gatekeeper" of a changing stratification system, and the
problems involved in the long-range social forecasting
and planning. They also concerned the relationship
between technology and politics in a democratic society, the role of the corporation, and the tension
between functional and substantive rationality. Finally, these ideas and themes concerned the role of the
intellectual and the scientist in modern society, the
emergence of the New Left, meritocracy and the problem
of equality, the nature of liberalism and its philosophical presuppositions, and the problem of legitimacy
as related to modern liberalism.

The Coming of Post-Industrial Society and The Cultural Contradictions of Capitalism are thus closely
linked in theme and purpose. This fact raises an
important possibility. The concept of the postindustrial society may have been crafted to project a set of
images that would make the articulation of the public
household along the lines specified by Bell in the
concluding chapter of The Cultural Contradictions of
Capitalism, titled "The Public Household," both necessary and logically irrefutable. The ultimate test of
the plausibility of this assertion rests with an examination of the functions served by the postindustrial
society. It is, however, essential that preparatory to
that task we examine closely the arguments advanced by
Bell in support of the public household. Some of the
arguments will by now be quite familiar, others are
new. But they are all developed with the purpose of
highlighting the major conclusion drawn by Bell in "The
Public Household," which is that while the United
States has a mechanism for the satisfaction of public
needs and wants as against private wants, it lacks the
wisdom to use this redistributive mechanism effectively. Hence the need for a philosophy of the public
household. Similarly, it is important to trace the
evolution of this concept. Ultimately, it is only by
understanding what the concept of the public household

means as a response to the crisis of liberalism that Bell wrote about so prolifically during the 1960s that we can structure our analysis of the functions served by his use of the postindustrial society.

The Public Household: The Call for a New Public Philosophy

Like the concept of the postindustrial society, the public household is a concept whose construction emerges from Bell's earlier work. Indeed, if the concept of the postindustrial society originates, as Bell acknowledges, out of a set of ideas discussed in "The Breakup of Family Capitalism" the concept of the public household originates in an even earlier work,[9] Bell's 1949 essay "America's Un-Marxist Revolution."

It will be remembered that, in assessing the implications of the New Deal in "America's Un-Marxist Revolution," Bell wrote of America's lack of an integrative moral philosophy and of the failure of its policymakers to recognize that government planning presupposes some overall mechanism for making crucial decisions that balance the economy. These processes would result in an agenda of problems that the American body politic would have to begin solving if the United States were to survive as a democratic society.

In "The Public Household" Bell issues exactly the same warning. The tone, however, is very different. In the earlier essay Bell suggests that America was in the midst of a deep-seated moral crisis, but in "The Public Household" Bell is more definite. In that essay he warns, in very explicit language, that the United States is in the midst of a moral crisis, a "crisis of belief."

Bell again argues that modern liberalism has failed to come to terms with the realities of American life. It has failed to come to grips with the consequences of the liberal reforms of the last 40 years. This failure was reflected in the absence of a new public philosophy. It has also failed to recognize the preconditions for maintaining order in society.

In order to come to terms with the consequences of the last 40 years, modern liberalism, argues Bell, must recognize that the ideology of economic growth to which it has committed itself since the 1930s no longer serves as the basis for solving political problems.

Furthermore, it must recognize the reasons why the ideology of growth fostered in the West by the Keynesian revolution can no longer serve this function.

Because of that "revolution," the United States has undergone a transformation that has witnessed the preeminence of the public household, the national budget, over the domestic household and the market economy. The federal budget now came before these other sectors of the American economy and the motor force that drives them. The federal government committed itself in the 1930s to the establishment of a normative economic policy. In the 1950s it committed itself to a policy of underwriting the majority of scientific and technological research in the United States; and in the 1960s the federal government was committed to establishing normative social policies in the fields of health, education, and income maintenance.

The significance of these transformations is that it has given rise to a revolution of rising entitlements for all groups in the United States and a political state that in adjudicating the conflicting claims of the different constituencies that it serves "is at worst an arena of power and is at best a normative umpire."[10]

The public household rests in an understanding of the basic economic fact that in relation to productivity, wage increases, unit costs, and inflation there has been in the United States "a structural imbalance between the technological (industrial and scientific) sector and the human and governmental services sector."[11] The significance of this imbalance is that while automobile workers may demand and receive a 10 percent wage increase, that escalation need not represent an inflationary increase, while the same wage increase when extended to police officers or other municipal workers would more likely be inflationary. This is because labor costs in the service sector represent a significantly higher proportion of the total costs of services than do labor costs in the productive sector. The wage cost proportion is generally so much higher in service industries that it cannot be readily made up through increased productivity as in the productive sector.

Finally, economic growth can no longer serve as a political solvent because of double digit inflation. In contrast to the steady, albeit manageable inflation of 4 to 5 percent a year, which is an inevitable concomitant of growth, double digit inflation weakens the middle class and creates class war. This class war is "not primarily between employers and workers but between the middle class and the working class, in the arena of the state budget."12 Double digit inflation promotes political instability, intellectual uncertainty, and discontent, especially among groups favored in the past whose income instability makes them vulnerable to the erosion of purchasing power caused by inflation.

Modern liberalism must start thinking of the public household as being more than just the federal government or as a public sector alongside the market economy and the domestic household, that is, alongside the primary and secondary sectors of the American economy. It must, argues Bell, start thinking of the public household as a mechanism for reallocation and redress that can be effective only when it is based on sound principles of household management. But that thinking cannot take place in a vacuum. Ultimately, what America lacks most is "a political philosophy of the public household that provides rules for the normative resolution of conflicting claims and a philosophical justification of the outcome."13

If modern liberalism is to provide American with that philosophy, it must do its homework. It must start rethinking what the public household means. The problem of unbalanced growth and the revolution of rising entitlements demand no less. The demands made upon the federal government as a political marketplace cannot now be easily matched by the revenues available to it or by available sociological knowledge, and the politically unstable situation that the revolution of increasing entitlements has given rise to has been substantially reinforced by cultural tendencies that promote debt as a common way of life. At the same time, the intellectual establishment has contributed to the growing crisis. In its "loss of nerve" the university and the literati have shown, when confronted by the radical left, an eagerness to repudiate their own existence with the result that many college students who would normally move into elite positions now question the legitimacy of Western institutions.

If it is to face this growing crisis of authority, modern liberalism must start with the public household. That concept will help it to think of the problem of management in terms of needs and limits. It will help liberals to recognize that the only way to curb infla-

tion is to curb appetites, to set limits on acquisitive
behavior. Ultimately, the concept of the public household may help modern liberalism face the painful truth:
just as families have to learn to live within their
means, so does the economy. But even more is required.

If modern liberalism is to stem effectively the
tide of inflation and at the same time deal with the
crisis of authority that it faces, then it must create
a philosophy of the public household that states who
gets what, when, and where. In order to establish such
a philosophy, modern liberalism cannot look with much
help to classical political theory, laissez-faire liberalism or to Marxian socialism. Rather, given the
nature of the United States as a pluralistic society,
it must "accept the differences between men and establish which differences are relevant and legitimate for
the normative functioning of the public household."14
It must, in short, develop a philosophy of the public
household on the basis of the "principle of relevant
differences."15

Modern liberalism, Bell argues, must recognize the
sociological preconditions for maintaining order in a
society. It must recognize that all societies are
moral orders that, in the end, have to justify their
"allocative principles and the balances of freedoms and
coercions necessary to facilitate or enforce such
rules."16 Furthermore, modern liberalism must recognize that "the point of philosophy is that it states a
rational standard, provides for consistency of application so that actions are not arbitrary or capricious,
and establishes a normative justification which satisfies men's sense of fairness."17 Finally, modern liberalism must recognize that the preeminence of the
public household in American life has created new and
deep dilemmas for modern liberal society that require a
normative theory of the fiscal state that can, on a
"renegotiable basis," reconcile the faith common to
both classical liberalism and to socialist utopianism,
a faith in humanity's power to remake through reason
itself and society "with the knowledge of its
limits."18

"The Public Household," thus, sees Bell rework and
articulate more fully the "Un-Marxist Revolution" essay. In its emphasis on both the limits of reason and
on the temporal limits of any normative theory of the
state, Bell also extends the "End of Ideology" essay in
terms that reflect the sustained influence of both

Reinhold Niebuhr and John Dewey on his sociological work.

Yet, "The Public Household" is more than these extensions. It is also an attempt to develop, largely as a result of a polemic against John Rawls that he developed in The Coming of Post-Industrial Society and of his long-standing distrust of socialist utopianism, the conceptual groundwork upon which a philosophy of the public household can be developed that:

1. though "renegotiated in the renewable present, does not, [and] cannot, ignore the past";[19]

2. restates what the grounded values of the society are, and hence what it considers to be, legitimate claims;

3. provides decision rules for the normative resolution of conflicting claims made upon the public household by multiplicity of interest groups which make the United States a pluralistic society," and a justification of the outcome";[20]

4. provides some agreement upon "balance between equity and efficiency in the competition between social claims and economic performance";[21]

5. accepts "the tension of the public and the private, the dual roles of person and citizen, individual and group";[22]

6. provides the need for some "transcendent tie to bind individuals sufficiently for them to make, when necessary, the necessary sacrifices of self-interest."23

In this list of functions to be served by the philosophy of the public household, we have Bell's formal program for a system of Welfare State liberalism that will limit the inflationary thrust in the Welfare State created rising entitlements and make the federal

budget responsive to both the productive capacities of
the primary and secondary sectors of the economy. It
also may serve to limit the claims of less-productive
segments of the economy.

Bell's program is one that grows out of his assessment of the "crisis of liberalism" and his desire
to have a public household that can provide a definition of the common good and a system for the satisfaction of the private rights and wants claimed by individuals and groups on the basis of scarcity rather than
abundance.24

The fact that "The Public Household" can be
defined in these terms is a function of Bell's efforts
to specify, on the basis of the principle of relevant
differences, the dimensions upon which the determination of who gets what, when, and where can be made.
Ultimately, one might question the efficacy of that
distributive principle. One might also ask who will
determine what differences are "legitimate" for the
normative functioning of the public household and what
criteria they will use to make that determination.
Those questions are left unanswered. They are important questions, but it is not our purpose to pursue
them here.

Our purpose is to understand how much the concept
of the public household permeates Bell's work in the
1960s. Bell may have still thought that the end of
ideology was complete but he was not satisfied that
that was enough. Marxian socialism no longer posed a
threat, but threats to freedom and civility remained.
Indeed, with modernism those threats became more intense. In the 1960s nihilism and antinomianism threatened to do what Marxian socialism could not: destroy
the foundations upon which a philosophy of the public
household could be constructed. It threatened to
destroy liberalism. Herein lies the story of the
public household, the development of which can be
traced through a reconstruction of Bell's thought in
the 1960s.

Toward a Reconstruction of Bell's Thought in the 1960s

"No idea ever emerges full-blown from the head of
Jove, or a secondary muse."25 Bell uses these words in
The Coming of Post-Industrial Society to initiate a
discussion of the history of the postindustrial society

as a conceptual idea. Had he been considering the public household's history he might very well have used the same words.

Like the postindustrial society, the idea of the public household is one that slowly evolves in Bell's writings. It was an idea that was grounded in his analysis of modern liberalism. That analysis focuses upon America's need for a new national style and for a new public philosophy. At the same time, his analysis highlights modern liberalism's need for a new set of normative and planning guidelines.

The need of modern liberalism for a new set of normative and planning guidelines is an implicit theme of his 1962 essay, "The National Style and the Radical Right." The context for his elaboration of that theme was the "immediate crisis of nerve" produced by the fall of China, the frustrating stalemate in Korea, the proliferation of anti-American sentiment in third world countries, and the decline in American economic growth relative to the growth of the Western European economies.26 Shattered in the wake of these developments was American's classic national style with its view that "life was tractable, the environment manipulable and anything [was] possible."27 Each of these developments tested the principal assumptions upon which that style was based, namely, that experience would provide solutions for all future problems and that rising material wealth would dissolve all strains resulting from inequality.

What concerned Bell most about that style was its emphasis on the individual and its specification of a problem-solving approach that emphasized ad hoc compromise and day-to-day patching up of problems to the exclusion of long-range policy perspectives or appeals to first principles. America's classical national style was totally deficient. It was deficient because it no longer provided a realistic view of America. Rather than the individual being the chief unit of social action, one from which all planning must emanate, it was now the corporations, the labor unions, the farm organizations, and the pressure groups in general that had become the principal forces in American society. To the extent that individual rights exist as a factor in the political process they derive from group rights or have become fused with them. Yet "other than the thin veil of the 'public consensus' we have few guidelines, let alone a principle of distribu-

tive justice, to regulate or check the arbitrary power
of many of these collectivities."[28]

Given the inadequacy of America's national style
there was, implies Bell, a strong need for a new national style, one that could adequately respond to the
changing character and structure of postwar American
society.

> Styles of action reflect the character of
> a society. The classic style was worked
> out during a period when America was an
> agrarian, relatively homogeneous society,
> isolated from the world at large, so that
> ad hoc measures were a realistic way of
> dealing with new strains. As an adaptive
> mechanism, it served to bring new groups
> into society. But styles of action, like
> rhetoric, have a habit of outliving in-
> stitutions. And the classic style in no
> way reflects the deep structural changes
> that have been taking place in American
> life in the past quarter of a century.[29]

The fact that America lacked an adequate national
style was no small matter. Ultimately, what it meant
for Bell was that America had no distinct, clearcut way
of meeting "the problems of order and adaptation, of
conflict and consensus, of individual ends and communal
welfare, that confront any society."[30] "The National
Style and the Radical Right" thus point to America's
need for a philosophy of the public household.

In 1967 Bell asserted the need of modern liberalism to create a new set of normative guidelines to an
explicit level. He did this through an analysis of the
changing needs of the United States that he constructed
when as the chairman of the Commission on the Year 2000
he edited a report that detailed the Commission's findings: Toward the Year 2000: Work in Progress.

Though he initially questioned the capabilities of
the Commission to meet the goals specified by its
founder Lawrence K. Frank, Bell nonetheless undertook
the task of marshalling its members to facilitate the
accomplishment of those goals, including, in Frank's
words, "the Promethean task" of renewing American's
"traditional culture" and reorienting its "social order
as a deliberately planned process."[31] That task would

involve the formulation of a new and comprehensive political philosophy, one that, in Frank's words, "would formulate the assumptions of the pluralistic economy and the service society that is emerging."32 The agenda for the Year 2000 would constitute the first step toward meeting this need.

As part of his work for the Commission, Bell assessed the task that was required of him and its other members. He balanced the responsibilities that its implementation involved against his predeliction toward planning and his skepticism about any commission being able to accomplish the kinds of goals that Frank had in mind. He also made it very clear that his orientation was less directed toward renewing America's traditional culture and developing a new political philosophy on that basis than it was with concrete policy problems and with the need for laying the intellectual and technical foundations for meeting them.

In no way was Bell apologetic about his response. It emerged as a reaction to the inability of American policymakers to appreciate the need for comprehensive research and planning. In the introduction to the Commission's report Bell indicates that it was a reaction to the weaknesses of America's style.

> Like many of my sociological colleagues, I was appalled by the fact that the Kennedy and Johnson Administration had "discovered" the problems of poverty, education, urban renewal, and air pollution as if they were completely new. In typical American fashion, tremendous energy was suddenly mobilized to "solve" the problems. Although action is typical of the American style, thought and planning are not; it is considered heresy to state that some problems are not immediately or easily solvable. . . . All these newly discovered problems were, in fact, anticipated many years ago. Intelligent research and planning could have laid the groundwork for more effective programs [more than those initiated under the Kennedy and Johnson administrations].33

While Bell was skeptical about the ability of any commission to develop a new "social" philosophy, he never questioned America's need for such a philosophy. Indeed, in the body of the Commission's report Bell later voices agreement with Frank about "the need for some new philosophy that can guide society in the twenty-first century."34   Bell also indicates that the development of such a philosophy should be based on a comprehension of the changing nature of American society and be geared to meeting those problems that changes in the nature of American society could be expected to produce.

Foreshadowed in Bell's prescriptive statement was an analysis of the changing needs of American society that he developed in "The Year 2000--The Trajectory of an Idea." The significance of that analysis is that it highlights many of the same themes that Bell would later elaborate upon in <u>The Coming of Post-Industrial Society</u> and <u>The Cultural Contradictions of Capitalism</u>. These included the growing preeminence of intellectual technology and the increasing importance of the university in facilitating research and development.   Other themes included the significance of the shift in employment from the productive to the service sector; a shift that signalled the advent of the "post-industrial society."35 The centralization of the American political system was yet another theme.   That theme was coupled with Bell's emphasis on the increasing diffusion of existing goods and privileges. Both themes served as cornerstones for yet another theme: America's emergence as a communal society. The basis for Bell's elaboration of this theme was the Commission's projection that the goods and services necessary for the maintenance of the cities, the environment, and for quality education and medical care will increasingly be purchased jointly by the federal government, local government, and the individual. A final theme was "the growing disjunction between the culture and the social structure."36

Each of these themes are pursued by Bell in "The Trajectory of an Idea" in order to elaborate upon his central thesis, namely, that time was running out on the United States. Certain problems had to be faced immediately in order to eliminate conflict and social tension, the chief among them being the problem of reconciling conflicting individual desires through the political mechanism. The fact that the United States was becoming an increasingly more communal society made both the resolution of that problem and the problem of balancing social choice against individual values and preferences critical.

Ultimately, what compounded these problems was the increased levels of expectations encouraged by the American value system with its emphasis on equality. If there has been any one thing that has defined the American experience with democracy it has been that "what the few have today, the many will demand tomorrow."[37] Another compounding factor was the impact of the disjunction between America's culture and its social structure. The conflict between the social structure's "technocratic" mode and American's increasingly hedonistic and antinomian culture was inevitable. What remained was whether the tension arising from that conflict would deal a death blow to the university as the citadel of intellectual freedom and civility.

It was these themes that provided the background against which Bell defined the nature of America's changing needs. Planning and the efficacy of existing political mechanisms headed his agenda.

It was his view that forethought must be given to the impact that the diffusion of existing goods and privileges will have on American society. When "diffusion begins to take rapid sway (as has recently been seen in higher education), it changes the size and scale of the servicing institutions and, consequently, that institution's character."[38] Because diffusion has this impact, the United States has a strong need for anticipating the future. Forethought must also be given to the consequences that attend America's emergence as a communal society. Because the public sector will come to have a greater importance in determining the allocation of goods and privileges, one of the most pressing tasks facing the United States is the need for it to consider the adequacy of its political mechanisms. Finally, forethought must be given to the adequacy of planning mechanisms, "for in the decisions we make now, in the way we design our environment and thus sketch the lines of constraints, the future is committed."[39] Because the future "begins in the present," the most basic need that confronts American society is for some systematic effort "to anticipate social problems, to design new institutions, and to propose alternative programs for choice."[40]

The major result that emerges for our summary of Bell's work for the Commission on the Year 2000 is the image of a social scientist whose approach to the

Commission's tasks were consistent with his earlier perspectives toward the problems of the future. His basic premise was that, ultimately, "the problem of the future consists in defining one's priorities and making the necessary commitments."41 It is the image of a social scientist who, through this perspective, expressed a growing concern about the importance of establishing new normative guidelines for planning in order to prevent potentially explosive situations from being left unattended.

It is also the perspective of a New Deal liberal who rejected laissez-faire liberalism in favor of planning. But his emphasis on planning was not the ad hoc piecemeal intervention that had characterized federal legislation during the postwar period. Instead, what Bell wanted was for American society to make explicit its commitment to planning and for it to establish the basis for democratic planning within a public philosophy that would provide the guidelines for allocation and priorities within which such planning would operate. The public philosophy, once made explicit and diffused, would be the basis of a new consensus that hopefully would legitimate, would gather public support for both the planning process and for the allocations and priorities that would democratically be negotiated. In hoping for this transformation from the individualistic, hedonistic calculus upon which classical liberalism was predicated to democratic planning, Bell was aware of the resistances and the restraints planning would entail, but he hoped that by creating and diffusing the new public philosophy these resistances could be overcome and self-restraint would be facilitated.

Initially, Bell had been skeptical that any one commission could self-consciously undertake to effect a fundamental change in social values that would reverse the entire tenor of America's classic national style; but as he warmed to the task, he apparently lost some of these reservations. Yet Bell was attempting to state "first principles" for New Deal-like democratic national planning despite both his knowledge of the American penchant for pragmatic ad hoc individual and unideological approaches to action and his own earlier reservations about total planning. If nothing else, Bell was trying to create through the Commission's report a revolution in the style and content of the national consciousness of the American citizenry.

If Bell was somewhat tentative in suggesting that

American liberalism required a new set of normative and planning guidelines in <u>Toward the Year 2000: Work in Progress</u>, by 1974, the year in which he wrote "The Public Household," that tentativeness was behind him. Indeed, as we have suggested in a number of places, Bell, through "The Public Household," seeks to lay the conceptual framework for the development of those guidelines. Bell does this by specifying the dimensions along which a new philosophy of modern liberalism could be articulated, a philosophy that would reaffirm the importance of certain principles central to his image of a sound liberal society.

Although the differences between Bell's stance in these two works may be attributed to his skepticism about the prospects of a commission being able to develop such a philosophy, it may also be reasonably attributed to a new set of demands and struggles that emerged after the completion of <u>Toward the Year 2000</u>. These were demands and struggles that Bell comments on in a number of articles that he wrote in the late 1960s and early 1970s.

The University and the Failure of American Liberalism

The late 1960s was a turbulent period for the United States in general, and for American universities in particular. Together, the black power movement, the student protests of the Vietnam War, the draft, and the participation of some universities in government-sponsored, war-related research projects transformed many college campuses into virtual battlegrounds. The fact that institutions with established liberal traditions like the University of California at Berkeley, Cornell University, and Columbia University became centers of confrontationist politics puzzled many liberal social scientists. But not Bell.

With Irving Kristol, Bell edited a book of essays on the student protest movement. Appropriately enough the book was titled <u>Confrontation</u>. In their brief introduction to that book they trace the "generalized" sources of student unrest and resentment toward modern liberalism and the university in the 1960s. They focus in that essay on the effects of mass higher education, increased scholarly and professional specialization, and the effect that government-sponsored research in the universities was having in transforming the Ameri-

can university. Highlighted in their analysis is the
"sense of the failure of American liberalism," one that
the students "shared with the liberals themselves."[42]
Ultimately, what conditioned that attitude was the
failure of the United States to develop effective social programs in the 1960s to tackle the problems of
poverty, urban deterioration, and racial discrimination.

Highlighted also by Bell and Kristol is the competitive anxiety students experience as a result of the
demands placed upon them to get into "good" graduate
schools. That anxiety contributed to their skepticism
about American liberalism. It made them responsive to
the New Left's rhetoric with its emphasis on the dehu-
manizing aspects of capitalism and competition. Their
justifiable sense of neglect by their college profes-
sors only served to reinforce their anxieties and the
appeal of the New Left.[43]

Each of these factors together with the Vietnam
War and the draft provided the basis for the students'
discontent and restlessness. Ultimately, what concerned Bell and Kristol most about that discontent and
restlessness was the "sense of the failure of American
liberalism" that inculcated those intense feelings. It
was telling that while the failure of the Kennedy and
Johnson administrations' domestic programs was seen by
liberals as the product of "the inherent complexity of
our social problems, the lack of detailed social science knowledge as to how to cut into them, and the
shortage of trained administrators," it was seen by the
students as an example of the government having "copped
out" on its responsibilities.[44]

Fed by their skepticism of the government, their
malaise was predictable. The rest, the progression
from student malaise to outright rage and to the questioning of the legitimacy of all existing authority,
Bell and Kristol argue, followed its own inherent logic; one that, paradoxically, was "legitimated" by the
culture of American society.

> . . . What was originally concern over a
> specific set of identifiable and specific
> political issues (e.g., Vietnam, civil
> rights) has been overwhelmed by an onrush
> of anger, rancor, and generational rage
> born of seeming impotence. And what
> began, often, as an attack against the

> way in which authority has been exercised
> turned into an attack against all exis-
> ting authority.   Here, that mood merges
> into a historic cultural tendency that,
> in the name of attacking repression and
> taboos, has been anti-institutional and
> even antinomian.   And this leads to a
> paradox, for the most important aspect of
> student behavior is that, while its so-
> ciology and politics are easily ridiculed
> in intellectual terms, its temperament
> and its style are actually legitimated by
> the culture of the society.   This schizo-
> phrenia has often made it difficult for
> professors, themselves the products of
> that culture, to oppose the student
> style.[45]

In addition to tracing the "generalized" sources
of the student's unrest and resentment, Bell and Kristol use their introduction to Confrontation to define
the underlying functions of the politics of confrontation as it was principally employed by the New Left.
Couched in the language of democracy, the New
Left's politics of confrontation betrayed the spirit
common to democracy and liberalism.   Unlike the politics of confrontation practiced by the black militants,
theirs was not rational politics whose goal was the
satisfaction of grievances.   Instead, the New Left's
politics, Bell and Kristol argue, was a form of the-
ater, the ultimate goal of which was the destruction of
authority itself.   Ultimately, "the sweeping demand for
participation" that was the credo of the radical student body, circa 1969, was one that served to "mask" a
distinct ideological function: "a desire to disestablish and render illegitimate all existing authority."[46]
Foreshadowed in the introduction to Confrontation
is Bell's historical account of the spring 1968 Columbia University siege, "Columbia and the New Left."
More than just a firsthand account of the turbulent
events that followed the April 23 student rally organized by the Students for a Democratic Society (the
occupation of school buildings by black militants and
student radicals and the confrontation between the
police and the students), "Columbia and the New Left"
offers a set of personal reflections concerning the
Columbia University crisis and the university admini-

stration's handling of that crisis. It is also a part
of an ongoing polemic that Bell developed in response
to both the Students for a Democratic Society (SDS) and
to Zbigniew Brzezinski who, in a New Republic article,
"Revolution and Counterrevolution (but Not Necessarily
about Columbia!)," offers his own analysis of Columbia's handling of the student protests and building
takeovers.

In "Columbia and the New Left" Bell characterizes
Brzezinski's article as "a rather Machiavellian essay
written from the balcony."47 He singles out Brzezinski
for defining the Columbia University siege in the same
terms that SDS had used to initiate the violence at
Columbia, namely, that the university was a microcosm
of American society. Bell's argument is that, while
Brzezinski's thesis on the university's handling of
events contains some critical insights into the failure
of the European democratic regimes in the 1930s to
effectively combat anarchy and fascism, it completely
misses the point about Columbia.

In drawing upon the European experience, Brzezinski attributes the deep "crisis of values" at Columbia
to the failure of the university administration to act
quickly and decisively to suppress the student revolution. In the course of developing this thesis, Brzezinski, at the time a colleague of Bell at Columbia,
also argues that in the revolutionary process "legiti-
mist reformers and intellectuals . . . objectively
became the tools of revolutionary forces."48 This was
characteristically the case, he argues, because intellectuals are inclined, when "interposing" themselves
into a revolutionary situation, "to apply most of their
pressure against the established authority, with which
they had many links, than equally against established
authorities and the revolutionary forces on behalf of
reformist appeals."49

If, argues Bell, the university were a microcosm
of the society, then Brzezinski's argument would have
some merit. The point, stresses Bell, is that "the
university is not the microcosm of the society; it is
an academic community with a historic exemption from
full integration into the society."50 There were,
argues Bell, two salient facts about the situation at
Columbia, the first of which was that "it was SDS which
initiated the violence at Columbia by insisting that
the university was the microcosm of the society, and
challenging its authority."51 The second was that

"after some confusion, the administration in its actions accepted this definition and sought to impose its
authority on the campus by resorting to force."[52]

In accepting the SDS logic the university made a
fundamental mistake that resulted in the radicalization
of hundreds of students: it called the police instead
of publicly debating SDS.   In doing so Columbia vio-
lated its status as a community.   In a community,
argues Bell, "one cannot regain authority simply by
asserting it, or by using force to suppress dissidents.
Authority in this case is like respect.   One can only
earn the authority--the loyalty of one's students--by
going in and arguing with them, by engaging in full
debate and, when the merits of proposed change are
recognized, taking the necessary steps quickly
enough."[53]

What led it to make this critical mistake, argues
Bell, was that in its conceptions of politics the
Columbia administration "was ill-equipped for either
the Machiavellianism of Brzezinski or the politics of
persuasion that . . . would have served the university
far better."[54]   Though "reputable political scientists," the administration leaders, Grayson Kirk and
David Truman, "were familiar only with the American
political system, in which one operates either legalis-
tically or by making deals."[55]   Hence, neither of them,
argues Bell, "had any feel for the volatility of social
movements, or for the politics of ideology."[56]   Trapped
by the shortcomings of their liberalism, they could not
"understand the dynamics of the student protest."[57]
They could not understand that

> whatever reason there may have been for
> early police action, when the buildings
> were seized by the hard-core SDS members,
> the subsequent surge of political support
> on the part of 500 other students--most
> of them liberal, moderate, pacifist, and
> not members of SDS--effectively changed
> the political character of the situation.
> The failure to make the necessary dis-
> tinction between these students and SDS,
> and thus to understand that these stu-
> dents were not wreckers but were now
> trying to express their inchoate griev-
> ances against the university, permitted
> SDS to call the tune--which, in the five

> crucial days of the occupation of the
> buildings it did.[58]

In the critical five days, five hundred students
had undergone a "conversion experience."[59] Bombarded
by SDS with "an extraordinary barrage of propaganda"
these students had been converted into "ideologists."
They had been converted into people who operate with a
"cognitive map," a map "with a built-in set of emotional judgments and rationalizations."[60] This was the
experience that was not challenged by the university's
administration. Rather, the students' conversion was
reinforced by the administration's use of the police to
suppress the protest. The conversion experience is one
that never occurs in a vacuum. The acquisition of any
new set of beliefs or judgments requires some confirmation of their validity by some "significant others"
(some testing of reality) and some confirmation at the
cognitive level. It requires some "real test of the
intellectual validity of the new conception."[61]
While members of the New York literary establishment provided one set of legitimations by throwing
large fund-raising parties in support of SDS and the
black militants, the administration never provided the
new converts with the intellectual debate that all new
converts seek in order to validate their new beliefs.[62]
In not challenging the charges of SDS that "Columbia
was the intersect of a corporate-military-CIA nexus to
advance American imperialism," and that it "was guilty
of institutional racism in its neighborhood policy,"
Columbia, unknowingly, left the "reality testing" to
the police. The "bust," argues Bell, had one ultimate
function: it confirmed the students' new beliefs.
"Whatever psychological guilt or unease was felt about
the demonstrators' coercive and disruptive tactics was
dissolved in the payment of broken heads and spilled
blood. As the students saw it, the administration
resorted to force because it could not answer them."[63]
In the final analysis, argues Bell, "with the
police action, the administration lost a large part of
its legitimacy--its moral authority--which had previously commanded the loyalty of students and faculty."[64]
Because it had this price attached to it, the police
action allowed SDS to prove to both itself and its new
converts "the truth of an old revolutionary adage that
no demonstration is successful unless it compels re-
pression."[65] By allowing SDS this opportunity, it

allowed SDS to achieve its goal of undermining the legitimacy of the university.

Ultimately, argues Bell, "SDS will be destroyed by its own style."[66] Impelled not to innovation but to destruction, SDS "lives on turbulence, but is incapable of transforming its chaotic impulses into a systematic, responsible behavior that is necessary to effect broad societal change."[67] Chiliastic in nature and temperament, its "desperado tactics" give evidence not of a coherent social movement, but rather of "the guttering last gasps of a romanticism soured by rancor and impotence."[68]

Nonetheless, argues Bell, the questions that SDS raises with their emphasis on the need to broaden participation in the institutions that affect people's lives are legitimate questions. Their questions "reflect the more generalized sources of student unrest which themselves arise out of world-wide structural changes in advanced industrial societies."[69] Ultimately, what makes both the university and the problem of legitimacy so important is that while in "the post-industrial societies of tomorrow . . . the problems of decentralization, of the balance between technical and political decision-making and of greater participation, will be pressing ones. . . . In the world of the university, as the experience of Columbia demonstrates, these problems have already come to the fore, and are now on the agenda."[70]

The way in which the university will deal with these problems cannot come, according to Bell, by invoking civil force. The university can only effectively deal with the disruptions that these problems will engender on college campuses "by rallying an entire community to establish common rules of common procedure."[71] The test of its ability to do this is, said Bell, the test of its ability to make "the fullest commitment to being a participatory institution, to an extent consonant with its full responsibilities."[72]

It was not until 1970 that Bell, in a Public Interest article titled "Quo Warranto? Notes on the Governance of Universities in the 1970s," specifies the universities' responsibilities and indicates the specific functions that they served in American society. These functions included the custodianship of the traditions of Western culture, the search for truth through inquiry and scholarship, the training of a large number of people as professionals in specific

fields, and the application of knowledge to social
use.73 But what is more important is that Bell raises
to a new level, in this essay, the problem of authority
and the New Left. He discusses that problem in terms
of both the "crisis of legitimacy" and the emergence of
the postindustrial society. While each would receive
considerable attention, it is the crisis of legitimacy
that would become the more important theme in his
subsequent work.

The Crisis of Legitimacy

In "Quo Warranto," as in a number of his other
essays up to and including "The Public Household," Bell
defines the crisis of legitimacy in terms of two overlapping developments: the "revolution of rising entitlements" and the emergence of a "new sensibility" in
American culture.

The product of a variety of forces, including a
"participation revolution" (generated by a poorly planned War on Poverty program), diffusion, and a shift in
the temper of the black protest movement (from an
emphasis on equality of opportunity to "equality of
results"), the revolution of rising entitlements reflected a deep shift in the character of Western society. The revolution of rising expectations or diffusion has been, Bell argues in "The Public Household,"
one of the chief features of American society since the
end of World War II. By the 1970s it was being transformed into a revolution of rising entitlements.74

For Bell this revolution reflected a broadening of
the demand for equality into "a demand for a wider set
of rights--political, civil, and social--as claims on
the community."75 It reflected not just the claims of
the minorities, the poor, or the disadvantaged; it
reflected "the claims of all groups in the society,
claims for protection and rights--in short, for entitlements."76

A major theme in his writings from 1965 on, the
emergence in American culture of a new sensibility is
viewed by Bell in "Quo Warranto" as "the most diffuse,
but in the long run the most potentially disintegrating
force in American society."77 Defined by him as anti-
institutional and antinomian, the primary features of
this new sensibility are a distinct distrust of criticism and a positive reliance on feelings as the touch

stone of human experience and judgment.

Based on the writings of the utopian socialist Charles Fourier and the anti-bourgeois writings of Pierre Baudelaire, Arthur Rimbaud, and Friedrich Nietzsche, the "new sensibility" had its origins in the nineteenth century. The 1960s version of this anti-bourgeois sensibility found, according to Bell, its distinct anti-institutional and antinomian coloration in the work of Herbert Marcuse, Norman O. Brown, and R. D. Laing. "A new trinity for a New Left," as Bell puts it in "Charles Fourier: A Prophet of Eupsychia," their work provides "a new recipe for Eupsychia--the psychological utopia of individual release far beyond the utopia of material plenty and freedom that nineteenth century prophets (including Marx . . .) had foretold for the future."[78]

Though he defines the crisis of legitimacy in The Cultural Contradictions of Capitalism largely in terms of the revolution of rising entitlements and the emergence of the "new sensibility," the dangers that each of these developments posed concerned Bell less than their relationship to America's emergence as a postindustrial society. The cultural contradictions set off by the interplay of these developments represented for Bell the largest problem for the legitimacy of American liberalism. It was a problem that Bell directs himself to in his 1970 essay "The Cultural Contradictions of Capitalism"; he would continue to address that problem in The Coming of Post-Industrial Society.

Bell argues in "The Cultural Contradictions of Capitalism" that the crisis of legitimacy faced by contemporary liberalism and American society could only be understood in relation to changes in both the culture and the social structure of American society; changes that dated back to 1915 and that embodied shifts in both the value structure and moral foundations of American life.

Written originally as an article for The Public Interest and later included as part of a book of essays on capitalism that Bell edited with Irving Kristol called Capitalism Today, "The Cultural Contradictions of Capitalism" is an extremely important essay. In it Bell joins with Kristol in repudiating liberals who attributed the emergence of the New Left and the counterculture to liberal capitalism's failure to realize its ideals.79 Instead, he locates the source of the counterculture to changes in the very development of capitalism, and the New Left's emergence to the failure of liberalism in the 1950s and 1960s to provide a new "viewpoint" to take the place of the older political ideas of an exhausted radical movement.

Bell's major thesis is that, because it calls itself a counterculture, the postmodernist culture has been incorrectly interpreted "as defying the Protestant ethic, heralding the end of Puritanism, and mounting a final attack on bourgeois values."80 Such an interpretation, he argues, misses the mark. Both the Protestant ethic and the Puritan temper as regulative codes that emphasized work, sobriety, frugality, sexual restraints, and a forbidding attitude toward life, "were eroded long ago."81 What caused their erosion was capitalism's adoption in 1920 of the installment plan.

Bell's argument is that with installment buying the seduction of the consumer generated sometime earlier through mass consumption and the efforts of the advertising industry became total; with that seduction both the Protestant ethic and the Puritan temper were completely undermined. By the mid-1920s capitalism was left with no "moral or transcendent ethic."82

Having promoted its own contradiction, capitalism served to place itself and bourgeois society in an intellectual bind. "Bourgeois society, justified and propelled as it had been in its earliest energies" by the Protestant ethic and the Puritan temper, could not readily admit to the fact that while it promoted a hedonistic way of life it could no longer justify it.83 Ultimately, bourgeois society "lacked a new religion or value system to replace the old, and the result was disjunction."84 Yet in the short run at least, capitalism was able to make the necessary adjustments and gain from the situation.

Under this disjunction, the "new capitalism continued to demand a Protestant ethic in the area of production--that is in the realm of work--but to stimulate a demand for pleasure and play in the area of consumption."85 But the disjunction between work and play, production and consumption, reflected a profound historical change in human society, a change that witnessed the primacy of culture over economics.86 This disjunction was bound to widen, resulting in the erosion of the moral foundations of bourgeois society. It was also inevitable that the older value system of bourgeois society would lose its social authority.

The fact that this loss of social authority did not generate any major disruptions before the early 1960s was because managerial capitalism was able to promote productivity and wealth as the new justification of the American economic system. Though this glorification of plenty was highly incongruent with the sociological foundations of the American value system, the incongruence mattered little. The incongruity was "eschewed with the blithe assurance that there was a consensus in the society on the moral verity of material abundance."87

Such assurances came in different forms, the most significant being the sophisticated rhetoric in the 1950s of the Luce magazines, _Time_, _Life_, and especially _Fortune_. Its theme was that "the secret of productivity and the permanent revolution of change that was the contribution of the American economic system to the coming prosperity of the world."88 It was a rhetoric that was able "to take the traditional American values, the belief in God, in work, in achievement, and to translate these, through the idiom of the coming urban civilization, into the creed of American destiny [the American century] on a wide scale."89 Thus, while American business was the dynamic agency tearing up small-town life and catapulting America into world economic dominance, the Luce publications encouraged its ability to do these things "within the language and cover of the Protestant ethic."90 But there was trouble in paradise; the new rhetoric did not resolve the problems of the underlying realities.

While the success of the new capitalism has long been in evidence, "the overt contradictions in the language and ideology" of American business and of American bourgeois society, "the lack of any coherent moral or philosophical doctrine, have only become manifest today."91 The contradictions between ideology and society and the lack of a philosophical doctrine provoked a crisis for American liberalism. While that crisis, the crisis of authority, was generated by the corporate class's abdication of its moral and political responsibilities, it was fueled by the fact that a politically dominant liberalism was unable to define, in the face of the assaults from the counterculture, the limits of modernism. The two failures were thus directly related.

"The fact that the corporate economy had no unified value system of its own . . . meant that liberal-

ism could go ideologically unchallenged."92   But while
liberalism had become dominant as an ideology in the
field of culture from the 1920s on, it never resolved
in its own terms the struggle between tradition and
modernity that was the distinct cultural feature of
American politics from the 1920s to the 1960s.   Left
alone in the fields of culture and politics to combat
the counterculture, liberalism found itself in an uneasy and tenuous position that was the direct result of
its internal struggle between tradition and modernity.

The counterculture, argues Bell, embodied only an
extension of several tendencies initiated in 1910 by
political liberalism and modernist culture, principally
through the works of Walter Lippman, Van Wyck Brooks,
John Reed and Harold Stearns.   It represented a split
in the camp of modernism.

The counterculture "sought to take the preachments
of personal freedom, extreme experience, and sexual
experimentation to a point in life style that the
liberal mentality--which would approve of such ideas in
art and imagination--is not prepared to go" when applied to personal life.93 Yet despite its strong reservations about personal libertarianism, liberalism
could not explain to the counterculture why it chose
not to go in the directions that the counterculture and
the New Left were taking it.

That liberalism still finds itself uneasy in
trying to explain its objections to the counterculture
and the New Left is a problem that could not go away.
It exists because modern liberalism "approves a basic
permissiveness, but cannot with any certainty define
the bounds."94 This, concludes Bell, is its dilemma.
It is liberalism's new crisis of nerve and legitimacy:
"in culture, as well as in politics, liberalism is now
up against the wall."95

The Public Household: Public Philosophy or Ideology?

Heretofore, a considerable amount of time has been
spent reviewing "The Household" and the ideas and social developments that gave rise to that work.   It has
been treated as a summation of a number of trends in
Bell's thought: his difference with neo-Marxist theorists over the problem of legitimacy in industrial
society; his efforts to reconcile the tension between
the optimism of socialism and classical liberalism with

the pessimism of Reinhold Niebuhr; his emphasis on America's need for new planning and allocative mechanisms; his emphasis on America's need for a new normative theory; his reaction to the student and black protest movements; and, finally, his emphasis on the cultural contradictions of capitalism.

The following chapters will undertake the problem of determining the degree to which "The Public Household" and the ideas that it is reflective of guide Bell's construction and use of the concept of postindustrial society. Again, it is ultimately through the resolution of this problem that the question that has prompted this study can be addressed: is Bell an ideologist of the end of ideology who is attempting through the development of the theory of the postindustrial society to rationalize the ideological perspectives embedded in the end of ideology?

As with the resolution of any problem, the problem of determining the degree to which "The Public Household" and the end of ideology are prefigured into Bell's construction of the postindustrial society rests with a common agreement on terms. It is with this in mind that it must be understood that Bell's work at the end of the 1960s is marked by a glaring contradiction that involves the way in which he uses the term ideology.

It will be remembered that in the introduction to Confrontation Bell and his coauthor, Irving Kristol, lash out at the Weathermen faction of SDS. In the process they charge that SDS's demand for democratization of institutions through increased citizen participation masked the desire of the radical left to undermine and render illegitimate the authority of the university in particular and the state in general. It may be, however, what is salient to this analysis is the fact that Bell and Kristol, characteristically, use the term ideology differently from established usage. Instead of referring to ideologies as distortive modes of thought that are used to rationalize predetermined points of view (points of view that can be conservative, liberal, or radical), they use it exclusively to mean the attempt by radicals to undermine established ideas and institutions.

Characteristically, Bell and Kristol used ideology the way Karl Mannheim uses utopia, that is, as ideas that are designed to shatter the existing order of things in a society. The point is that ideologies can and have been used to conserve institutions and patterns of authority just as much as to disestablish them.

Ultimately, what is ironic about Bell and Kristol's dismissal of the radical left as ideologists is that at virtually the same time that they were constructing their critiques of the New Left Bell was attempting to create a "public philosophy" that would devalue or transform the American classic national style, and "legitimate" intellectually a new stance toward democratic national planning.

The use of terms like first principles and national style does not alter the fact that the public philosophy to which Bell devotes himself to laying the foundations for in "The Public Household" could just as easily be called an ideology as a public philosophy. Ultimately, what terms are used hinges on what side of the fence one is on. It may well be that the only objective test of the principles outlined in "The Public Household" is the extent to which they falsely distinguish the impossible from the possible. The test, in other words, may rest in the extent to which those principles exclude from public debate policy alternatives that might otherwise be considered.

Notes

1. Bell, The Coming of Post-Industrial Society, p. 114.

2. Ibid., p. 119.

3. Ibid.

4. Ibid., p. 483.

5. Bell defines the postindustrial society in these terms in a number of places. For his definition of the postindustrial society as a knowledge society see The Coming of Post-Industrial Society, p. 212. For his definition of the postindustrial society as a service society see The Coming of Post-Industrial Society, p. 127. For his definition of the postindustrial society as a communal society see pp. 128, 364.

6. Bell, The Coming of Post-Industrial Society, p. 409.

7. Ibid., pp. 480-81.

8. Peter Steinfels, The Neoconservatives (New York: Simon and Schuster, 1979), p. 164.

9. Bell, The Coming of Post-Industrial Society,

p. 34.

    10. Daniel Bell, "The Public Household," in *The Cultural Contradictions of Capitalism* (New York: Basic Books, 1976), p. 232.

    11. Ibid., p. 234.

    12. Ibid., p. 240.

    13. Ibid., p. 252.

    14. Ibid., p. 256.

    15. Ibid., p. 257.

    16. Ibid., p. 250.

    17. Ibid., p. 252.

    18. Ibid., p. 282. The tone here is distinctly Niebuhrian, a fact that is confirmed when Bell says "within limits, men can remake themselves and society, but the knowledge of power must coexist with the knowledge of its limits. This is, after all, the oldest and most enduring truth about the human condition." Bell, "The Public Household," in *The Cultural Contradictions of Capitalism* (New York: Basic Books, 1976), p. 282.

    19. Ibid.

    20. Ibid., p. 252.

    21. Ibid.

    22. Ibid., p. 279.

    23. Ibid., p. 281.

    24. Ibid., p. 254. In elaborating this position Bell argues that modern liberalism must face one "inelectable" fact: "there is no escape from economics." Within this context he argues that "men constantly redefine needs so that former wants become necessities. The constraints of resources are tangible, and while the amounts needed may not become physically exhausted, the costs of using these rise, and relative costs, not physical quantities, become the measure of scarcity." Bell, "The Public Household," in *The Cultural Contradictions of Capitalism* (New York: Basic Books, 1976), p. 254.

    25. Bell, *The Coming of Post-Industrial Society*, p. 33.

    26. Bell, "The National Style and the Radical Right," *Partisan Review*, Fall 1962, p. 521.

    27. Ibid., p. 520.

    28. Ibid., p. 522.

    29. Ibid., p. 523.

    30. Ibid., p. 519.

    31. Daniel Bell, ed., *Toward the Year 2000: Work in Progress* (Boston: Beacon Press, 1969), p. 9.

32. Ibid.
33. Ibid., p. 10.
34. Ibid., pp. 367-68.
35. Ibid., p. 5.
36. Ibid., p. 7.
38. Ibid.
39. Ibid., p. 1.
40. Ibid., p. 10.
41. Ibid., p. 8.
42. Daniel Bell and Irving Kristol, eds., <u>Confrontation</u> (New York: Basic Books, 1969), p. x.
43. Their argument is that the shift in professorial attention from undergraduate to graduate students was the result of the sheer increase in the number of students produced by mass higher education and poor educational planning.
44. Bell and Kristol, <u>Confrontation</u>, p. x.
45. Ibid., p. x-xi.
46. Ibid., p. xi.
47. Bell, "Columbia and the New Left," in <u>Confrontation</u>, p. 99.
48. Ibid., p. 100.
49. Ibid.
50. Ibid., p. 101.
51. Ibid.
52. Ibid.
53. Ibid.
54. Ibid.
55. Ibid.
56. Ibid.
57. Ibid.
58. Ibid.
59. Ibid., p. 102.
60. Ibid., p. 97.
61. Ibid., p. 98.
62. ". . . The acquisition of new beliefs or judgments also requires confirmation at the cognitive level, some real test of the intellectual validity of the new conception. This can--in more neutral areas and in quieter times--take the form of intellectual debate about the consistency of the argument, the quality of evidence, the congruity with other beliefs, its place within a larger theoretical or intellectual structure, and so on; reality testing also take the form or prediction, and falsification of such judgments becomes the basis for the beginning of disbelief. Where emotions are deeply involved, such testing is

never wholly persuasive, of course, but it is still
necessary. . . . The accusations--and beliefs--of the
students were never challenged by the administration. .
. ." Bell, "Columbia and the New Left," in <u>Confronta-
tion</u>, pp. 98-99.

     63. Bell, "Columbia and the New Left," in <u>Con-
frontation</u>, p. 99.

     64. Ibid.

     65. Ibid., p. 102.

     66. Ibid., p. 106.

     67. Ibid.

     68. Ibid.

     69. Ibid.

     70. Ibid.

     71. Ibid., p. 107.

     72. Ibid.

     73. Bell, "Quo Warranto?" <u>The Public Interest</u>,
Spring 1970, p. 62.

     74. Bell, "The Public Household," p. 232.

     75. Ibid., p. 233.

     76. Ibid.

     77. Bell, "Quo Warranto?" p. 59.

     78. Bell, "Charles Fourier: Prophet of Eupsy-
chia," <u>American Scholar</u>, Winter 1968-1969, p. 41.

     79. Bell, "The Cultural Contradictions of Capi-
talism," <u>Capitalism Today</u>, ed. Daniel Bell and Irving
Kristol (New York: Basic Books, 1970), p. 24. This
essay also appears in <u>The Cultural Contradictions of
Capitalism</u>. All subsequent references to this essay
will be to its appearance in this later work.

     80. Bell, "The Cultural Contradictions of Capi-
talism," in <u>The Cultural Contradictions</u>, p. 55.

     81. Ibid.

     82. Ibid., p. 74.

     83. Ibid., pp. 74-75.

     84. Ibid., p. 75.

     85. Ibid.

     86. To quote Bell, "for thousands of years, the
function of economics was to provide the daily necessi-
ties--the subsistence--of life. For various upper-
class groups, economics has been the basis of status
and a sumptuary style. But now, on a mass scale,
economics had become geared to the demands of culture.
Here, too, culture, not as expressive symbolism or
moral meanings but as life-style, came to reign su-
preme." <u>The Cultural Contradictions</u>, p. 75.

     87. Ibid.

88. Ibid., p. 76.
89. Ibid.
90. Ibid.
91. Ibid.
92. Ibid., p. 79.
93. Ibid.
94. Ibid.
95. Ibid.

7

The Postindustrial Society
in Perspective

Competing Realms

The postindustrial society is an elusive concept. What makes it difficult to pin down is that Bell uses that concept in four different ways in The Coming of Post-Industrial Society. Originally he uses it as an ideal-type construction that, in contrast to preindustrial and industrial societies, specifies a new "design," a new pattern and mode of interaction.[1] Bell also uses the postindustrial society concept as a way of articulating a theory of social change and as a way of describing an emergent reality, a reality that justifies the establishment of a new set of philosophical legitimations.

The theory of social change outlined in The Coming of Post-Industrial Society (and the one that Bell continues to elaborate upon in The Cultural Contradictions of Capitalism) is based on a loosely drawn analytical scheme in which the postindustrial society was defined as both a "knowledge" and a "communal" society. As a knowledge society the postindustrial society revealed the preeminence of theoretical knowledge and a profound shift in employment that was reflected in the growing importance of occupations dealing with the husbanding, distribution, and expansion of knowledge as measured in the United States by the Bureau of Labor statistics.[2] As a communal society, the postindustrial society reflects the response of the United States and other technologically advanced societies to the realities of modern life, namely, that given the prohibitive costs involved in maintaining essential services, protecting

the environment, extending public education, and impro-
ving the quality of life, the costs can only be absorbed communally.

In contrast to the holistic images of society
stressed by both Marxian and structural-functionalist
social theory, Bell's theory of social change emphasizes an image of society whose characteristic feature
is disjunction and conflict. While both Marxism and
structural-functionalism were joined in their belief
that society is a structurally interrelated system and
that, therefore, all social actions can only be understood in relation to that unified system, Bell's theory
makes no such claims. It does not claim to see societies as organic or integrated social systems. Rather,
Bell's theory is based on an analytical scheme in which
the workings of contemporary society are understood to
fall within three institutional realms--the techno-
economic order or social structure, the polity, and
culture--with each being organized around their own
organizing or "axial" principles and structures.

Developed, then, as a conflict theory, Bell's
theory of social change provides a framework for analyzing the tensions that framed the 1960s and conditioned
the black and student protest movements. Bell's theory
views those tensions as the result of a set of historical contradictions that were deeply embedded in the
value structure of Western society. His theory locates
the structural sources of those tensions in the axial
principles that underlie and define the social structure, the polity, and the culture of modern Western
society.

Bell considers the axial principle of Western
social structure to be functional rationality. He
defines the "regulative mode" of the social structure
as "economizing," by which he means "the science of the
best allocation of scarce resources among competing
ends."3 He considers the axial structure of the
techno-economic order of all modern societies, socialist and capitalist, to be bureaucracy and hierarchy.

Bell considers the axial principle of the polity
(society's arena for the regulation of conflict and the
delegation of social justice and power) to be legitimacy. He defines the axial principle of the modern
democratic polity as "the principle that power can be
held and grievances exercised only with the consent of
the governed."4 Bell considers the axial structure of
the modern democratic polity to be participation, by

which he specifically means "the existence of political parties and/or social groups to express the interests of particular segments in the society."5

Bell considers the axial principle of modern culture to be the desire for self-fulfillment and enhancement. He defines this principle as a style of thought that encourages the denial of any limits or boundaries to experience. It is a principle that encourages "a reaching out for all experience"; a reaching out in which "nothing is forbidden" and "all is to be explored."6

The key to Bell's theory of social change is the idea that the United States was undergoing a set of transformations that intensifies the discordances between its social structure, its polity, and its culture because it was increasingly becoming a postindustrial society.

Ultimately, what makes postindustrialism a catalytic agent, according to Bell, is that "the post-industrial society, in its initial logic, is a meritocracy."7 It is a society in which "differential status and differential income are based on technical skills and higher education."8 Because it is a society in which few high places are attainable without those skills, it is a society that breeds considerable insecurity, especially given the history of discrimination against blacks and women. This insecurity has been chiefly evidenced in the university primarily because in the postindustrial society it is the university that increasingly becomes "the arbiter of class position."9 It is the university that provides the necessary skills and knowledge for entrance into the postindustrial society. In short, the university is both the "gatekeeper" of the postindustrial society and the center of unrest and insecurity because "it has gained a quasi-monopoly in determining the future stratification of the society."10

Within this context, the demand for equality that was part of the "populist" reaction to the postindustrial society in the early 1970s represents a defense against exclusion from that society. This demand for inclusion is one that is reinforced by a political system, Western democracy, that, through its axial principles, encourages equality and participation. Formally based on equality and participation, the democratic polity stands in sharp contradiction to an industrial order that is based on functional rationality and to a stratification system that assigns power and distributes rewards on the basis of technical skill and knowledge.   Based on the principle of representation, the democratic polity is one that encourages participation in decision making about the distribution of goods and services.

The demand for equality encourages adversary relationships that question the existing legitimations of the American industrial and political systems.   The adversary culture ultimately rejects the claims and ends of both those systems.   It acts out the anti-bourgeois values that were given initial impetus by Charles Baudelaire, Arthur Rimbaud, and Friedrich Nietzsche and promotes ends that are antagonistic toward the ends of the industrial and political systems: purity, personal freedom, and self-fulfillment.

Ultimately, postindustrialism is the spark that raises these historically conditioned contradictions to the surface.   It intensifies them by raising new insecurities and demands that become disjunctive elements in the value structure of American society.

Bell's Theory of Social Change

In focusing on the disjunction between the social structure, the polity, and the culture of American society, Bell develops a theory of social change that stresses changes in the class structure of American society, particularly the emergence of a new technical elite.   Made up of scientists and engineers, this new elite consists of individuals listed in the National Register of Scientific and Technological Personnel maintained by the National Science Foundation.   Largely, although not exclusively, employed in the universities and government, the new technical elite numbers some three hundred thousand persons.

The emergence of this new elite was largely the result of the revolution in knowledge.   This revolution involved a change in the character of knowledge, one that reflected the centrality of theoretical knowledge in modern industrial societies.   It involved the pre-eminence of theory over empiricism and the codification of knowledge into abstract systems of symbols as the basis for the organization of decisions and the direction of change in production and management in the postindustrial society.

The revolution in knowledge also reflected the growing preeminence in modern society of the science-based industries: computers, electronics, optics, and polymers. It reflected the growing preeminence of industries "which increasingly dominate the manufacturing sector of the society and which provide the lead, in product cycles, for the advanced industrial societies."11 In short, the scientific-technical revolution reflected a shift in the thinking of twentieth-century society away from the indifference to science and abstraction that was the credo of many of the nineteenth-century inventors. In both the public and the corporate worlds abstract or theoretical knowledge was adopted as the "strategic" and necessary resource.

Another major factor that led to the emergence of the new technical elite was the close relationship that developed in the postwar period between the federal government and science. This relationship during the Eisenhower and Kennedy administrations was the product of federal research and development expenditures that increased by an average of 15 to 16 percent a year. During those years the federal government became the largest single sponsor of scientific and technological research in the United States.

Bell's theory of social change as it is projected, particularly in the "Cultural Contradictions of Capitalism," relates the tensions in American society during the late 1960s and early 1970s to historical shifts in its social structure and culture. It ascribes the undermining of the Protestant ethic to capitalism's ability in the 1920s to promote through mass production and mass consumption hedonism as a dominant way of life. His theory also locates the source of bourgeois society's lack of a transcendent ethic to capitalism's lack of a unifying ideology.

Bell's theory of social change ultimately emphasizes the failure of modern liberalism and the democratic polity to mediate the conflict between the social structure and the culture of American society. It attributes this failure, on the one hand, to the inability of the United States to develop planning and allocative mechanisms to meet the demands made necessary by America's emergence as a communal society. It attributes the failure of liberalism, on the other hand, to its inability to create a philosophy of the public household, its lack, in short, of a "common framework of values" that can guide the setting of

political policy.   Ultimately, Bell's theory locates
the failure of modern liberalism with its failure to
respond to his programmatic injunctions.
     Bell's theory of social change thus acknowledges
the triumph of an "adversary ideology" within the Welfare State and the collapse of an older value system
based on Puritanism and restraint.   In doing so, Bell's
theory of social change asserts a disquieting message:
because of capitalism's absence of a transcendent
ethic, the "cultural paradox" that it fostered in the
1920s will remain "a continuing crisis of capitalist
society."12   Hence, Bell's theory of social change is a
prediction that "in a post-industrial society the disjunction of culture and social structure is bound to
widen."13   This disjunction is made inevitable in the
Western democracies because modern Western society is
experiencing a crisis of legitimacy, a crisis that both
underlies the cultural contradictions of capitalism and
frames the future of the postindustrial society.

> The historic justifications of bourgeois
> society--in the realms of religion and
> character--are gone.   The traditional
> legitimacies of property and work become
> subordinated to bureaucratic enterprises
> that can justify privileges because they
> can turn out material goods more effi-
> ciently than other modes of production.
> But a technocratic society is not enno-
> bling.   Material goods provide only tran-
> sient satisfaction or an invidious supe-
> riority over those with less.   Yet one of
> the deepest human impulses is to sanctify
> their institutions and beliefs in order
> to find a meaningful purpose in their
> lives and to deny the meaninglessness of
> death.   A post-industrial society cannot
> provide a transcendent ethic--except for
> the few who devote themselves to the
> temple of science.   And the antinomian
> attitude plunges one into a radical aut-
> ism which, in the end, dirempts the cords
> of community and the sharing with others.
> The lack of a rooted moral belief system
> is the cultural contradiction of the
> society, the deepest challenge to its
> survival.14

The Post-Industrial Society as the Preamble to The Public Household

In addition to using the concept of the postindustrial society to develop a theory of social change, Bell uses it to describe an emergent reality. This is a description of an American society beset by a number of overlapping social and political problems, the great bulk of which were the product of America's emergence as a knowledge and as a communal society. In turn, his description of American society justifies the establishment of a new set of philosophical legitimations.

Bell's image of America is of a society questioning the values of the private enterprise system and its basic institution, the business corporation. One of these endangered values is the emphasis on individual private consumption through the increased production of material goods. This value is summarized by the notion that all that is required to satisfy people in a society is the increased availability of more and more goods at relatively stable prices.

Another of these values is summarized by the term economizing. Based on the proposition that individual satisfaction is the best unit upon which costs and benefits can be calculated, economizing reflects a strong advocacy of the principles of functional rationality, the notion that "all aspects of organization are single-mindedly reduced to becoming means to the goals of production and profit."15 Economizing also reflects an atomistic view of society. It is this view that conditions its approach to management and production. The principal assumption upon which it rests is the idea that the most appropriate mix of humans in the organization of production can be established through a calculus of monetary costs within a framework of relative costs. Ultimately, economizing suffers the weaknesses of its atomistic view of society, the central one of which is the "utilitarian fallacy that the sum total of individual decisions is equivalent to a social decision."16

In the tradition of "The End of Ideology," Bell's description of current social reality is of people questioning these older values in a new way, one that is different from the way in which socialists and radicals questioned them in the 1930s. No longer were those values being questioned because they were being achieved only at the cost of the exploitation of the

worker.   Instead, they are questioned at the more basic
levels.

Questioned are the creation of private goods at
the expense of social values like clean air and water.
This new emphasis on social, collective values has
emerged despite the fact that, since the end of the
Second World War, the corporation has been moving
steadily toward the "sociologizing mode," that is,
toward the view that corporations are more than institutions for economizing; they are also ways of life for
their members.   Hence, the corporation must provide
services, the coordination of which both tests the
limits of the economizing mode and challenges its most
basic assumptions.   Thus, Bell's description is of an
American society in which, paradoxically, the legitimation of corporate capitalism is being challenged on the
same grounds that in the 1950s were used to justify it
ideologically.   The challenge is on the basis of its
performance.

Bell's description is of an American society that
finds itself in the midst of a cultural crisis.   In
part, this crisis is the product of a social structure
that is directed toward functional rationality and
technocracy and a culture that is anti-institutional
and antinomian.   In part, it is also a crisis that
stems from modern liberalism's use of "intellectual
concepts and paradigms that are products or summations
of an older order of experience."17   Hence, Bell's
description is of a society in which people in discussing its governmental structure "still use the language
and often the assumptions of two hundred years ago."18
They still use the language and the assumptions of
laissez-faire capitalism and of seventeenth-century
liberalism; the language and assumptions of Adam Smith
and John Locke.19   Yet Bell's description is more than
a picture of a society wedded to an outdated worldview;
it is a description of a society that in facing up to
the limits of that worldview must face one of its most
pressing problems: reconciling the logic of the economizing mode with the logic of the sociologizing mode.

Equally important is the fact that Bell's description is of a "great society" in which more and more
goods necessarily have to be purchased communally.   It
is a description of a communal society in which,
"defense apart, the planning of cities and the rationalization of transit, the maintenance of open spaces
and the extension of recreational areas, the elimina-

tion of air pollution and the cleaning up of the rivers, the underwriting of education and the organization of medical care, all are now public institutions."20

In a related way Bell's description is of a society in which the rise of the new post-World War II claimants on the political system, scientists, educators, intelligentsia, black, youth, and the poor, had disrupted the power of the old political coalitions. The result of both postindustrialism and the revolution of rising expectations, the rise of these new claimants to political power had disrupted the kinds of coalitions that had given interest-group politics its force. On the national level these coalitions involved big business, labor, and farm organizations; on the state and city levels, they involved ethnic groups. Bell's description is thus of a society that will, he asserts, require more conscious decision making. The salient fact is that ultimately the postindustrial society is a society in which "the clash of individual interests, each following its own whim, leads necessarily to a greater degree of coercion (with a reduction of personal freedom) in order to have effective communal action."21

Bell's description is of a society that, despite its emergence as a communal society, lacks both an allocative mechanism for the distribution of goods and services and for the adjudication of claims to scarce resources: it lacks a communal ethic. Individuals have their respective scale of values that they utilize to make purchases; yet the society as a whole lacks a mechanism, a scale of values, that enables its political leaders to consider, "in terms of costs and benefits, the varying combinations of private consumption and public purchases of goods."22 It is, in other words, a description of a society that lacks a philosophy of the public household.

Finally, Bell's description is of an emerging knowledge society that is being confronted with a new set of costs or scarcities the management of which both confounds the utopian visions of the postindustrial society envisaged by nineteenth-century writers and tests the limits of modern liberalism: the costs of information, the costs of coordination, and the costs of time.

Foreshadowed in Bell's various descriptions is the pronounced fear that American society may ultimately realize the fate Michael Young assigns English society

in his fable The Rise of Meritocracy; a violent revolution stemming from popular opposition to meritocracy
and exclusion. Ultimately, it is this fear that sparks
the urgency of Bell's descriptions of American society:
descriptions that collectively and individually point
to America's need for a new philosophy of the public
household.

The Fork in the Road

The theory of social change and the descriptions
of the emergent reality projected through the concept
of the postindustrial society are telling, but they are
not, in and of themselves, conclusive. To be sure,
they create an image of the United States at a critical
crossroad in its history; they portray the United
States as a society that requires a new legitimacy and
a new philosophy of the public household from which
that legitimacy can be derived. Yet they do not con-
clusively tell us whether Bell is an ideologist. More
importantly, they do not tell us of what Bell is an
ideologist.

Ultimately, Bell's theory of social change and the
images of American society projected through the concept of the postindustrial society point to Bell being
an ideologist who is trying to promote through his
construction and use of that concept the ideas and
values embodied in his "Public Household" essay. Yet
the best measure of whether Bell is an ideologist rests
with a discussion of the problems that he poses through
his construction and use of the concept of the post-
industrial society. In the final analysis, Bell's
theory of social change and his descriptions of American society may reflect ongoing realities, or they may
reflect, perhaps at the same time, a personal or political ideology that is largely independent of the
answers he gets to the problems he poses. But it is
the nature of the way that he poses those problems that
is conclusive. If nothing else, ideologists are people
who try to influence other people, and, ultimately, as
Bell acknowledges in quoting John Dewey in The Coming
of Post-Industrial Society, the setting of a problem
"is the most effective way of influencing subsequent
thought."[23]

The Problems Subsumed in the
Postindustrial Society Concept

While there was some overlap in the problems that
Bell articulates through the concept of the postindustrial society they can be understood to fall within
five broad categories or types of problems.   These
categories include problems related to Americans emergence as a knowledge society; problems that stem from
America's emergence as a communal society; problems of
corporate capitalism; problems of political philosophy
and planning; and problems concerning the relationship
between America's new adversary culture and its social
structure.

Problems of the Knowledge Society

Under the first category, problems related to
America's emergence as a knowledge society, we can
delineate two sets of problems that Bell articulates
through the concept of the postindustrial society.   The
first set concerns the problems generated by the meritocracy principle.   The second set concerns problems
that arise "from the historic independence of the scientific community and the contradictory problems generated by its tradition of autonomy, its increasing dependence on government research funds, and the service
it is called upon to perform."[24]
The first set of problems attends the switch from
equality of opportunity to the equality of result standard generated by the affirmative action policies of
the great society.   For Bell this switch constitutes
the "central value problem" of the postindustrial society.   This problem underlies what Bell considers the
chief problem of the emerging postindustrial society:
"the conflict generated by a meritocracy principle
which is central to the allocation of position in the
knowledge society."[25]
In the second set of problems that Bell relates to
America's emergence as a knowledge society, he identified five specific problems: the problem of defining
the relationship between science and government; the
problem of what constitutes a policy of science; the
problem of creating representative structures for science; the problem of defining the legitimate functions
of science in the postindustrial society; and the prob-

lem of whether the technicians and engineers in the
postindustrial society will become a "new working
class" as the socialist theoreticians Serge Mallet and
Andre Gorz had predicted.[26]

The Problems of the Communal Society

Under the second category, problems that stem from
America's emergence as a communal society, we can delineate two problems that Bell articulates through his
concept of the postindustrial society. The first problem concerns what the socialist writer James J. O'Con-
nor called "the fiscal crisis of the state."[27] This is
the problem of how wealth is to be redistributed in a
society in which the government has become the single
largest employer and in which the multiplication of
government functions that are the result of a combination of forces creates a continuous need for new revenues.

The second concerns how the claims on the political system are to be settled. This for Bell is a
central problem for two reasons, one of which is that a
postindustrial society is by definition "a communal
society wherein public mechanisms rather than the market become the allocators of goods, and public choice,
rather than individual demand, becomes the arbiter of
services."[28] The other reason is that "a communal
society by its very nature multiplies the definition of
rights--the rights of children, of students, of the
poor, of minorities--and translates them into claims of
the community."[29] Ultimately, in a democratic society
the solution to this problem rests in a determination
of what criteria it will use to adjudicate the competing claims placed upon it as a result of its emergence
as a communal society.

The Problems of Corporate Capitalism

Under the third category, the problems of corporate capitalism, we can delineate several problems that
Bell articulates through the concept of the postindustrial society, the bulk of which derive their force
from his analysis of the changing character of American
capitalism in the twentieth century.

In his analysis Bell assesses the significance of

the new wave of criticism that has been directed toward American industry. This criticism centers on environmental issues and raises questions concerning the social responsibility of the corporation in protecting the environment from the effects of industrial waste and pollution, from the effects of what welfare economists call "externalities," or costs of production that are passed on to the public in the government expenditures for cleaning polluted rivers and lands. The significance of this criticism is that it raises key questions about the authority and legitimacy of the corporation in American society.

By the end of the 1950s corporate capitalism, Bell argues, had established a new legitimacy in American life. This legitimacy was not based on the natural right of property that from Adam Smith's time to the 1930s had been capitalism's traditional basis of legitimacy. Rather, its new legitimacy was based on performance. It was based on the role of the corporation "as an instrument for providing more and more goods to the people."[30] That performance could serve as the new basis of legitimacy for corporate capitalism was, argues Bell, a function of several factors. One of the most important was a change in ideology.

This was a change in which "the idea took hold that size was less relevant than performance."[31] It was a change in which the corporation no longer had to defend itself against the charge that the bigness of business represented an economic and political threat to democracy. This charge, going back to 1890 when Congress passed the Sherman Antitrust Act, had been the credo of the populist movement. Buoyed by John Kenneth Galbraith's argument that bigness enables the large corporation to underwrite technological progress, corporate capitalism in the 1950s was able to make a convincing case for itself. Ultimately, "a vigorous large government could present its case to the public that size was immaterial, so long as the corporation displayed those hallmarks of dynamism that added up to performance."[32]

The major factor in its success in making performance the new basis of its legitimacy was the fact that by the end of the 1950s corporate capitalism seemed to be performing its role as an instrument for providing more and better goods to the American people very adequately.[33] The fact that it had achieved a new basis of legitimacy was, notes Bell, reflected in the

fact that by the end of the 1950s criticism of corporate capitalism had become so muted that the criterion
of performance went virtually unchallenged. With the
new wave of criticism that grew out of the late 1960s
all that changed.

Ironically, corporate capitalism was challenged by
environmentalists and by citizens concerned with the
price of externalities that had been passed on the
public, precisely on the grounds of performance.
Instead of the quiet acceptance of the legitimacy of
corporate capitalism, "a feeling has begun to spread in
the country that corporate performance has made the
society uglier, dirtier, trashier, more polluted, and
noxious."34 The significance of this turnabout, argues
Bell, is that "the sense of identity between the self
interest of the corporation and the public interest has
been replaced by the sense of incongruence."35

There are two basic problems that Bell poses that
fall into the category of the problems of corporate
capitalism. The first concerns the obligation of the
corporation to society and deals with the need to
establish a balance of obligations between the public
and the private in a liberal society. It is the problem of determining whether the corporation should be
viewed as an instrument of the stockholders or as "an
autonomous enterprise which, despite its particular
history, has become--or should become an instrument for
service to society in a system of pluralistic pow-
ers."36 The second problem concerning corporate capitalism centers on the limits of the economizing mode.
It is the problem of establishing a balance between the
logic of the economizing and the sociologizing modes.

Bell also raises a number of problems that not
only test the limits of the economizing mode but press
the issue of the corporation's obligations to the fore-
front. Among them are the problems of worker satisfaction, minority employment, and environmental pollution.
The last problem is one of private versus social costs.
Another related problem is that of determining the role
of the corporation in dealing with such moral issues as
private investment in South Africa.

Problems of Political Philosophy and Planning

Under the fourth category, problems of political
philosophy and planning, we can delineate two problems

that Bell articulates through the concept of the post-industrial society. The first is the problem of formu-lating a normative theory of the public household: "a normative theory, which--taking into account the in-eluctable elements of centralized decision-making, the extension of social or communal choices, and the need for conscious social planning (not to direct the soci-ety, but to facilitate desired social changes)--can set forth rational criteria consonant with the values of a free society."37 The second is the problem of devel-oping a system of social accounts, a system whereby social changes can be charged, political demands anti-cipated, and the effectiveness of present social poli-cies tested.

The Adversary Culture and the Social Structure

Under the fifth category, problems concerning the relationship between the new adversary culture and America's social structure, we can delineate two major problems that Bell articulates through the concept of the postindustrial society. The first is the tension that exists in the United States because of the clash in values between its adversary culture and its social structure. The second is whether postindustrial Ameri-ca can survive without a transcendental ethic.

The question that remains to be answered is, in what contexts does Bell pose all of these problems? Does he pose them as solvable or unsolvable problems? The answer is that he poses them in different contexts.

Bell on Corporate Capitalism and Liberalism

If we start with the problems of corporate capi-talism that Bell poses through the concept of the postindustrial society we find him posing them within two overlapping contexts. He poses them through his repudiation of classical liberalism, the core of which is his attack on the inviolability of private property, and within the context of justifying American's need for a new ordering mechanism and a new public philo-sophy.

Behind each of these problems one finds the same set of intentions. There is, first of all, the desire to demonstrate that the problems are complex and tech-

nical. Bell's reminder is constant: because they are
complex problems they do not yield to "ideological"
solutions. They can only be effectively approached
following the creation of an ordering mechanism and a
system of social accounts that measures costs against
responsibilities for all sectors of society. Bell also
desires to demonstrate to the corporate managers the
new realities that give weight to the criticisms of the
New Left against corporate capitalism. And, finally,
his intention is to demonstrate that because of the
preeminence of the public sector in American life comprehensive government planning is not just necessary,
it is inevitable if something resembling a liberal
society is to survive. These are the host of intentions that give rise to Bell's critique of corporate
capitalism.
     Bell's critique is multi-faceted. It embodies a
polemic against the defenders of private property and
the economizing mode and attacks their underlying assumptions. In nature and purpose this polemic closely
resembles the one that John Dewey develops in Liberalism and Social Action. It should be remembered that in
this book Dewey locates "the crisis of liberalism" in
liberalism itself. He locates that crisis in liberalism's failure to rise beyond its special and historically relative interpretation of liberty and deal with
the new problem that its very success precipitated.
This problem, as discussed in Chapter 2, was of legitimacy. It was the problem of how to establish within
the framework of a democracy the moral foundations for
a new integrating philosophy.
     The thrust of Bell's critique is that the problems
of environmental pollution, minority employment, and
the moral responsibility of the corporation on racial
issues can only be approached when they are placed into
a larger context, one that permits us to recognize that
the concepts through which we have traditionally approached them are inadequate. Pollution is a case in
point. It is easy to blame the business corporation
and to stop there, but the inescapable reality is that

> all sections of the society are at fault:
> the farmer who, by seeking to increase
> food production, uses more nitrate ferti-
> lizer and thus pollutes the rivers of the
> country; the individual automobile owner
> who, seeking greater mobility, spews

noxious gas into the atmosphere; the Atomic Energy Commission which, in seeking to expand nuclear power, may be responsible for thermal pollution of the waters; and the corporation whose smokestacks emit smog-creating gases in the air, or whose waste products pollute the lakes.[38]

But where does this realization leaves us? Bell's answer is that it leaves us with a fuller understanding of the dimensions of the problem that the pollution problem presents to American society as a whole. It presents us with

the fact that the allocative mechanism of society, the proper distribution of costs and resources is not working. In a free society, the socially optimal distribution of resources and goods exists where the market reflects the true economic cost of an item. But where private costs and social costs diverge, then the allocation of goods becomes skewed. When the owner of a factory has no incentive to take account of costs to others of the pollution he generates because these costs are not charged to him, factory output (or automobile mileage in the case of a car owner) will be at a higher level than is socially optimal.[39]

The fact that this increasing divergence of private costs and social costs constitutes a growing problem for modern society is for Bell indisputable. The fact that it is a problem that necessitates the development of a new allocative mechanism is for Bell equally indisputable. The underlying problem is whether such a mechanism can be developed within the framework of the traditional conceptions of private property and liberty that corporate capitalism continues to find itself trapped by. The answer Bell offers is that it cannot.

The development of a new allocative mechanism requires a system of social accounts, one that can go beyond the individualistic utilitarian fallacy promoted by classical liberalism and legitimated by the economi-

zing mode: the fallacy that a social decision represents the sum of individual decisions. The development
of a new allocative mechanism, thus, requires a commitment on the part of the United States to go beyond the
limits of the economizing mode with its commitment to
economic growth at the exclusion of the costs involved
in unplanned and uncoordinated growth. Above all, it
requires the recognition that what is required from
government is a commitment to planning; not single
purpose planning but comprehensive social and technological planning. The development of a new allocative
mechanism requires, in other words, that the government
must make a commitment to the kind of planning that can
calculate the secondary and tertiary costs of social
and technological change and develop adequate support-
ing systems to offset the negative effects (the hidden
costs) of social and technological change.40

The development of a new allocative mechanism in
the exact sense that it requires a system of social
accounts requires, argues Bell, the recognition that
the business corporation is not just an economic instrument or an institution of private property. The
business corporation, in addition to being an economic
instrument, is now a lifetime experience for many of
its employees; it is not that for the stockholders. As
the growth of mutual funds, pension funds, and trust
funds indicate, the stockholder is "often an in-and-out
person with little continuing interest in the enterprise."41 Hence, the balance of obligations between
the business corporation, its employees, and society
will have to be defined in a very different way than
the one that is legitimated by the economizing mode.
We must also recognize that private property is a legal
fiction. That recognition makes the conservative position that the business corporation is a private property institution whose sole function should be the pursuit of profit for its stockholders, the position legitimated by the economizing mode, completely untenable.

The unmasking of the self-serving myths, the repudiation of the conservative position should be understood for what they are: they provide the stage from
which one could generate an appeal to corporate capitalism to accept the new realities of American life.
Bell wanted the champions of corporate capitalism to
accept the fact that "the consumer-oriented free enterprise society no longer satisfies the citizenry as it
once did," and to adjust itself to those new reali-

ties.[42]

> The private enterprise system has been
> the primary institution of Western soci-
> ety not because of its coercive power but
> because its values--economizing and in-
> creasing output of material goods-- were
> congruent with the major consumer values
> of the society. With all its obvious
> imperfections the system worked.   Today,
> however, those values are themselves
> being questioned, not in the way social-
> ists and radicals questioned them a gen-
> eration ago . . . but at the very core,
> the creation of more private goods at the
> expense of other social values. . . . No
> one, meeting collectively voted in our
> market economy. But now votes are being
> taken.[43]

Bell's appeal is in part an appeal for corporate
capitalism to recognize a larger set of social obligations than it has in the past and to include on its
boards of directors not just stockholders but also
workers and consumers. Yet, it is more than an appeal.
Ultimately, Bell's critique is a warning to corporate capitalism that, unless it seeks out such representation, serious questions about the legitimacy of
managerial power will continue. It is at the same time
a statement that exhorts corporate capitalism to recognize that the adoption of a new allocative mechanism
provides both capitalism and liberalism with something
that is absolutely indispensable. A new allocative
mechanism, one that grants the subordination of the
corporation to the public interests, provides for a
system of countervailing power that would safeguard
liberalism and guarantee the stockholders their due:
"not as owners but as legitimate claimants to some
fixed share of the profits of a corporation."[44]
It is Bell's push for that system that permits us
to understand his critique of corporate capitalism as a
rationalization of Welfare State liberalism that was
developed less to counter the claims of Milton Friedman
and other conservatives about the inviolability of
private property than to press for the creation of a
new ordering mechanism that can reconcile the logic of
the economizing mode with the logic of the sociologi-

zing mode.

Bell on Politics and the Limits of Democratic Planning

If we take the problems of political philosophy and planning that Bell poses through the concept of the postindustrial society, what we find is Bell posing the problem of formulating a normative theory of the state within a very specific context. We find him posing that overarching problem through an analysis of the limits of interest group theory for understanding the changing nature of American politics.

Bell's analysis is marked by his criticism of V. O. Key's characterization of the politician in a democratic society as a "broker," a characterization in which the politician is viewed as an umpire whose role "is to maintain a working balance between the demands of competing interests and values."[45] The thrust of Bell's criticism is that Key's characterization is "astonishingly" out of date for an understanding of postwar politics because it fails "to take into account the three most decisive characteristics, or shaping elements, of national policy today: the influence of foreign policy, the future orientation of society, and the increasing role of technical decision-making."[46] Because of them the president has to coordinate a wide variety of functions that are new to the presidential office. In emphasizing this point Bell argues that a more adequate picture of American politics than the one projected by interest group theorist "would have to see the presidency as a system capable of free action, even choosing which interests it allows to become inputs, and the executive itself bargaining--on the basis of technocratic decisions--with various interest groups in the society."[47]

The significance of Bell's argument is that it is far from being a legitimation of the broker state, a fact that stands out when Bell's views on the problem of developing a system of social accounts are closely reviewed. The two are hardly compatible.

What we find when we examine Bell's views on the problem of developing such a system is that it poses that problem in terms that parallel his views on utopianism. This is to say that he poses the problem as an inherently unsolvable problem; but one that we must nonetheless struggle with if there is to be any hope of achieving a more rational and hence a better society. Bell's position is that although the United States can develop a system of social accounts that will give us some truer measure of our needs, it is very doubtful that we will ever reach the point that we can in a completely rational fashion make choices between which needs we should give precedence to.

Two presuppositions underlie Bell's statement of this problem. The first is his conviction that because the United States is becoming a communal society it must now create an ordering mechanism whereby the choices between different normative and economic policies can be weighed. To this end, a system of social accounts would serve to "broaden our concept of costs and benefits, and put economic accounting into a broader framework," one against which we can eventually "create a balance sheet that would be useful in clarifying policy choices."[48]

The second is his acceptance of Kenneth J. Arrow's "impossibility theorem," a theorem that demonstrated to many welfare economists' satisfaction the impossibility of any society achieving a truly rational system of social choice through democratic means.[49] The theorem calls for the recognition that, although it fulfills more of the conditions of "fairness" than any other principle (and hence, is infinitely more desirable morally than its alternatives) the principle of majority rule cannot be viewed as a rational principle. This is to say that it cannot be viewed as a principle upon which we can predict what a majority will choose when there are at least three alternatives that the individual members of a society are free to order in any way they choose.

If the ordering of alternatives is to be rational, it must, Arrow argues in Social Choice and Individual Values, meet two formal conditions or axioms of rationality. First, it must be "connected," which is to say that of any two alternatives (x and y) either one is preferred to the other or else they are regarded as indifferent. Second, the ordering has to be "transitive," which is to say that when choices x, y, and z are presented in a set to be voted on by the consumer, it must yield a predictable ordering. It must, in other words, produce an ordering in which we can say that "if x is either preferred or indifferent to y and y is either preferred or indifferent to z then x must be either preferred or indifferent to z."[50]

Can a rational social welfare function (that is, a process or rule that for every set of individual preferences or ordering determines a social ordering) be constructed through democratic processes? This is the central question that Arrow devotes himself to in his analysis of the "impossibility theorem" His answer is that doubts about a rational social welfare function being constructed under democratic processes are raised by the "paradox of voting."[51] The paradox is that if we can predict that the majority in a group will opt for one choice over the other we cannot infer from that what the majority will choose when given a third alternative to choose from freely.

The proof of this paradox can be demonstrated if we construct a scale based on the following three inputs: three individuals stating their preferences on the three issues they think are most important. Suppose after surveying their preferences on these three issues, call them issues x, y, and z, we find that the following pattern emerges:

VOTERS

PREFERENCES	A	B	C
First	x	z	y
Second	y	x	z
Third	z	y	x

We can see that x is preferred to y by a majority (A and B). We can also see from the data that y is preferred to z by a majority (A and C). Given these facts and the principle of transitivity (the principle that says that if an individual prefers x to y and y to z then he would also logically prefer x to z) we would assume, in seeking to predict what the majority would be, that x would also be preferred by the majority over z. Yet, as we can see, z is preferred over x by a majority, that is, by voters B and C. Hence, no majority can be formulated on these three issues.

There is something that is very striking about Bell's acceptance of the Arrow impossibility theorem (apart from his failure to discuss in any detail the questions raised by some economists, namely, Paul Samuelson and Richard B. Brandt, about its methodological soundness) especially when we consider his views on the problem of developing a normative theory of the state.

In his acceptance of the implications of the impossibility theorem (the fact that when accepted at face value it both denies the possibility of any democratic society developing a truly rational ordering mechanism and sets limits on what can be achieved through democratic planning), Bell develops a two-part argument that legitimates the broker state. The first part of that argument is that the impossibility theorem undermines the authority of both liberal and conservative political theory because it strikes "at the assumption of those who think that the general will emerges out of necessity in democratic debate and those rationalists . . . who assume that the public interest is discoverable simply by a summation of preferences."[52] The second part of that argument is that one need not shed tears over this development. The fact that the impossibility theorem challenges these basic rationalist assumptions reinforces the ideal common to the American democratic tradition "that differences between persons are best settled, as are so many differences, by bargaining."[53]

Bell on Equality, Meritocracy, and Justice

When we consider the problems of equality and meritocracy that Bell poses through the concept of the postindustrial society, what we find is that he raises them as problems that underscore the need in the West for a reaffirmation of Welfare State liberalism and the principles of liberal education developed by John Dewey in his philosophy of education. Within this context, it is very important to understand that Bell poses these problems as a preamble to both a vigorous defense of meritocracy and an equally vigorous polemic against the New Left. This polemic is ultimately designed to illustrate the limits of socialism and the virtues of Welfare State liberalism in view of a set of larger problems, the problem of scarcity and the problem of consensus.

Because it is designed to serve that function, Bell's polemic has a heavy impact on Benjamin Kleinberg's argument that Bell is an ideologist of the end of ideology. This is an issue that shall be discussed later. The fact of the matter is that without a detailed elaboration of Bell's polemic that discussion has no reference point. The detailed elaboration begins with the "Coda" to The Coming of Post-Industrial Society.

It is in the "Coda" that Bell posed the problem of meritocracy and equality and in the process focuses on meritocracy in a way that was calculated to highlight the urgency of the problems that he posed. He introduces the subject with a brief summary of Michael Young's fable The Rise of Meritocracy, a book that, as mentioned earlier, outlines the tumultuous demise of meritocracy in England. He then poses a question, the analysis of which dominates much of the "Coda"; a question that is made relevant through his observation that "the post-industrial society, in its initial logic, is a meritocracy."[54] The question that he raises is whether the fate of the meritocracy described by Young is also to be the fate of the postindustrial society.

Bell made it very clear that this is not an academic question. In the fashion of "Columbia and the New Left," he argues that the rise of the New Left and the student and black protest movements have made the fate of the postindustrial society a contemporarily relevant question.

> Any institution which gains a quasi-monopoly power over the fate of individuals is likely, in a free society, to be subject to quick attack. Thus, it is striking that the populist revolt, which Michael Young foresaw several decades hence, has already begun, at the very onset of the post-industrial society. One sees this in the derogation of the IQ and the denunciation of theories espousing a genetic basis of intelligence; the demand for open admission to universities on the part of minority groups in the large urban centers; the pressure for increased numbers of blacks, women, and specific minority groups such as Puerto Ricans and Chicanos in the faculties of universities, by quotas if necessary; and the attack on credentials and even schooling itself as the determinant of a man's position in the society.[55]

In discussing this issue, Bell makes it very clear that it opposed the affirmative action policies of the Johnson and Nixon administrations. He also makes it very clear that he views these policies as having dangerous implications for American society in general and the university in particular. With respect to the former, the adoption of quotas and preferential hiring has reversed the progressive movement of Western society from universalism and achievement back to ascription and particularism. We have seen an extraordinary change, argues Bell, one in which, "without public debate," there has been both a switch from equality of opportunity to equality of result and a substitution of professional qualification and individual achievement for a "new ascriptive principle of corporate entity."[56] This new principle is membership in an ethnic or racial group. "The historic irony" of this change is that it constitutes a "complete reversal of radical and humanist values."[57] Historically, the liberal and radical attack on discrimination has always been based on the denial of group criteria. Now one finds liberals and radicals demanding that "one must have a place primarily because one possesses a particular group attribute."[58]

In extending this argument to the university Bell makes it equally clear that he thinks that the use of quotas in the hiring of faculty and research personnel could only have negative effects for the university and those minority persons it hires on the basis of ascriptive criteria.

> . . . Quotas and preferential hiring mean that standards are bent or broken. The inescapable assumption of the ascriptive criterion as regards tenured university positions is that minority persons are less qualified and could not compete with others, even if given a sufficient margin. What effect does this have on the self-esteem of a person hired on second class grounds? And what effect does it have on the quality of a university, its teaching and research and morale, if its faculties are filled on the basis of quotas?[59]

Bell makes it equally clear that the extension of

affirmative action policies to the universities was the product of a misguided assumption, one that, in effect, makes no distinction between mental and physical labor and no distinction between talent and credentials.

> By focusing on group identity rather than the person, by making the mechanical equation of number of women Ph.D.s to number of positions they should hold, the government assumes that educated labor is homogeneous--that individual talent or achievement is less important than the possession of the credential. This may be true in many occupations, but not in university teaching and research, where individual merit is the singular test. Putting someone in a tenured position, which is capitalized at three quarters of a million dollars, is very different from hiring a black rather than a white plumber; simply having the degree is not necessarily the qualification for the high position.[60]

Bell also makes it very clear that while the affirmative action programs of the Nixon administration posed one threat to the principle of meritocracy, the New Left assertion that "all schooling is being subordinated to the demands of technocratic thinking and that the school is assuming a disproportionate influence in the society" posed another.[61] Within this context, he calls into question Ivan Illich's demand for the elimination of the university and the substitution, in its place, of an informal system of "learning webs made up of skill-exchanges, peermatching and Educators-at-Large."[62] Bell's argument is that in his efforts to recreate a Rousseauian state of nature through the elimination of existing educational institutions, Illich makes the same fundamental mistake that one finds in so much of modernism: the confusion of "experience, in all its diversities, with knowledge."[63]

The modernists are right, the role of experience is important, but it does not, argues Bell, gain from the rejection of the old or the existent.

> Experience has to be made conscious, and this is done, as Dewey remarked, "by

means of that fusion of old meanings and
new situations that transfigures both."
Knowledge is the selective ordering--and
reordering--of experience through relevant concepts. Reality is not a bounded
world, out there, to be imprinted on the
mind as from a mirror, or a flux of
experience to be sampled for its novel-
ties according to one's inclination (or
its relevance for me), but a set of meanings organized by mind, in terms of categories, which establishes the relations
between facts and infers conclusions.[64]

While granting that the postindustrial society
imposes certain constraints on education, Bell argues
that one need not abandon the university as a viable
institution of learning. "One need not defend the
technocratic dimensions of education--its emphasis on
vocationalism and specialization--to argue that schooling becomes more necessary than ever before."[65] All
that one has to realize is that "by the very fact that
there are now many more differentiated ways in which
people gain information and have experiences, there is
a need for the self-conscious understanding of the
processes of conceptualization as the means of organizing one's information in order to gain coherent perspectives on one's experience."[66]

Within this context, Bell defines the function of
the university in the postindustrial society as one
that involves the ability

to relate to each other the modes of
conscious inquiry: historical consciousness, which is the encounter with a tradition that can be tested against the
present; methodological consciousness,
which makes explicit the conceptual
grounds of inquiry and its philosophical
presuppositions; and individual self-
consciousness, which makes one aware of
the sources of one's prejudgments and
allows one to re-create one's values
through the disciplined study of the
society.[67]

To this set of Hellenistic prescriptions, Bell

concludes his polemic with Illich with his philosophy of education, a philosophy that at the same time bears the imprint of his Hebraism and his Hellenism.

> Education is the reworking of the materials of the past, without ever wholly surrendering its truths or bending to its pieties. It is a continuing tension, "the tension between past and future mind and sensibility, tradition and experience, [which] for all its strains and discomforts, is the only source for maintaining the independence of inquiry itself." It is the affirmation of the principle of intellectual and artistic order through the search for relatedness of discordant knowledge.[68]

Bell continues his polemic against the New Left in the "Coda" by challenging John Rawls's theory of justice. Bell's interest in Rawls stemmed, in part, from the fact that under Rawls "the concept of equality of result has become the Archimedean point of a major new effort to provide a philosophical foundation--a conception of justice as fairness for a communal society."[69] In greater part it stemmed from the fact that through a critique of Rawls's theory Bell could provide himself with a vehicle for reasserting, through the Arrow impossibility theorem, the indispensability of the principle of relevant differences in constructing a fair and intellectually viable philosophy of the public household.

Bell's critique of Rawls's theory of justice is fundamentally an extension of his critique of the limits of utility theory. It is an extension of this thesis that Arrow's impossibility theorem demonstrates the fallacy of the rationalist assumption that the public interest is discoverable simply by a summation of preferences. The fact that it can be understood in these terms is a function of Bell's criticism of Rawls's notion that there can be a generalized social norm that is truly rational. The problem, as Bell puts it, is not so much the development of a social norm that expresses our interest in achieving a society based on fairness, that is, the principle of helping the least fortunate as the prior obligation of society. The problem is, can we develop a social norm that is at the same time both fair and rational?

Rawls makes the claim, Bell argues, that a generalized social norm can be constructed that corresponds to the sum of the individual's preferences on what the norm should be. He also makes the claim that this social norm can be rational; but he avoids the central question that a democratic society must seek to come to terms with. The question is: if rationality is the basis of the social norm, can we have, given Arrow's impossibility theorem, "a social welfare function that amalgamates the discordant preferences of individuals into a combined choice which recapitulates the rationality of the individual choice?"[70]

We can choose to avoid the difficulties imposed by the impossibility theorem as Rawls does by rejecting the principle of majority rule on the grounds that the action of a majority does not, a priori, make any decision just. But if we do we face an overriding problem: "is there, as a consistent rule, any better method than majority vote, subject to the democratic check of a minority having the right and ability to change the decision and become a majority, in reaching consensus."[71] This, argues Bell, is but one of the problems that we find in Rawls's work.

Rawls's theory also suffers, argues Bell, from the fact that while his proposal that the maximization of the minimum sounds equalitarian because it moves the distribution of such primary social goods as income and self-respect to the mean, it, as Lester Thurow, has demonstrated, need not be equalitarian at all. Thurow's argument is that what Rawls presumes in this proposal is that the trickle-down effect would be "so large that it would be impossible to design economic activities that concentrated income gains among high income groups."[72] What he rejects is the fact that "there are many economic activities with marginal amounts of trickle-down."[73] He thus skirts, argues Bell, the essential problem of distribution, which is the fact that "some coercive device may be necessary to achieve the desired outcome of a set of rules that will maximize the minimum prize, or give priority to the disadvantaged."[74]

Barring the rejection of the principle of majority rule, what we are faced with, given the Arrow impossibility theorem, is the fact that what the social norm will be is ultimately a political question that is "subject either to consensus or to conflict--extortion by the most threatening, or collective bargaining in which people eventually accept some idea of trade-off."[75] We are faced, in other words, with the realization that "we may want a social norm for reasons of fairness, but in the structure of rational choice procedures we cannot define one."[76]

Because this is the case we are faced with another binding truth: the fact that "the principle of helping the least fortunate as the prior social obligation may mean--in a sociological sense as well as statistical sense--a regression toward the mean."[77] The problem here, argues Bell, is that

> if it is assumed that we have reached a post-scarcity stage of full abundance, this may be a desirable social policy. But if this is not so--and it is questionable whether it can ever be so--and if one defines society, as Rawls does, "as a cooperative venture for mutual advantage," why not, just as logically, allow greater incentives for those who can expand the total social output and use this larger social pie for the mutual (yet differential) advantage of all?[78]

Bell concludes his polemic against Rawls with a spirited defense of meritocracy and equality of opportunity.

> The United States today is not a meritocracy; but this does not discredit the principle. The idea of equality of opportunity is a just one, and the problem is to realize it fairly. The focus, then, has to be on the barriers to such equality. The redress of discrimination by representation introduces arbitrary, particularistic criteria which can only be destructive of universalism, the historic principle, won under great difficulty, of treating each person as a person in his own right.[79]

To this observation, Bell adds, in a remark that he would soon elaborate into the principle of relevant differences, that "the difficult and thorny question, in the end, is not just priority--who should be helped first--but the degree of disparity among persons."[80] This is the question of how much difference there should be "in income between the head of a corporation and a common laborer, between a professor at the top of the scale and an instructor?"[81] As economic decisions became politicized, "and the market becomes replaced by social decisions the question that will be one of the most 'vexing' for the United States as a post-industrial society is what shall be 'the principle of fair reward and fair differences.'"[82]

What, of course, we hear in these set of remarks (remarks that we cite because they as much as anything else constitute the context in which Bell ultimately poses the problems of meritocracy and equality) is what we hear when we examine the context in which he poses the problems of social structure and culture. We hear a call made on the basis of the principle of relevant differences for a philosophy of the public household; the call for a new public philosophy.

The Repeated Call for a New Public Philosophy

The context in which Bell poses the problems of social structure and the adversary culture is one that was designed to dramatically illustrate America's need for a public philosophy that can restore the legitimacy of Welfare State liberalism. The context is Bell's portrait of American society experiencing a crisis of authority made inevitable by its inability to define the limits of protest.

The fact that Bell poses the problems of social structure and culture in order to substantiate his claims about America's need for a new public philosophy is confirmed by his advancement at the end of The Coming of Post-Industrial Society of the very same assessment of the crisis of liberalism that he formulates in "The Cultural Contradictions of Capitalism": inculcated by the adversary culture, liberalism, though repelled by the tendencies of the counterculture, "finds itself at a loss to explain its reticence" about them.[83]

Trapped by the fact that it approves a basic permissiveness, liberalism, argues Bell, "cannot with any certainty define the bounds" of that permissiveness.[84] What is significant about this assessment is the conclusion that he derived from it: liberalism's failure to define the limits of the disruptive behavior that it will tolerate "leaves the moral order in a state of confusion and disarray," one from which liberalism "may yet suffer a reaction."[85]   The reason why such a possibility could not be ruled out, argues Bell in a statement that (if not explicitly, then certainly implicitly) represents, in the image that it evokes, a call for a philosophy of the public household, is that while "ideas and cultural styles do not change history --at least, not overnight . . . they are the necessary prelude to change, since a change in consciousness--in values and moral reasoning--is what moves men to change their social arrangements and institutions."[86]

Toward a Conclusion

The problems that Bell poses through the concept of the postindustrial society makes certain conclusions about The Coming of Post-Industrial Society inevitable.

The first is that Bell poses several problems especially the problems of meritocracy and equality, in a way that serves to rationalize an image of the world that is implicit in his concept of the postindustrial society.   In this image the world is a game between people in which, given the limits of planning and reason, there can be no perfect set of rules concerning the distribution of rewards and services.   This image ultimately serves to justify the development of a philosophy of the public household on both the same grounds specified in "The Public Household" and foreshadowed in "The End of Ideology" essay, that is, on the grounds that scarcity and the insatiableness of human appetites prohibits anything more than the achievement of Welfare State liberalism in the United States.   But does this make Bell an ideologist?

The answer is "yes" if we understand by that term someone who seeks to rationalize an image of the world that conceals a predetermined articulated end.   There can be no doubt given the ways in which Bell both articulates and uses the concept of the postindustrial society that the message of the public household was self-consciously prefigured into its construction.   The answer is also "yes," if scarcity and restraint of human appetites are to be on a priori grounds applied to some groups and not to others.   The fact that Bell never specifies what interests will be represented in

the final construction of the normative philosophy of
the public household tends to promote the view that
Bell ultimately treats this issue as a technological
problem rather than as an ideological problem. And
yet, as Bell would concede, it is a distinctly ideological problem.

Ultimately, the restatement of a society's
grounded values implies a set of weights attached to
those values. What weights are attached to what values, and what lessons from the past are to be used to
balance the scales, are problems that are not resolvable in fixed administrative terms. They imply the
existence of an overarching set of philosophical and
political impulses that are themselves the logical
outcome of a set of perceptions and images grounded in
the selective reconstruction of reality. That reconstruction is never value free: it is always reduction-
ary and, hence, ideological.

Bell's omissions are glaring but they are not out
of character. Bell's calls for a public philosophy are
always calls, they are never articulated philosophy.
They are always a set of calls that imply the guidelines for the construction of a new public philosophy.
Those guidelines are the grounded values of a social
scientist whose work is marked by a tremendous intellectual and emotional investment in demonstrating to an
audience which he believes does not have his vivid
recollections of Kronstadt, the Moscow trials, and the
Nazi-Soviet Peace Pact, that ideological politics has
no constructive place in a world whose complexities
require technical and administrative solutions rather
than ideological ones.

Bell's concept of the postindustrial society, in
the sense that it promotes an image of the world in
which there are no fixed absolute solutions (a world
subject to the constraints demonstrated by the Arrow
"impossibility theorem") reflects his message about the
limits of ideological politics. More than anything
else this concept served as a vehicle by which Bell
could promote against the New Left a message that,
again, is implicit in the concept's very construction.

Yet this image of ideology as being the absolutism
of the left is as we have noted not a unique one; it is
the idea embodied in Mannheim's utopianism, the notion
that utopias always aim to shatter the prevailing order
of things. Under Bell's conception one could not be a
liberal ideologist or a conservative one, but one

could, we imagine, be of the radical right. Obscured in Bell's use of the term is what it took Alexis de Tocqueville's genius to recognize: historically, intellectuals on both the left and right ends of the political spectrum have served with equal passion as legitimators of ideas. They can and frequently do define the parameters of political planning and discussion for very often it is they who are given the reins to distinguish the possible from the impossible.

We have reached another fork in the road. If we are to stop here and conclude that Bell is ultimately an ideologist whose work is only designed, as some of his critics would have us believe, to rationalize technocracy, we would be making a grave error. Not only would such a conclusion be intellectually wrong it would also be irresponsible. One need not have to be an apologist for Bell to recognize that just as The Coming of Post-Industrial Society serves to rationalize the message of his "End of Ideology" essay it also, in the fashion of Thorstein Veblen's The Price System and the Engineers, provides a strong argument against technocracy.

Bell's argument, which is elaborated in the sixth chapter of The Coming of Post-Industrial Society, "Who Will Rule?," is that given the technical complexities of planning and decision making in advanced industrial societies both the politician and the political public will have to become increasingly versed in the technical character of policy. They will have to become "aware of the ramified impact of decisions as systems become extended."87 This argument, especially when taken in conjunction with Bell's assertion that "the technical intelligentsia must learn to question the often unanalyzed assumptions about efficiency and rationality which underlie their techniques" discredits the principle of technocracy.88 It discredits technocracy on grounds that were first specified in "Adjusting Men to Machines" and "Work and Its Discontents"; grounds that qualify Bell as a radical critic of managerial absolutism. But is Bell's radicalism enough?

The demand that politicians should become versed in technology and technologists become aware of their assumptions is a programmatic hope that they can do so. It is a hope upon which, like other of Bell's hopes, one bases current policy. The hope is taken as a fact; and the possible nonachievement of the hope is discounted or not considered.

One might entertain the possibility that politicians can take over the technocrat's view, including the technical, bureaucratic rationality and the authoritarianism of the technologist. Conversely, one might imagine that in sacrificing princple for expedience technologists might (in the fashion of the Adolph Eichman that emerges from Hannah Arendt's _Eichman in Jerusalem_) take over the larger "irrationalities" of the politicians and implement them rationally. All of these are possibilities within the assumption of the future convergence of the perspective of democratic politics and managerial rationality. Yet Bell only considers one possibility. If he is an ideologist-- even for democratic planning--he accomplishes his ideological argument by excluding alternatives, not by polemic advocacy and achieves the same purposes that a manifest ideologist would.

But again Bell's opposition to technocracy and to the claims of purely functional rationality suggests that he is more than just an ideologist. Bell's real concern is about developing a conceptual groundwork against which liberalism can generate a new integrative philosophy: a philosophy of the public household. Bell's opposition to technocracy and the misplaced reliance on functional rationality that the technocratic mind-set produces gives evidence to his ability to map out against the excesses of both the political left and the right the first steps of a highly reasoned defense of rational planning. His defense succeeds in building on the spirit common to classical liberalism and utopian socialism: faith in humanity's capacity to transform the world through reason.

It may well be that when all is said and done, when all the questions about Bell's standing as an ideologist recede into the background, his work will be remembered as providing the paradigm for the final construction of that public philosophy. The question as to whether he is an ideologist will, then, be viewed as a purely academic one. It will have relevance only to the extent that efforts to resolve it provide a useful and (probably) necessary framework for discerning the contradictions and tensions that frame his efforts to develop a philosophy of the public household that serves to legitimate the thrust toward rational planning made necessary by both the success of liberal capitalism and the failure of liberal political theory to anticipate OPEC and the exigencies of limited growth in an economy traditionally given to unplanned growth.

Notes

1. Bell, _The Coming of Post-Industrial Society_, p. 116.
2. Ibid.
3. Bell, _The Cultural Contradictions of Capitalism_, p. 275.
4. Ibid., p. 11.
5. Ibid., p. 12.
6. Ibid., p. 14.
7. Bell, _The Coming of Post-Industrial Society_, p. 409.
8. Ibid.
9. Ibid., p. 410.
10. Ibid.
11. Ibid., p. 25.
12. Ibid., p. 480.
13. Ibid.
14. Ibid.
15. Ibid., p. 288.
16. Ibid., p. 283.
17. Ibid., p. 301.
18. Ibid.
19. Ibid., p. 303.
20. Ibid., p. 304.
21. Ibid., p. 475.
22. Ibid., p. 304.
23. Ibid., p. 10.
24. Ibid., p. 44.
25. Ibid.
26. Ibid., p. 150.
27. Ibid., p. 157.
28. Ibid.
29. Ibid.
30. Ibid., p. 272.
31. Ibid., p. 271.
32. Ibid., p. 272.
33. Ibid.
34. Ibid.
35. Ibid.
36. Ibid., p. 293.
37. Ibid., p. 313.
38. Ibid., p. 273.

39. Ibid.

40. In calling for this commitment from the national government, Bell argues that "the major sociological problem ahead will be the test of our ability to foresee the effects of social and technological change and to construct alternative courses in accordance with different valuations of ends, at different costs." Bell, The Coming of Post-Industrial Society, p. 284.

41. Ibid., p. 294.

42. Ibid., p. 298.

43. Ibid., p. 297.

44. Ibid., p. 295.

45. Ibid., p. 310.

46. Ibid.

47. Ibid.

48. Ibid., p. 326.

49. For a further discussion see Sidney Hook, ed., Human Values and Economic Policy (New York: New York University Press, 1967).

50. I. M. Copi, review of Social Choice and Individual Values by Kenneth J. Arrow (New York: John Wiley & Sons, 1951) in Ethics 62, April 1952, p. 221.

51. Bell, The Coming of Post-Industrial Society, p. 306.

52. Ibid., p. 307.

53. Ibid.

54. Ibid., p. 409.

55. Ibid., p. 410.

56. Ibid., p. 419.

57. Ibid.

58. Ibid.

59. Ibid., p. 418.

60. Ibid.

61. Ibid., p. 419.

62. Ibid., p. 422.

63. Ibid.

64. Ibid.

65. Ibid., p. 423.

66. Ibid.

67. Ibid.

68. Ibid.

69. Ibid., p. 433.

70. Ibid., p. 448.

71. Ibid., p. 449.

72. Ibid.

73. Ibid.

74. Ibid.
75. Ibid.
76. Ibid.
77. Ibid.
78. Ibid., pp. 449-50.
79. Ibid., p. 450.
80. Ibid.
81. Ibid., pp. 450-51.
82. Ibid., p. 450.
83. Ibid., p. 479.
84. Ibid.
85. Ibid.
86. Ibid.
87. Ibid., p. 365.
88. Ibid.

8

Conclusion

The Final Fork in the Road

Once again we have reached another fork in the road. We have stated that because of his critique of managerial absolutism Bell is more than just an ideologist. But that begs the question. Is he an ideologist? More specifically, is he an ideologist on the grounds specified by Benjamin Kleinberg? Is he an ideologist of the end of ideology who has attempted through the development of the theory of the postindustrial society to rationalize the ideological perspectives embedded in the end of ideology? What are these perspectives?

They, as noted earlier, include the disavowal of the ideological politics of the left in favor of a kind of administrative or technical rationality which requires that no action be undertaken unless its costs and benefits are specified. It also includes an assessment of social conditions in the United States that obviates the need for radical reform or socialism, namely, the view that the fundamental political problems of the industrial revolution have been solved.

The best way to resolve the problem is to start with "The Public Household." Ultimately, The Coming of Post-Industrial Society serves as the proof against which "The Public Household" is also the summation of Bell's 1960s writings. If there is any one single work that represents the continuities in Bell's thinking it is "The Public Household"; that work, again, has its origins in his 1949 essay "America's Un-Marxist Revolution." Thus, it would seem that if one work embodies the perspectives embedded in the end of ideology it would be "The Public Household." But does it?

The answers are maybe and no. Maybe one could read into Bell's call for a public philosophy that does not and "cannot ignore the past" an implicit reference to Kronstadt, the Moscow trials, and the Nazi-Soviet Peace Pacts--events that underscored the naivete of ideological politics. Characteristically, these events dominated Bell's image of the past and dictated his emphases on utopias being legitimate when and only when they can specify their costs in advance. The War on Poverty programs and the affirmative action initiatives of the Johnson and Nixon administrations only served to reinforce the lesson derived from each of these events: there are some problems that are not resolvable in fixed and absolute terms, hence planning must be tempered to accommodate reality. However, nowhere in Bell's design for the new public philosophy is there expressed the view so typical of the end of ideology that the fundamental problems of the industrial revolution have been solved.

Where then does this analysis leave us? If Bell is an ideologist he is an ideologist because he has self-consciously worked to rationalize an image of the world (the image of scarcity and cultural crisis projected in <u>The Coming of Post-Industrial Society</u>) that justifies the establishment of a new public philosophy on the lines detailed in "The Public Household." Certainly one cannot fault Bell for trying to develop the principles around which a theory of justice fitted to the needs of a liberal society can be developed. He can, however, be faulted for trying to pass on as a scientific fact an image of American society that is designed to legitimate the moral authority of those principles and the claims they make. The use of science for that end is self-serving and ideological.

But Bell to the extent that he is an ideologist is a strange kind of ideologist. At the same time that Bell devotes himself to rationalizing "The Public Household" with its emphasis on the limits of social policy and planning he devotes himself to rationalizing the radicalization of the corporation and the democratization of work. He is, on the one hand, carrying out John Dewey's mandate of creating the new public philosophy liberalism requires to get out of the crisis of authority it has been thrust into by capitalism. But he ironically carries out that mandate along the lines specified by Reinhold Niebuhr's moral injunctions against the faith common to liberalism and socialism; the faith in the inevitability of progress through science and reason. He, in other words, carried out Dewey's mandate by expounding a philosophy of the public household whose principles are based on limits rather than possibilities.

One might conclude, then, that if Bell is an ideologist because he excludes possibilities and thus accomplishes the same goals a manifest ideologist would, namely, limiting the range of alternatives available against which policy choices can be made through the political process, through the making of the possible possible. The only problem with such a conclusion is that when rendered as a final overarching conclusion it excludes other more salient characterizations.

Let us be very clear on this point. The case has been made that Bell is an ideologist. But the results do not support the charges made by Benjamin Kleinberg and foreshadowed in C. Wright Mill's "Letter to the New Left." The results indicate that Bell is an ideologist because his writings up to and including The Coming of Post-Industrial Society serve to rationalize the necessity for creating a new public philosophy along the lines specified in "The Public Household." The theory of the postindustrial society developed over the course of those writings was, again, written to furnish the proof against which "The Public Household" could be made to derive its intellectual authority.

Terms like ideologist and neoconservative are credible terms. They can provide a useful way of seeing things but not when they are used to exclude, be it in the name of science or in the interests of ideology, a fuller understanding (and perhaps even appreciation) of a writer's work and the forces that serve to shape that work. The task is to find a means of classification that can facilitate the ultimate purposes of a study such as this, one that is aimed less toward the resolution of the problem of whether Bell is an ideologist and more toward understanding the contradictions and tensions that frame his work; one that thus tries to locate Bell's work within some kind of intellectual tradition.

Again, let us be clear. This is not to say that the problem of whether Bell is an ideologist is insignificant. It is not in any sense an insignificant

problem. In addition to the reasons previously specified there is still yet another reason why it is a
problem that demands serious attention. The analysis
it requires serves as the necessary prerequisite for
locating the tensions and contradictions in Bell's
writings. Ultimately, a critique of concept constructions should do more than determine whether a theorist's work is ideological; as both Max Weber and Karl
Mannheim recognized it should provide the mechanism for
defining the Weltanschuung out of which the theorist's
thinking emerges. It should arouse a fuller comprehension of the ideas that humans struggle to realize by
making explicit not only the values and assumptions
that underlie the construction of those ideas but the
Weltanschuung that ultimately produces and legitimates
those values and assumptions.

So Nu? The Bottom Line

Nu is a Yiddish word and like all Yiddish words it
evokes more than its literal translation into English
can convey. It means more than "come give me the final
point." Intolerant of pilpulisms and equivocations nu
means "hurry up with your point in spades." It is a
fitting word, one which resonates through the term
neoconservatism.

While it recognizes the place of ambivalence and
contradictions, the term neoconservatism says that a
Bell should be held accountable for what is preeminent
in his writings, his cultural conservatism. The work
that gives this term its greatest authority is Peter
Steinfels's Neoconservatives.

But Steinfels's Neoconservatives does more than
explicate this long-lingering inchoate term. It makes
good use of images to dramatize the careers of Daniel
Patrick Moynihan, Irving Kristol, Daniel Bell, and
Nathan Glazer. One of them is the image of the centaur.[1]

Like the word nu, centaur has a fitting place in
this discussion for ultimately Bell is as much, if not
more, the conciliator as the ideologist, and this
brings us to the nub of the issue.

The classification of Bell as an ideologist is
deficient. It misses more than it explains. Ultimately, its chief value is that it leads us, when we ask
what Bell is an ideologist of, to the contradictions

and tensions evident in his work.   Limited also is the term neoconservatism.

The term as used by Steinfels bears the sins of its virtues.   Under neoconservatism it is possible for a Bell to be a "socialist in economics, a liberal in politics, and a conservative in culture."[2]   The term, in other words, permits for complexities and contradictions.   Indeed, the term serves as a benchmark against which contradictions can be gauged in relation to the predominance of certain fixed themes; themes that are at the same time conservative and new, and which emerge from liberal, conservative, and socialist traditions.[3]

And yet the term neoconservatism is flawed.   It implies a greater degree of cohesion of ideas and themes then one finds evidenced in Bell's work.   The term when applied to Bell's work is too narrow, too facile.   To belong to a group where socialist and conservative affinities alike are tolerated is not to take into account the tension that one brings to the reconciliation of those affinities.   This is not to say that one cannot be a liberal in politics, a socialist in economics, and a conservative in culture.   It is to say that one can hardly wear these different hats without some struggle, without some tension.

Ultimately, then, what is Bell?   He is, above all, a conciliator.   He is a Jewish intellectual who sees his mission as that of developing the ultimate grounds upon which some reconciliation between the economizing and the sociologizing mode can be effected in a world that he perceives as being divided on the right by conservatives, who, like Milton Friedman, would see the United States return to the world of Adam Smith and on the left by those consumed by an adversary culture that would threaten the standards upon which Bell's political philosophy is constructed.   These are the standards of a social scientist who, in his own fashion, has remained faithful to his own "revisionist" conception of socialism yet who, at the same time, has ruled out the feasibility of a socialist victory in the United States.

Bell's conception is one that springs out of the British socialist tradition as articulated by the former British Labour party leader Clement R. Attlee who, in his treatise on socialism in England, The Labour Party in Perspective and Twelve Years Later, declared that in order for socialism to succeed in countries with a democratic tradition, it must be adapted to the particular exigencies of the country in which it seeks to occupy a dominant role. Bell's conception, like Attlee's, rules from socialism the membership of theorists or revolutionaries so absorbed by "utopian dreams" that they are "unwilling to deal with the actualities of everyday life."[4] Bell's conception is one that would seek to reconcile the faith of socialism with the American pragmatic "national style" with the necessities of limited planning and with the limits of man as a rational being.

In this regard, it is not without significance that Bell could end The Coming of Post-Industrial Society with the same argument about utopianism with which he ended "The End of Ideology in the West: An Epilogue." His ultimate argument is that utopia represents an unrealizable idea that men can and should strive for but one that they, given the nature of things, can never achieve.

> Utopia has always been conceived as a design of harmony and perfection in the relations between men. In the wisdom of the ancients, utopia was a fruitful impossibility, a conception of the desirable which men should always strive to attain but which, in the nature of things, could not be achieved. And yet, by its very idea, utopia would serve as a standard of judgments on men, an ideal by which to measure the real.[5]

Nor is it without significance that Bell directed this admonition to the New Left:

> The modern hubris has sought to cross that gap and embody the ideal in the real; and in the effort the perspective of the ideal has diminished and the idea of Utopia has become tarnished. Perhaps it would be wiser to return to the classic conception.
>
> Men in their imagination will always seek to make society a work of art; that remains an ideal. Given the tasks that have to be solved, it is enough to engage in the sober construction of social reality.[6]

But what of Bell's own work? What about a public
philosophy that is based on achieving an agreement on
ultimate values and that will limit the demands of all
groups on the public household? What about a public
philosophy that will be the basis of the rational
allocation of societal rewards and that will secure the
consent of all parties to the allocations and to the
mechanism of allocation? Within Bell's framework such
a public philosophy is itself utopian.

Bell's scheme, his prescription for the new public
philosophy, is also utopian in the Enlightenment sense
that the mere announcement of the reasonable solution
to a problem (in his case a reasonable program for the
solution of the problem) is the basis of its acceptance. His rationality thus assumes the rationality of
others. Yet there is nothing in Bell's program to
suggest that his hopes that politicians, businessmen,
and technologists will be reasonable (as New Left ideologues are not) are any more than hopes. In converting
programmatic hopes to facts, based perhaps on the idea
that the necessary will be rationally perceived, Bell
may be both a utopian and unlikely dialectician. The
future inevitably reaches out and guides the blind to a
higher reason that only the dialectician foresees.

The salient problem is how useful is the concept
of the postindustrial society in providing a sober
construction of social reality. If by "sober" Bell
means a construction of social reality that reinforces
the end of ideology thesis that the problems of modern
industrial society transcend (utopian) ideology and can
only be dealt with through planning, the answer is that
Bell's concept does provide a sober construction of
reality. But a sober construction of reality must also
deal with the problem of how planning is legitimated
and who legitimates it. A sober construction of reality must, in other words, try to determine when planning, political and otherwise, becomes an end in itself. And in this the concept of the postindustrial
society fails. It also fails to go beyond the formal
statement of the need for planning. The specific substantive goals, priorities, and allocations are left to
the future as are the plans to work out a mechanism for
goal allocation and the decision as to who does the
actual planning.

Ultimately, all that Bell's concept of the postindustrial society succeeds in doing is to specify the
programmatic or formal dimensions along which humans

can plan for a better world. These dimensions, in effect, represent attempts at a reconciliation of Dew-eyian instrumentalism with its optimism about the in-evitability of progress through science and planning and the pessimism of Reinhold Niebuhr with its emphasis on the limits of planning and reform. But the concept succeeds at doing this at the price of sacrificing, in the name of a sober image of humanity, what it took Karl Mannheim's genius to recognize: that utopias can-not always specify their costs in preestablished terms. Nor should they have to, especially when the insistence that they do, in effect, guarantees the virtual perpe-tuation of the status quo. Bell's image of humanity is one that stresses the duality that encompasses humani-ty's existence and the ineradicable tension under which it lives. It stresses, on the one hand, a murderous aggression from primal impulse, to tear apart and des-troy, and on the other, humanity's "search for order, in art and life, as the binding of the will to harmo-nious shape."7

Ultimately, it is this image of humanity, an image forged over a lifetime, that makes The Coming of Post-Industrial Society the work of a synthesizer, a moral-ist, dedicated after the fashion of the nineteenth-century English critic Matthew Arnold, to the tempering of the radical idea with the conservative impulse.

It is not accident that we have identified Bell with Matthew Arnold rather than with Edmund Burke, the figure that Bell's critics generally compare him with in their efforts to characterize him as a neoconserva-tive. This is not to say that there is not some basis in using Burke as a model for analyzing Bell's work. Burke's Reflections on the Revolution in France bears the strain of his knowledge of the danger of modern abstraction and ideologies when they are allied with modern politics. So too does Bell's work up to and including The Coming of Post-Industrial Society and The Cultural Contradiction of Capitalism show evidence of this strain, and often with the same result; the failure to recognize that "the moral imagination can easily smother and destroy valuable ideas as [it can] humanize dangerous abstractions."8 Yet the use of Burke as a model upon which to discuss Bell's work is fundamentally wrong.

What makes it wrong is that it misses the complex-ities of Bell's work. The use of Burke as a model for analyzing Bell's work misses the fact that from a left-

liberal perspective Bell's work is that of a social
scientist dedicated to making an irrefutable case to
the corporate managers and the defenders of laissez-
faire capitalism for accepting both the subordination
of the corporation to society and the necessity of
reconciling the economizing mode to the exigencies of
the sociologizing mode. It misses the fact that on the
right his work is that of a man dedicated to showing
the limits of the "adversary culture" embraced by the
New Left. Ultimately, the Burke analogy obscures the
fact that Bell's work is rich in the kind of contradictions that one would expect of a man who seeks to
reconcile for himself the optimism of a John Dewey with
the pessimism of a Reinhold Niebuhr. Bell is an intellectual who, in effect, seeks to reconcile the Hellenic, the "spontaneity of consciousness," with the Hebraic, "the strictness of conscience."[9]

The advantage of using Matthew Arnold as a model
for discussing Bell's work is that it permits us to
focus on the contradictions in his work without ever
losing a sense of the original impulses that gave rise
to them. The Arnold analogy thus gives us a sense of
the grounding of the contradictions that frame his work
in intellectual history.

Contradictions and Reconciliations

What are the contradictions that frame Bell's
work? Certainly the most basic and overriding one is
the acceptance of what he himself, when discussing the
limits of growth argument developed by exponents of the
Jay Forrester model, rejected in principle: the view
that the world is a closed system of fixed resources.
The fallacy of the Forrester model as Bell recognized
is that it assumes that "no qualitative change in the
behavior of the system takes place or is even possible."[10] Yet, paradoxically enough, Bell accepts a
Niebuhrian image of the world that presumes that man
lives in a world of immutable boundaries. This is an
image of the world that is bound by a fixed set of
limits; limits that by definition preclude the search
for utopia. In this image man is destined to live in a
permanent state of anxiety unless he, in accepting his
limits as a creature of nature, can operate between
those limits and his own aspirations in effecting a
balance between the finiteness and the freedom that

both bounds his life and makes him, in the final analysis, a creature of necessity. Ultimately, Bell's acceptance of the Niebuhrian worldview is part of a larger contradiction.

The most striking thing that one finds in Bell's work from the mid-1940s to the present is that it is guided by the desire to effect some balance between the seventeenth-century rationalism of the Enlightenment with its faith in the inevitability of progress and what he calls the "wisdom of the ancients": the realization that life must be bound by "halakah," that is, by "the law" or "the way."[11] The desire to strike a balance between these two perspectives constitute the basis of Bell's polemic against Marxian socialism. It is the reason why he invokes, against the Chiliasm of the old left, Max Weber's distinction between the ethics of responsibility (or the acceptance of limits) and the ethics of conscience (or the dedication to absolute ends). That desire is also the basis of his polemic against the New Left and modernism.

The counterpart to Bell's efforts to strike a balance between seventeenth-century Enlightenment rationalism and the moral injunctions of Judaism and Pauline Christianity is Matthew Arnold's critique of mid-nineteenth-century English life, Culture and Anarchy. In that work Arnold analyzes the philosophical defense of anarchism as a precondition for trying to establish "a principle of authority in England sufficiently strong to judge and control the excesses of doing as one likes" that he associates with the Hyde Park riots: one that would constitute a balance between the Hellenic and the Hebraic.[12] Although it was not explicitly mentioned by him Arnold's subject was John Stuart Mill's essay On Liberty; a work that he respected but that he viewed as rationalizing the anarchic tradition that he associated with Benthamism and nonconformism.[13]

For Arnold the distinction between these two categories of intellectual development is that where Hebraism is concerned primarily with conduct and with obedience to a law of conduct--with "strictness of conscience"--Hellenism is concerned with seeing things as they are. It is concerned with "spontaneity of conscience."[14] It is a distinction between a conception of human nature that "speaks of thinking clearly, seeing things in their essence and beauty, as a grand and precious feat for man to achieve [Hellenism]" an another, Hebraism, that "speaks of becoming conscious of sin, of awakening to a sense of sin, as a fact of this kind."[15] The distinction between the two is, as Lionel Trilling notes, a distinction between the basic assumptions of rationalism and Christianity.

The basis of comparison between Arnold and Bell rests upon the fact that while Arnold could weave a philosophy of history around the distinction between the Hebraic and the Hellenistic to analyze the merits of quantity and quality in English society, Bell could do the same with respect to American society. This is to say that while Arnold could say in referring back to Hebraism and Hellenism "here is too much a good thing, or too little and [thus be] spared the offense of saying here is a bad thing," Bell could do the same with respect to rationalism and religion in analyzing American society. The comparison between the two also rests in the fact that each in his own fashion attempted to find in the balance between the Hebraic and the Hellenistic a foundation for order and authority in society. The difference between the two men of course is that while Arnold argued that mid-nineteenth-century England required more Hellenism to achieve a balance between the two extremes, Bell took the opposite position. For him what is required in order for contemporary American to achieve such a balance is more Hebraism, more order. Yet what joins Arnold and Bell together are their efforts to effect a reconciliation between these two discordant worldviews in response to their own perceptions of the "crisis of liberalism." They can be defined in each case as the efforts of men committed to tempering the radical idea with the conservative impulse.

In the final analysis, Bell is an intellectual who operates out of a very distinctly Jewish socialist tradition, a tradition that seeks to reconcile the Hellenistic and Hebraic worldviews. It is a tradition, a Weltanschauung, that can be traced back to Moses Hess. The struggle that resonates through works like The End of Ideology and The Coming of Post-Industrial Society is both a legitimate and painful one; ultimately it is that struggle that distinguishes Bell from Moynihan, Kristol, and Glazer.

Bell and Neoconservatism

To distinguish Bell from "neoconservatives" like Moynihan, Kristol, and Glazer is not as difficult a task as one might imagine. The key rests in the extent to which each struggles with their own past.

Neoconservatism is defined by Peter Steinfels as the fork in the road taken by liberals who can no longer align themselves with socialism in the struggle to restructure American society. The fork in the road is the crisis of authority evoked in the 1960s. Distrustful of the New Left, they are the people who have come to align themselves with the moderate right but the baggage they bring with them on their travels is mixed with remnants of a well-traveled past, among them the socialism of their youth. Never a socialist, Moynihan is the exception not the rule: he is the neoconservative for whom there is no radical past to struggle against or to justify one's claims to prior experience.

There is little in Glazer's and Kristol's writings to suggest any struggle. The moral injunctions against the hedonism of the adversary culture are never counterbalanced by pointed critiques of capitalist institutions. No claim to a just or necessary socialism is ever exercised. It would be rhetorical for us to ask whether the same can be said for Bell.

Aside from the obvious attacks against capitalism as evidence in "The Cultural Contradictions of Capitalism" the place of Bell's socialism remains constant. As we have gone to considerable lengths to show, Bell's socialism leads him to a place in which Moynihan, Kristol, and Glazer would have a difficult time establishing more than a summertime home; it leads him to espouse both the subordination of the corporation to the greater society and the subordination of the economizing mode to the sociologizing mode.

One may legitimately question whether Bell's socialism goes far enough. One may even argue that Bell repeatedly comes out on the wrong side of the struggle that his efforts to reconcile Hellenism with Hebraism makes necessary. But there is no denying the struggle.

We have previously referred to this struggle in terms of a Jewish socialist tradition that can be traced back to Moses Hess. It is time to expand that thesis for ultimately it is that tradition that is the Weltanschauung that produces a Bell; it is that tradition that makes the passages to be traveled winding and

uncertain. The tradition to which we refer is that of
the twice born. It is the tradition of the Jewish
intellectual in the diaspora; the prodigal son who
travels the distance between the Pale and Camelot seeking to reconcile for himself and the world at large
Hellenism with Hebraism. It is, as Hans Kohn notes,
the tradition that all analytical and self-conscious
Jews bring to bear upon their entrance into Western
life.[16] The tradition then is the task itself. But
this in nothing new.

Ultimately, every generation--Jew and Gentile
alike--has its own responsibility to manage that burden.[17] The extent to which Bell has handled the burden
imposed by his struggle to reconcile the universal
aspirations embodied in Hellenism with Hebraism may be
argued. But like the struggle the burden is not the
mark of a neoconservative.

It may be that Bell is something like a Moses for
ultimately the position that his right-wing socialism
takes him is that of the holder of the faith; the
reluctant and troubled leader against whom "those who
would strike in new directions to achieve the same ends
must test their visions and faith."[18] His responsibility then is not to obscure that vision and faith with
moral injunctions that, while perhaps useful, tend to
emphasize the limits of political action to the exclusion of any real analysis of its possibilities. The
subordination of the corporation is a part of that
analysis; but it is only a part.

To paraphrase Bell, facts are harsh masters.[19]
There is nothing wrong with being a Moses, but every
Moses, every preserver of the faith, must lay claim to
a set of commandments. History does not demand that
commandments be tested, it demands that they be made
explicit and this is the iron cage that a Bell finds
himself trapped by.

The use of analogies can be dangerous. Ultimately, they can lead to oversimplification. But they can
be useful. While the Arnold analogy permitted us to
locate Bell within a distinctly Jewish socialist tradition, the iron cage analogy permits us to see him as an
intellectual who is as well versed in Deweyian instrumentalism as he is in the more conventional dictums of
scientific value relativism yet who cannot find an
intellectual resting place in either.

Utopianism and the Limits of Pragmatism: An Epilogue

Time and time again we have found Bell groping for
a way of establishing through Deweyian pragmatism some
way of measuring values, some way of developing a
scientific approach to planning that does not negate
the principles of a free and liberal collective society. The End of Ideology is one example. The Coming
of Post-Industrial Society is another. The Cultural
Contradictions of Capitalism is yet a third.   Indeed,
facts can be harsh masters. Two "facts" can scarcely
be neglected. The first is that Bell's work almost
always fails to realize his programmatic intentions.
The second is that this failure may be inevitable. It
rests in a basic methodological deficiency of Deweyian
pragmatism.

The salient feature of Deweyian pragmatism is that
in rejecting absolute values Dewey expresses the hope
that one can judge one's values by the consequences of
the application of those values in practice. Yet to
judge the application of values in practice one must
use values as the basis for one's standard of judgment.
The act of judgment thus implies a priori values: if we
are to judge values we have to judge them in terms of
other values. Those other values, if accepted as the
criteria for judgment, are at least for the moment
accepted as absolute values. At the most, Dewey may
be saying that we postpone the act of judgment of
values until that time when the judgment of values is
necessary and appropriate. If this is Dewey's argument, he "solves" the problem by postponing final judgment and rendering any complete acceptance of ultimate
values into a series of discrete judgments that may,
when viewed with the passage of time, be seen as contradictory, reversible, and expedient. But if this is
the case Dewey does not solve the problem of what
values are to be the criteria of judgment. Dewey
postpones the problem but does not rule it out of
existence. If one wishes to support Dewey's position
one can say that "that's life." There is no other
solution in human existence than the fact that our
ultimate values are always emergent and, socially, are
based on consensus.

Ultimately then, it is not without some irony that
Bell, the most commonly associated with the end of
ideology, remains a utopian in his belief in reason.
He is trapped by the same ultimate optimism that one

finds in Karl Marx and John Dewey. Theirs is not the
utopianism of fools but of intellectuals whose faith in
reason can find a home only outside of science. But
this is a conclusion they refuse to accept. Science
will assure their quest for certainty; their own values
do not.

Again, facts are harsh masters. There is nothing
wrong with being a Moses. There is nothing ignoble
about leading others to a promised land that one can
never enter. But there is something wrong if all that
an unsettled people are given is a pragmatism with no
moral reference point. It was ultimately Chester
Bowles's wisdom to recognize that if democracy is to be
made more than a fruitful impossibility, then more is
required of its leaders than pragmatism.

> The question which concerns me most about
> this new Administration [the Kennedy
> administration] is whether it lacks a
> genuine sense of conviction about what is
> right and wrong. . . . Anyone in public
> life who has strong convictions about the
> rights and wrongs of public morality,
> both domestic and international, has a
> very great advantage in times of strain,
> since his instincts on what to do are
> clear and immediate. Lacking such a
> framework of moral conviction or sense of
> what is right and what is wrong, he is
> forced to lean almost entirely upon his
> mental processes; he adds up the pluses
> and minuses of any question and comes up
> with a conclusion. Under normal condi-
> tions, when he is not tired or frus-
> trated, this pragmatic approach should
> successfully bring him out on the right
> side of the question.
>
> What worries me are the conclusions
> that such an individual may reach when he
> is tired, angry, frustrated, or emotion-
> ally affected. The Cuban fiasco demon-
> strates how far astray a man as brilliant
> and well intentioned as Kennedy can go
> who lacks a basic moral reference
> point.[20]

Ultimately, the road to utopia is a long one. But

there is no pragmatic utopia. To dream of its existence is to suffer more than the programmatic injunctions of a restless vanity; it is to ensure the permanence of one's journey. It is to guarantee the permanence of one's winding passages.

Notes

1. The image of the centaur is evoked by Steinfels to characterize the public perception of Moynihan.
"The odd beast, half politician, half professor, yet
unlike the mermaid or the centaur never successfully
joined." Peter Steinfels, The Neoconservatives. (New
York: Simon and Schuster, 1979), p. 112.

2. Bell, 1978 Foreword to The Cultural Contradictions of Capitalism, p. xi.

3. Steinfels, The Neoconservatives, p. 3.

4. Attlee, The Labour Party in Perspective, p.
29.

5. Bell, The Coming of Post-Industrial Society,
pp. 488-89.

6. Ibid., p. 489.

7. Ibid., p. 488.

8. Richard Chase, The Democratic Vista (Garden
City, N.Y.: Doubleday Anchor Books, 1958), p. 124.

9. Matthew Arnold, Culture and Anarchy, p. 45.

10. Bell, The Coming of Post-Industrial Society,
p. 464. Some years after The Coming of Post-Industrial
Society, Bell would direct a similar criticism toward
contemporary economic theory with its emphasis on viewing the world as being subject to a set of "economic
laws" that have both an a priori existence and life of
their own. See Bell's "Models and Reality in Economic
Discourse" in his The Crisis in Economic Theory (1981).
In that essay Bell argues in a tone that resonates with
George Lukacs's critique of reification that "Economic
theory, unlike physics, is not constitutive of a single
underlying reality. Nor can it be, pace Alfred Mar-
shall (and Gary Becker), timeless generalizations about
human behavior. In consequence, economics cannot be,
as its model in classical mechanics, a 'closed system'
which ignores change or the effort to discern specific
patterns of change."

11. Bell, The Cultural Contradictions of Capitalism, p. 162.

12. Arnold, Culture and Anarchy, p. 45.

13.   See Lionel Trilling, Matthew Arnold (New York: W. W. Norton and Company, 1939) for a discussion of the relationship between the two.

14.   Arnold, Culture and Anarchy, p. 124.

15.   Ibid., pp. 135-36.

16.   For a further elaboration of this point see Hans Kohn, "The Teaching of Moses Hess," The Menorah Journal 18 (May 1930), pp. 399-409.

17.   One is reminded here of the verdict rendered by Irving Howe in his review of Isaac Rosenfeld's Passage from Home, "The Lost Young Intellectuals": "to each age its own burdens." Implicit in that verdict is the call for the rejection of self-pity and the exercise of responsibility in managing one's grief and alienation.

18.   Peter Gay, The Dilemma of Democratic Socialism, p. 311.

19.   Bell, review of "Dated Socialist-Liberalism," New Leader, 5 December 1942, p. 2. The exact quote is "facts are stubborn masters."

20.   As quoted by David Halberstam in The Best and the Brightest (New York: Fawcett Crest, 1972), p. 88.

Bibliography

Aiken, Henry David. "Sidney Hook as Philosopher."
    Commentary, February 1962, pp. 143-51.
------. "American Pragmatism Reconsidered: John Dew-
    ey." Commentary, October 1962, pp. 334-44.
Arnold, Matthew. Culture and Anarchy. New York: Mac-
    millan and Co., 1883.
Arnold, Thurman. The Folklore of Capitalism. New
    Haven, Conn.: Yale University Press, 1938.
Aron, Raymond. The Opium of the Intellectuals. New
    York: Doubleday and Co., 1957.
Arrow, Kenneth J. Social Choice and Individual Values.
    2d. ed. New York: John Wiley & Sons, 1963.
Attlee, Clement Richard. The Labour Party in Perspec-
    tive and Twelve Years Later. London: Victor Gol-
    lancz, 1949.
Beard, Charles. America Faces the Future. Boston:
    Houghton Mifflin, 1932.
Beer, Samuel H. British Politics in the Collectivist
    Age. New York: Alfred A. Knopf, 1965.
Bell, Daniel. "Memo to Mrs. Roosevelt: A.Y.C. Destroys
    Chances for a Progressive Youth Organization."
    New Leader, 6 July 1940, p. 4.
------. "OPM Puts Gov't in Aluminum, Magnesium, Air-
    craft Business." New Leader, 31 May 1941, p. 3.
------. "Business Plans to Defy Gov't Efforts to Con-
    trol War Industries." New Leader, 28 June 1941,
    p. 2.
------. "Defense Monopoly Hits Small Business, Chokes
    Production." New Leader, 2 August 1941, p. 1.
------. "Captive Mine Decision to Settle Lewis Role at
    CIO Parley." New Leader, 8 November 1941, p. 1.

------. "Lewis Unions May Provoke Clashes in Organizing Drives." New Leader, 29 November 1941, p. 1.

------. "Political Intrigues Balk New Moves for Labor Peace-Settling of Jurisdiction Key to Permanent Peace." New Leader, 24 January 1941, p. 1.

------. "Standard Oil-Nazi Firm Tie-up Halted Rubber Production; I. G. Farben Patents Held by Jasco Balked U.S. Efforts--Full Story Told." New Leader, 31 January 1942, p. 1.

------. "Pro-Fascist Heads 'Free Hungary' Group, Seeks Official Recognition; Czech, Yugoslav Gov'ts Protest Activity of Tibor Eckhart Here." New Leader, 21 February 1942, p. 1.

------. "Lack of Vigilance Permits Fascists to Grab Strategic Defense Posts; Chicago Group, Eds. Lodge Curran Spread Defeatism." New Leader, 7 March 1942, p. 1.

------. "Technocracy Rides Again in New High-Powered Campaign." New Leader, 14 March 1942, p. 1.

------. "Scott, Ex Woobly, Makes Fancy Appeal with Catch-all Program," New Leader, 21 March 1942, p. 1.

------. "AFL-CIO Actions Refute Tory Cry on Labor's Slowdowns." New Leader, 28 March 1942, p. 1.

------. "Urge Probe of Int'l Cartels Balking Production, Foreign Ties of U.S. Firms; Farben Patents Worth Millions Sold to Standard for Song." New Leader, 4 April 1942, p. 1.

------. "Labor Wants 'Win the War' Congress; Tory Drives Hit Production Morale." New Leader, 25 April 1942, p. 1.

------. "New CIO Wars Loom over Lewis Break; Murray to Repeat AFL Peace Feelers." New Leader, 30 May 1942, p. 1.

------. "Senate to Probe Hi-Octane Sales to Axis." New Leader, 27 June 1942, p. 1.

------. "Fascist Papers--A Checklist of Danger." New Leader, 18 July 1942, p. 1.

------. "Sterling--A Story the Senate Fears to Hear." New Leader, 8 August 1942, p. 1.

------. "Clippings and Comment." New Leader, 19 September 1942, p. 2.

------. "Clippings and Comment." New Leader, 24 October 1942, p. 2.

------. "Clippings and Comment." New Leader, 7 November 1942, p. 2.

------. "Clippings and Comment." New Leader, 28

November 1942, p. 2.

------. "The Strange Case of Stuart Chase." New Leader, 5 December 1942, p. 2.

------. "Clippings and Comment." New Leader, 12
December 1942, p. 2.

------. "Clippings and Comment." New Leader, 9 January 1943, p. 2.

------. "Communist Forces Losing Hold in CIO Elec-
tions, Survey Shows." New Leader, 13 February
1943, p. 1.

------. "Planning by Whom for What? Business Menaces
FDR Schemes, Vested Interests Plan Own Board for
Economic Control." New Leader, 20 March 1943, p.
1.

------. Review of Business as a System of Power by
Robert Brady. Partisan Review, July-August 1943,
pp. 377-80.

------. "UAW Parley to Show Labor's Mood towards FDR
Policies; Report Phil Murray to Force Compromise
in Reuther-Addes Fight." New Leader, 2 October
1943, p. 1.

------. "Clippings and Comment." New Leader, 23 October 1943, p. 2.

------. "Business Plans for Business: CED; Free Enterprise in a Controlled Economy." Common Sense,
December 1943, pp. 427-31.

------. "Washington '44--Prelude to the Monopoly
State." New Leader, 29 January 1944, p. 4.

------. "Two Steps toward Monopoly State." New Leader, 26 February 1944, p. 5.

------. "Pipeline to Imperialism." Common Sense,
April 1944, pp. 130-33.

------. "The Face of Tomorrow." Jewish Frontier, June
1944, pp. 15-20.

------. "The Balance Sheet of the War." New Leader,
21 October 1944, p. 8.

------. "Dangers Ahead for the Unions." Common Sense,
February 1945, pp. 7-11.

------. "The Political Economy." Common Sense, January 1946, pp. 35-37.

------. Review of Reveille for Radicals by Saul Alinsky. Commentary, March 1946, pp. 92-94.

------. Review of Economic Mind in American Civilization: 1606-1965 by Joseph Dorfmann. Commentary,
July 1946, pp. 91-94.

------. "A Parable of Alienation." Jewish Frontier,
November 1946, pp. 12-19.

------. "Adjusting Men to Machines: Social Scientists Explore the World of the Factory." <u>Commentary</u>, January 1947, pp. 79-88.

------. "Preventing Economic Breakdown." Review of <u>The Coming Crisis</u> by Fritz Sternberg. <u>Commentary</u>, May 1947, pp. 492-95.

------. Review of <u>The Eternal Light</u> by Morton Wishengrad. <u>Commentary</u>, November 1947, pp. 495-97.

------. "Screening Leaders in a Democracy." <u>Commentary</u>, April 1948, pp. 368-75.

------. "American Socialist: What Now?" <u>Modern Review</u>, January 1949, pp. 345-53.

------. "America's Un-Marxist Revolution," <u>Commentary</u>, March 1949, pp. 207-15.

------. "Has America a Ruling Class?" Review of <u>Strategy for Liberals: The Politics of the Mixed Economy</u>. <u>Commentary</u>, December 1949, pp. 603-7.

------. Review of <u>Jewish Labor in the USA: 1882-1914</u> by Melech Epstein. <u>Commentary</u>, July 1950, pp. 186-88.

------. "Last of the Business Rackets." <u>Fortune</u>, June 1951, pp. 89-91.

------. "The Language of Labor." <u>Fortune</u>, September 1951, p. 86.

------. "Labor's Coming of Middle Age." <u>Fortune</u>, October 1951, p. 114.

------. <u>Marxian Socialism in the United States</u>. Princeton, N.J.: Princeton University Press, 1952.

------. "Hometown Revolutionists." Review of <u>The American Communist</u> by Morris Ernst and David Luth. <u>Saturday Review of Literature</u> 35, December 1952, p. 17.

------. "Prospects of American Capitalism." Review of <u>American Capitalism</u> by John Kenneth Galbraith. <u>Commentary</u>, December 1952, pp. 602-12.

------. "Rosenberg Case." <u>New Statesman</u>, January 1953, pp. 120-21.

------. "The Next American Labor Movement." <u>Fortune</u>, April 1953, pp. 120-23.

------. "Crime as an American Way of Life." <u>Antioch Review</u> 13, June 1953, pp. 131-54.

------. "Labor's New Men of Power." <u>Fortune</u>, June 1953, p. 148.

------. "Hard Times for the Intellectuals." <u>New Republic</u>, August 1953, pp. 8-10.

------. "Scandals in Union Welfare Funds." <u>Fortune</u>, April 1954, pp. 140-42.

------. "What Crime Wave." _Fortune_, January 1955, pp. 96-99.

------. "Bolshevik Man: His Motivations." _Commentary_, February 1955, pp. 179-87.

------. "America Loses Its Innocence." Review of _Part of Our Time_ by Murray Kempton. _Saturday Review of Literature_, May 1955, pp. 13-14.

------. "Beyond the Annual Wage." _Fortune_, May 1955, pp. 92-95.

------. "Out of the Fight for Warsaw." Review of _The Seizure of Power_ by C. Milosz. _The New Republic_, May 1955, pp. 41-42.

------. "Letter from New York: Passion and Politics in America." _Encounter_, January 1956, pp. 54-61.

------. "No Boom for the Unions." _Fortune_, June 1956, pp. 136-37.

------. "Great Back-to-Work Movement." _Fortune_, July 1956, pp. 90-93.

------. "Theory of Mass Society." _Commentary_, July 1956, pp. 75-83.

------. "The Worker and His Civil Functions." _Monthly Labor Review_ 71, July 1956, pp. 62-69.

------. "Breakup of Family Capitalism." _Partisan Review_, Spring 1957, pp. 317-20.

------. "Once-Born, Twice-Born, and the After-Born." _New Leader_, 1 April 1957, pp. 16-17.

------. "Yale Man as Revolutionist." Review of _Memoirs of a Revolutionist_ by Dwight MacDonald. _New Leader_, 9 December 1957, pp. 22-24.

------. "Where Does Labor Go from Here?" _Fortune_, December 1957, pp. 152-55.

------. "Invisible Unemployed." _Fortune_, July 1958, pp. 105-11.

------. "Call Me Ishmael." _Harpers'_, June 1959, pp. 78-81.

------. "Rediscovery of Alienation." _Journal of Philosophy_ 56, November 1959, pp. 933-52.

------. "The Subversion of Collective Bargaining." _Commentary_, March 1960, pp. 64-65.

------. "In Search of Marxist Humanism: The Debate on Alienation." _Survey_ 32, April-June, pp. 21-31.

------. "The Future of the Left." _Encounter_, May 1960, pp. 59-61.

------. "Vulgar Sociology." _Encounter_, December 1960, pp. 54-56.

------. "Reflections on Jewish Identity." _Commentary_, June 1961, pp. 471-78.

------. "The National Style and the Radical Right."
Partisan Review, Fall 1962, pp. 519-34.

------. "Alphabet of Injustice." Partisan Review,
Fall 1964, pp. 417-29.

------. "The Ethnic Group." Review of Beyond the
Melting Pot by Daniel Moynihan and Nathan Glazer.
Commentary, January 1964, pp. 74-76.

------. "Twelve Modes of Prediction." Daedalus 93,
Summer 1964, pp. 845-80.

------. The End of Ideology. New York: Free Press
Paperback Edition, 1965.

------. "Symposium on Morality." American Scholar 34,
Summer 1965, pp. 347-69.

------. The Reforming of General Education. New York:
Doubleday and Co., 1966.

------. "The Writer as Public Figure." Saturday
Review, 4 June 1966, pp. 18-19.

------. "Sociodicy." American Scholar 35, Autumn
1966, pp. 696-714.

------. "The Modern Review: An Introduction and Ap-
praisal." Labor History 9, Fall 1968, pp. 380-83.

------. "Charles Fourier: Prophet of Eupsychia."
American Scholar 38, Winter 1968-1969, pp. 41-58.

------. "The Idea of a Social Report." Public Interest, Spring 1969, pp. 72-84.

------. "Quo Warranto?" Public Interest, Spring 1970,
pp. 53-68.

------. "Technocracy and Politics." The China Quarterly 44, October-December 1970, pp. 1-24.

------. "Post-industrial Society: The Evolution of an
Idea." Survey 17, Spring 1971, pp. 102-68.

------. The Coming of Post-industrial Society. New
York: Basic Books, 1973.

------. "Technology, Nature, and Society." In Techno-
logy and the Frontiers of Knowledge. The Frank
Nelson Doubleday Lectures, no. 1. Garden City,
N.Y.: Doubleday and Co., 1973, pp. 25-70.

------. "The Moral Vision of The New Leader." New
Leader, 24 December 1973, pp. 9-12.

------. "Modern Review, New York, 1947-1950." In The
American Radical Press 1880-1960. Vol 2. Ed.
Joseph R. Conlin. Westport, Conn.: Greenwood
Press, 1974, pp. 644-47.

------. "The Public Household." Public Interest, Fall
1974, pp. 29-68.

------. The Cultural Contradictions of Capitalism.
New York: Basic Books, 1976.

------. "The Intelligentsia in American Society." In
    Tomorrow's American. Ed. Samuel Sandmel. New
    York: Oxford University Press, 1977, pp. 26-46.
------. "Foreword: 1978." The Cultural Contradictions
    of Capitalism. New York: Basic Books Harper Colo-
    phon Book, 1978.
------. The Winding Passage. New York: Basic Books,
    1980.
Bell, Daniel, ed. The Radical Right. Rev. ed. Garden
    City, N.Y.: Anchor Books and Doubleday and Co.,
    1964.
------. Toward the Year 2000: Work in Progress. Bos-
    ton: Beacon Press, 1969.
Bell, Daniel, and Virginia Held. "The Community Revo-
    lution." Public Interest, Summer 1969, pp. 142-
    77.
Bell, Daniel, and Irving Kristol. Capitalism Today.
    New York: Basic Books, 1970.
Bell, Daniel, and Irving Kristol, eds. Confrontation.
    New York: Basic Books, 1969.
Bell, Daniel, and Irving Kristol, eds. The Crisis in
    Economic Theory. New York: Basic Books, 1981.
Bendix, Reinhold. Max Weber: An Intellectual Portrait.
    Garden City, N.Y.: Anchor Books, 1960.
Bensman, Joseph, and Arthur J. Vidich. The New Ameri-
    can Society. Chicago: Quadrangle Books, 1971.
Bensman, Joseph, and Robert Lilienfeld. Craft and Con-
    sciousness. New York: John Wiley and Sons, 1973.
Berle, Adolph, A., Jr., and Gardiner C. Means. The
    Modern Corporation and Private Property. New
    York: Macmillan Co., 1933.
Berlin, Isaiah. "The Life and Opinions of Moses Hess."
    In Against the Current. New York: Penguin Books,
    1982, pp. 213-51.
Bershady, Harold J. Ideology and Social Knowledge.
    New York: Halsted Press, 1973.
Berger, Peter. The Sacred Canopy. Garden City, N.Y.:
    Anchor Books, Doubleday and Co., 1969.
Birnbaum, Norman. "America: A Partial View." Commen-
    tary, July 1958, pp. 42-46.
Bondy, Francois. "Berlin Congress for Freedom." Com-
    mentary, September 1950, pp. 245-251.
Bourricaud, Francois. "Post-industrial Society and the
    Paradoxes of Welfare." Survey 16, Winter 1971,
    pp. 43-59.
Brady, Robert. Business as a System of Power. New
    York: Columbia University Press, 1943.

Brandt, Richard. "Personal Values and the Justification of Institutions." In Human Values and Economic Policy. Ed. Sidney Hook. New York: New York University Press, 1967, pp. 22-40.

Braunthal, Alfred. "Blueprints, but Not in a Vacuum." New Leader, 26 December 1942, p. 2.

Brecht, Arnold. Political Theory: The Foundations of Twentieth Century Political Thought. Princeton, N.J.: Princeton University Press, 1959.

Brenda, Julien. The Betrayal of the Intellectuals. Boston: Beacon press, 1955.

Brinton, Crane. The Shaping of the Modern Mind. New York: Mentor Books, 1959.

Brooks, Van Wyck. America's Coming of Age. New York: B. W. Huebsch, 1915.

Brzezinski, Z. "America in the Technotronic Age." Encounter, January 1968, pp. 16-26.

Burke, Edmund. Reflections on the Revolution in France. Baltimore, Md.: Penguin Books, 1969.

Burnstein, Alexander J. "Niebuhr, Scripture, and Normative Judaism." In Reinhold Niebuhr: His Religious, Social and Political Thought. Ed. Charles W. Kegley and Robert W. Bretall. New York: Macmillan Co., 1956, pp. 411-28.

Burtt, E. A. The Metaphysical Foundations of Modern Science. Garden City, N.Y.: Doubleday and Co., 1954.

Chamberlain, John. "Carl Dreher: Totalitarian Liberal." Common Sense, November 1942, pp. 369-72.

Chase, Richard. The Democratic Vista. Garden City, N.Y.: Doubleday Anchor Books, 1958.

Chase, Stuart. "Socialist-Liberalism Is Out of Date." Common Sense, December 1942, pp. 418-19.

Cohen, Bernard. Sociocultural Changes in American Jewish Life as Reflected in Selected Jewish Literature. Rutherford, N.J.: Fairleigh Dickinson University Press, 1972.

Cohen, Eliot. "The Intellectual and the Jewish Community." Commentary, July 1949, pp. 20-30.

------. "What Do the Germans Propose to Do?" Commentary, September 1950, pp. 225-28.

Cohn, Norman. Pursuit of the Millennium. London: Secker & Warburg, 1957.

Comte, Auguste. "Plan of the Scientific Operations for Reorganizing Society." In On Intellectuals. Ed. Philip Rieff. Garden City, N.Y.: Anchor Books, 1970, pp. 269-305.

Conford, F. M. From Religion to Philosophy: A Study
    in the Origins of Western Speculation. New York:
    Harper Torchbooks, 1957.
Coser, Lewis. "What Shall We Do?" Dissent, Spring
    1956, pp. 156-65.
Crosland, C. A. R. The Future of Socialism. London:
    Jonathan Cape, 1950.
Dahl, Robert A., and Charles E. Lindblom. Politics,
    Economics and Welfare. New York: Harper Torch-
    books, 1963.
Davis, Harry R., and Robert C. Good. Reinhold Niebuhr
    on Politics. New York: Scribner's Sons, 1960.
DeToledano, Ralph. Lament for a Generation. New York:
    Farrar, Straus and Cudahy, 1960.
Dewey, John. Democracy and Education. New York: Mac-
    millan Co., 1916.
------. Reconstruction in Philosophy. New York: Henry
    Holt and Co., 1920; reprint ed., Boston: Beacon
    Press, 1967.
------. The Public and Its Problems. New York: Henry
    Holt and Co., 1927.
------. Individualism: Old and New. New York: Minton,
    Balch, 1930.
------. Art as Experience. New York: Capricorn Books,
    1934.
------. Liberalism and Social Action. New York: G. P.
    Putnam, 1935.
------. The Quest for Certainty. 10th ed. New York:
    Capricorn Books, G. P. Putnam's Sons, 1969.
Diggins, John. P. The American Left in the Twentieth
    Century. New York: Harcourt Brace Jovanovich,
    1973.
Dittberner, Job Leonard. "The End of Ideology and
    American Social Thought, 1930-1960." Ph.D. dis-
    sertation, Columbia University, 1974.
Dreher, Carl. "John Chamberlain: Prophet of Reaction."
    Common Sense, November 1942, pp. 366-68.
Drucker, Peter F. The End of Economic Man. New York:
    John Day Co., 1939; reprint ed., New York: Harper
    & Row, 1969.
------. The Age of Discontinuity. New York: Harper &
    Row, 1969.
Dubofsky, Melvyn. "Success and Failure of Socialism in
    New York City, 1900-1918: A Case Study." Labor
    History 9, Fall 1968, pp. 361-75.
Eastman, Max. "Socialism and Human Nature." New
    Leader, 24 January 1942, pp. 5-6.

Ellul, Jacques. _The Technological Society_. New York:
    Vintage Books, 1964.
Engels, Frederich. _Ludwig Feuerbach and the Outcome of_
    Classical German Philosophy. Ed. C. P. Dutt. New
    York: International Publishers, 1941.
Epstein, Joseph. "The New Conservatives: Intellectuals
    in Retreat." In _The New Conservatives_. Ed. Lewis
    A. Coser and Irving Howe, New York: Quadrangle/New
    York Times Book Co., 1974, pp. 9-28.
Etzioni, Amitai. _The Active Society: A Theory of Soci-_
    etal and Political Processes. New York: Free
    Press, 1968.
------. "Columbia in Turmoil: Challenge to Liberal-
    ism." _New Leader_, May 1968, pp. 16-19.
"Ex-Socialists Join 'Old Guard' Party." _New York_
    Times, 4 June 1936, p. 1.
Galbraith, John Kenneth. _American Capitalism_. Boston:
    Houghton Mifflin Co., 1952.
------. _The New Industrial State_. Boston: Houghton
    Mifflin Co., 1967.
------. _The Affluent Society_. 2d. ed. New York:
    Mentor Books, 1970.
Girvetz, Harry K. _The Evolution of Liberalism_. Lon-
    don: Collier Books, 1963.
Goldscheid, Rudolf. "A Sociological Approach to Public
    Finance." In _Classics in the Theory of Public_
    Finance. Ed. Richard A. Musgrave and Alan T.
    Peacock. New York: St. Martin's Press, 1967, pp.
    202-13.
Goodman, Paul. _Utopian Essays and Practice Proposals_.
    New York: Random House, 1962.
Habermas, Jurgen. "What Does a Crisis Mean Today?
    Legitimation Problems in Late Capitalism." _Social_
    Research 40, Winter 1973, pp. 643-67.
Hacker, Andrew. Review of _Political Man_ by Seymour
    Martin Lipset. _Commentary_, June 1961, pp. 547-50.
Halberstam, David. _The Best and the Brightest_. New
    York: Fawcett Crest, 1972.
Hallowell, John H. _Main Currents in Modern Political_
    Thought. New York: Henry Holt and Co., 1950.
------. _The Decline of Liberalism as an Ideology_. New
    York: Howard Fertig, 1971.
Harrington, Michael. "The Welfare State and Its Neo-
    conservative Critics." In _The New Conservatives_.
    Ed. Lewis A. Coser and Irving Howe. New York:
    Quadrangle/New York Times Book Co., 1974, pp. 29-
    63.

Hegel, G. W. F. *Reason in History*. Indianapolis:
    Bobbs-Merrill, 1953.
Heidegger, Martin. *Being and Time*. Trans. John Mar-
    quarrie and Edward Robinson. New York: Harper,
    1962.
Herberg, Will. "The Stillborn Labor Party." *Common
    Sense*, May 1944, pp. 160-63.
------. "From Marxism to Judaism." *Commentary*, Janu-
    ary 1947, pp. 25-32.
Hofstadter, Richard. *The American Political Tradition*.
    New York: Vintage Books, 1957.
------. *Anti-intellectualism in American Life*. New
    York: Vintage Books, 1963.
Hook, Sidney. "Materialism." In *Encyclopedia of the
    Social Sciences*. Ed. E. R. A. Seligman and Alvin
    Johnson. New York: Macmillan Co., 1932, pp. 209-
    20.
------. *Reason, Social Myths, and Democracy*. New
    York: John Day Co., 1940.
------. "Social Change and Original Sin: Answer to
    Niebuhr." *New Leader*, 8 November 1941, p. 5.
------. "The New Failure of Nerve." *Partisan Review*,
    January-February 1943, pp. 2-23.
------. *From Hegel to Marx*. Ann Arbor, Mich.: Ann
    Arbor Paperbacks/University of Michigan Press,
    1968.
------. *John Dewey: An Intellectual Portrait*. 1939;
    reprint ed., Westport, Conn.: Greenwood Press,
    1971.
------. *Pragmatism and the Tragic Sense of Life*. New
    York: Basic Books, 1974.
Howe, Irving. Review of *Passage from Home* by Isaac
    Rosenfeld. *Commentary*, August 1946, pp. 190-92.
------. "The Lost Young Intellectual." *Commentary*,
    October 1946, pp. 361-67.
------. "The Critics of American Socialism." *The New
    International* 13, May-June 1952, pp. 115-52.
------. *Steady Work*. New York: Harcourt, Brace and
    World, 1966.
------. "The New York Intellectuals: A Chronicle and a
    Critique." *Commentary*, October 1968, pp. 29-51.
------. "The New York Intellectual." *Commentary*,
    January 1969, pp. 14-16.
------. *World of Our Fathers*. New York: Harcourt
    Brace Jovanovich, 1976.
Howe, Irving, ed. *The Idea of the Modern in Litera-
    ture and the Arts*. New York: Horizon Press, 1967.

Hughes, H. Stewart. "The End of Political Ideology."
    Measure 2, Spring 1951, pp. 146-58.
------. Consciousness and Society. New York: Vintage
    Books, 1961.
Jacobs, Mark. "Columbia in Turmoil: A Student View."
    New Leader, 20 May 1968, pp. 12-16.
Jacobs, Paul, and Saul Landau. The New Radicals. New
    York: Random House, 1966.
James, William. The Varieties of Religious Experience.
    New York: Modern Library, 1902.
Jencks, Christopher. Review of The Neoconservatives by
    Peter Steinfels. New York Times, 1 July 1979,
    sec. 7, p. 1.
Jencks, Christopher, and David Riesman. The Academic
    Revolution. Garden City, N.Y.: Doubleday and Co.,
    1968.
Kadushin, Charles. "Who Are the Elite Intellectuals?"
    Public Interest, Fall 1972, pp. 109-25.
Kaplan, Abraham. The Conduct of Inquiry. San Fran-
    cisco: Chandler Publishing Co., 1964.
Kelsen, Hans. What Is Justice. Los Angeles: Univer-
    sity of California Press, 1960.
Kleinberg, Benjamin S. American Society in the Post-
    industrial Age. Columbus, Ohio: Charles E. Mer-
    rill Publishing Co., 1973.
Kohn, Hans. "The Teaching of Moses Hess." The Menorah
    Journal 18, May 1930, pp. 399-409.
Kristol, Irving. "The New York Intellectuals." Com-
    mentary, January 1969, pp. 12-14.
------. "Memoirs of a Trotskyist." New York Times
    Magazine, 23 January 1977, p. 51.
Kuhn, Thomas S. The Structure of Scientific Revolu-
    tions. Chicago: University of Chicago Press,
    1970.
Kuhns, William. The Post Industrial Prophets. New
    York: Weybright and Talley, 1971.
Laidler, Harry W. History of Socialism. New York:
    Thomas Y. Crowell, 1968.
Lakoff, Sanford. Equality in Political Philosophy.
    Boston: Beacon Press, 1968.
Lane, Robert E. "The Decline of Politics and Ideology
    in a Knowledgeable Society." American Sociologi-
    cal Review 31, 1956, 149-62.
Lasch, Christopher. The Agony of the American Left.
    New York: Alfred A. Knopf, 1969.
Laski, Harold J. The Rise of Liberalism. London:
    Irwin Books, 1962.

Lawson, R. Alan. The Failure of Independent Liberal-
    ism. New York: G. P. Putnam's Sons, 1971.
Lee, Algernon. "On the Split of 1936." New Leader, 10
    May 1947, p. 3.
Lenin, V. I. What Is to Be Done? New York: Interna-
    tional Publishers, 1969.
Lerner, Abba P. "Collectivism and Freedom." New
    Leader, 29 November 1942, p. 2.
Lichtheim, George. The Concept of Ideology and Other
    Essays. New York: Vintage Books, 1967.
Lippman, Walter. The Public Philosophy. Boston: Lit-
    tle, Brown and Company, 1954.
Lipset, Seymour Martin. Political Man. Garden City,
    N.Y.: Anchor Books, 1960.
------. "The Changing Class Structure and Contemporary
    European Politics." Daedalus 93, Winter 1964, pp.
    271-303.
Lowi, Theodore J. The End of Liberalism. New York: W.
    W. Norton and Company, 1969.
Lukacs, Georg. History and Class Consciousness: Stu-
    dies in Marxist Dialectics. Cambridge, Mass.: M.
    I. T. Press, 1968.
Lyons, Eugene. The Red Decade. Indianapolis: Bobbs-
    Merrill, 1941.
MacDonald, Dwight. "The Future of Democratic Values."
    Partisan Review, August 1943, pp. 321-44.
------. Memoirs of a Revolutionist. New York: Farrar,
    Straus and Cudahy, 1957.
Mandelbaum, Maurice. The Problem of Historical Know-
    ledge. New York: Liverigest, 1938.
Mannheim, Karl. Ideology and Utopia: An Introduction
    to the Sociology of Knowledge. Trans. Louis Wirth
    and Edward Shils. New York: Harcourt, Brace and
    World, 1936.
------. Man and Society in an Age of Reconstruction.
    New York: Harcourt, Brace and Company, 1941.
------. "Conservative Thought." Essays on Sociology
    and Social Psychology. Ed. Paul Kecskemeti. New
    York: Oxford University Press, 1953, pp. 74-164.
Marcuse, Herbert. Reason and Revolution. 6th ed.
    Boston: Beacon Press, 1968.
Marris, Robin. The Economic Theory of Managerial Capi-
    talism. New York: Free Press of Glencoe, 1964.
Marx, Karl. Economic and Philosophic Manuscripts of
    1844. Ed. Dirk J. Struik. New York: Internation-
    al Publishers, 1964.
Marx, Karl, and Frederick Engels. The German Ideology.

New York: International Publishers, 1947.

Merton, Robert K. <u>Science, Technology and Society in
Seventeenth Century England</u>. New York: Harper
Torchbooks, 1970.

Mett, Ida. <u>The Kronstadt Uprising</u>. Montreal: Black
Rose Books—Our Generation Press, 1971.

Mills, C. Wright. "Collectivism and the Mixed Up Economy." <u>New Leader</u>, 19 December 1942, pp. 5-6.

------. <u>The New Men of Power</u>. New York: Harcourt,
Brace and Company, 1948.

------. <u>The Power Elite</u>. New York: Oxford University
Press, 1959.

------. "Liberal Values in the Modern World." In
<u>Power, Politics and People</u>. Ed. Irving Louis
Horowitz. New York: Oxford University Press,
1963, pp. 187-95.

------. "The Social Role of the Intellectual." In
<u>Power, Politics and People</u>. Ed. Irving Louis
Horowitz. New York: Oxford University Press,
1963, pp. 292-304.

Molner, Thomas. <u>The Decline of the Intellectual</u>.
Cleveland: Meridian Book—World Publishing Co.,
1961.

Monsen, Joseph R., Jr. <u>Modern American Capitalism:
Ideologies and Issues</u>. Boston: Houghton Mifflin
Company, 1963.

Morgenthau, Hans J. "The Perils of Political Empiricism." <u>Commentary</u>, July 1962, pp. 60-64.

------. <u>Scientific Man vs. Power Politics</u>. Chicago:
University of Chicago Press, 1946; reprint ed.,
Chicago: Midway, 1974.

Musgrave, Richard A. <u>The Theory of Public Finance</u>.
New York: McGraw-Hill, 1959.

Nettl, J. P. "Ideas, Intellectuals, and Structures of
Dissent." In <u>On Intellectuals</u>. Ed. Philip Rieff.
Garden City, N.Y.: Anchor Books, 1970, pp. 57-134.

Niebuhr, Reinhold. <u>Christianity and Power Politics</u>.
New York: Charles Scribner's Sons, 1940.

------. <u>The Nature and Destiny of Man</u>, 2 vols. New
York: Charles Scribner's Sons, 1941.

------. <u>The Children of Light and the Children of
Darkness</u>. New York: Charles Scribner's Sons,
1944.

------. "Will Civilization Survive Technics?" <u>Commen-
tary</u>, December 1945, pp. 2-8.

------. <u>The Irony of American History</u>. New York:
Charles Scribner's Sons, 1952.

------. _Christian Realism and Political Problems_. New
    York: Charles Scribner's Sons, 1953.
Nieburg, H. L. _In the Name of Science_. Chicago: Quad-
    rangle Books, 1966.
Nomad, Max. "White Collars and Horny Hands." _Modern
    Quarterly_, Autumn 1932, pp. 68-76.
Novak, George, _Pragmatism versus Marxism_. New York:
    Pathfinder Press, 1974.
"Old Guard Forms New Party." _New York Times_, 12 May
    1936, p. 1.
Oser, Jacob, and William C. Blanchfield. _The Evolution
    of Economic Thought_. New York: Harcourt Brace
    Jovanovich, 1973.
Parsons, Talcott. "Unity and Diversity in the Modern
    Intellectual Disciplines: The Role of the Social
    Sciences." In _Science and Culture_. Ed. Gerald
    Holton. Boston: Houghton Mifflin Co., 1965, pp.
    39-69.
------. "Value-Freedom and Objectivity." In _Max Weber
    and Sociology Today_. Ed. Otto Stammer. New York:
    Harper Torchbooks, 1971, pp. 27-50.
Phillips, William. "What Happened in the 30's." _Com-
    mentary_, September 1962, pp. 204-12.
Plato. _The Republic_. Trans. W. H. D. Rouse. New
    York: Mentor Books, 1956.
Podhoretz, Norman. "The Young Generation of U.S. In-
    tellectuals." _New Leader_, 11 March 1957, pp.
    8-10.
------. _Making It_. New York: Random House, 1967.
Polanyi, Karl. _The Great Transformation_. New York:
    Octagon Books, 1975.
Popper, Karl R. _The Open Society and Its Enemies_.
    Princeton, N.J.: Princeton University Press, 1950.
Rawls, John. _A Theory of Justice_. Cambridge, Mass.:
    Belknap Press of Harvard University Press, 1972.
------. "Concepts of Distributional Equity." _American
    Economic Association_ 64 (May 1974): 141-45.
Remmling, Gunter W. _The Sociology of Karl Mannheim_.
    Atlantic Highlands, N.J.: Humanities Press, 1975.
Rickert, Heinrich. _Science and History: A Critique of
    Positivist Epistemology_. Princeton, N.J.: D. Van
    Nostrand Co., 1962.
Riesman, David. _The Lonely Crowd_. New Haven, Conn.:
    Yale University Press, 1950.
Rose, Arnold. "Sociology and the Study of Values."
    British Journal of Sociology 7, 1956, pp. 1-17.
Rosenberg, Bernard. "The New American Right." _Dis-_

    <u>sent</u>, Winter 1956, pp. 45-50.
Rosenfeld, Isaac. <u>An Age of Enormity</u>. Cleveland:
    World Publishing Co., 1962.
------. <u>Passages from Home</u>. Cleveland: World Publish-
    ing Co., 1965.
Russell, Bertrand. <u>A History of Western Philosophy</u>.
    New York: Simon and Schuster, 1954.
Rustow, Dankwart A. "Columbia in Turmoil: Day of Cri-
    sis." <u>New Leader</u>, 20 May 1968, pp. 5-12.
Samuelson, Paul. "Arrow's Mathematical Politics." In
    <u>Human Values and Economic Policy</u>. Ed. Sidney
    Hook. New York: New York University Press, 1967,
    pp. 41-51.
Sartori, Giovanni. "Technological Forecasting and
    Politics." <u>Survey</u> 16, Winter 1971, pp. 60-68.
Schapiro, J. Salwyn. <u>Liberalism: Its Meaning and His-</u>
    <u>tory</u>. Princeton, N.J.: D. Van Nostrand Co., 1958.
Schlesinger, Arthur, Jr. "Reinhold Niebuhr's Role in
    American Political Thought and Life." In <u>Reinhold</u>
    <u>Niebuhr: His Religious, Social and Political Thought</u>.
    Ed. Charles W. Kegley and Robert W. Bretall. New
    York: Macmillan Co., 1956, pp. 125-50.
Schottland, Charles I., ed. <u>The Welfare State</u>. New
    York: Harper & Row, 1967.
Schumpeter, Joseph A. "The March into Socialism."
    <u>American Economic Review</u> 40, May 1950, pp. 447-56.
------. "The Crisis of the Tax State." Trans. W. F.
    Stolper and R. A. Musgrave. Reprinted in <u>Interna-</u>
    <u>tional Economic Papers</u> no. 4. New York: Macmillan
    Co., 1954, pp. 5-38.
------. <u>Capitalism, Socialism and Democracy</u>. 3d. ed.
    New York: Harper Torchbooks, 1962.
Shils, Edward. "The End of Ideology." <u>Encounter</u>,
    November 1955, pp. 55-58.
------. <u>The Torment of Secrecy</u>. Glencoe, Ill.: Free
    Press, 1956.
------. "Ideology and Civility: On the Politics of the
    Intellectual." <u>Sewanee Review</u> 66, Summer 1958,
    pp. 450-80.
Shklar, Judith. "The Political Theory of Utopia: From
    Melancholy to Nostalgia." <u>Daedalus</u> 94, Spring
    1965, pp. 367-81.
"Socialist Party Enters Campaign Badly Divided." <u>New</u>
    <u>York Times</u>, 31 May 1936, sec. 4, p. E7.
Soule, George. <u>A Planned Society</u>. Gloucester, Mass.:
    MacMillan and Co., 1932.
Spitz, David. <u>Patterns of Anti-democratic Thought</u>.

New York: Macmillan and Co., 1949.

Stankiewicz, W. J. _Political Thought since World War II_. New York: Free Press of Glencoe, 1964.

Steinfels, Peter. _The Neoconservatives_. New York: Simon and Schuster, 1979.

Stevens, Judith Peterson. _Daniel Bell and Kenneth Boulding on Social and Educational Theory_. Ann Arbor, Mich.: University Micro-Films International, 1977.

Stone, I. F. _The Truman Era_. New York: Monthly Review Press, 1953.

Stone, Ronald H. _Reinhold Niebuhr: Prophet to Politicians_. Nashville, Tenn.: Abingdon Press, 1972.

Strauss, Leo. _Natural Right and History_. Chicago: University of Chicago Press, 1953.

Swados, Harvey. _A Radical's America_. Boston: Little, Brown and Company, 1962.

Taylor, Stanley. _Conceptions of Institutions and the Theory of Knowledge_. New York: Bookman Associates, 1956.

Tawney, R. H. _The Acquisitive Society_. New York: Harvest Books, 1920.

------. _Equality_. London: Irwin Books, 1931.

Teller, Judd L. "A Critique of the New Jewish Theology." _Commentary_, March 1958, pp. 243-48.

Thoenes, Piet. _The Elite in the Welfare State_. London: Faber & Faber, 1966.

Thompson, Kenneth. "The Political Philosophy of Reinhold Niebuhr." In _Reinhold Niebuhr: His Religious, Social and Political Thought_. Ed. Charles W. Kegley and Robert W. Bretall. New York: Macmillan and Co., 1956, pp. 152-75.

Thurow, Lester. "Toward a Definition of Economic Justice." _Public Interest_, Spring 1973, pp. 56-80.

------. _The Zero-Sum Society_. New York: Penguin Books, 1981.

Tillich, Paul. _The Interpretation of History_. New York: Charles Scribner's Sons, 1936.

------. "Reinhold Niebuhr's Doctrine of Knowledge." In _Reinhold Niebuhr: His Religious, Social and Political Thought_. Ed. Charles W. Kegley and Robert W. Bretall. New York: Macmillan and Co., 1956, pp. 36-43.

Titmuss, Richard M. _Commitment to Welfare_. New York: Pantheon Books, 1968.

Tominaga, Ken'ichi. "Post-industrial Society and Cultural Diversity." _Survey_ 16, Winter 1971, pp. 69-77.

Trilling, Lionel. _Matthew Arnold_. New York: W. W. Norton and Company, 1939.

------. _Beyond Culture_. New York: Viking Press, 1965.

------. _Sincerity and Authenticity_. Cambridge, Mass.: Harvard University Press, 1974.

Tugwell, Rexford G. _The Industrial Discipline and the Governmental Arts_. New York: Columbia University Press, 1933.

Ulam, Adam. "Socialism and Utopia." _Daedalus_ 94, Spring 1965, pp. 382-400.

Unger, Roberto M. _Knowledge and Politics_. New York: Free Press, 1975.

"The United States in a New World: The Domestic Economy." _Supplement to Fortune_, December 1942, pp. 1-17.

Veblen, Thorstein. _The Engineers and the Price System_. New York: Viking Press, 1921.

------. _The Theory of the Leisure Class_. New York: Mentor Books, 1953.

------. _Absentee Ownership and Business Enterprise in Recent Times_. New York: Augustus M. Kelly, 1964.

------. "The Preconceptions of the Classical Economists." In _The Portable Veblen_. Ed. Max Lerner. New York: Viking Press, 1968, pp. 241-74.

von Weiser, Frederich. "The Theory of the Public Economy." In _Classics in the Theory of Public Finance_. Ed. Richard A. Musgrave and Alan T. Peacock. New York: St. Martin's Press, 1964, pp. 190-201.

Waldman, Louis. _Labor Lawyer_. New York: E. P. Dutton and Company, 1944.

Walling, William English. _The Larger Aspects of Socialism_. New York: Macmillan and Co., 1913.

Walzer, Michael. "In Defense of Equality." In _The New Conservatives_. Ed. Lewis A. Coser and Irving Howe. New York: Quadrangle/New York Times Books Co., 1974, pp. 107-23.

Waxman, Chaim I., ed. _The End of Ideology Debate_. New York: Funk and Wagnalls, 1968.

Weber, Max. _From Max Weber: Essays in Sociology_. Ed. Hans H. Gerth and C. Wright Mills. New York: Oxford University Press, 1946.

------. _The Methodology of the Social Sciences_. Trans. and ed. Edward A. Shils and Henry A. Finch. New York: Free Press, 1949.

------. _Ancient Judaism_. Trans. and ed. Hans H. Gerth and Don Martindale. New York: Free Press, 1952.

------. _The Sociology of Religion_. 4th rev. ed. Trans. Ephraim Fischoff. Introduction by Talcott Parsons. Boston: Beacon Press, 1956.

------. _The Protestant Ethic and the Spirit of Capitalism_. Trans. Talcott Parsons. New York: Charles Scribner's Sons, 1958.

White, Morton. _Social Thought in America_. Boston: Beacon Press, 1966.

Whitehead, Alfred North. _Science and the Modern World_. New York: Free Press, 1927.

Williams, Daniel D. "Niebuhr and Liberalism." In _Reinhold Niebuhr: His Religious, Social and Political Thought_. Ed. Charles W. Kegley and Robert W. Bretall. New York: Macmillan and Co., 1956, pp. 193-214.

Wirth, Louis. "American Sociology, 1915-47." _American Journal of Sociology_, Index to volumes 1-52, 1895-1947. Chicago: University of Chicago Press, June 1948, pp. 273-338.

Wrong, Dennis. "The Perils of Political Moderation." _Commentary_, January 1959, pp. 1-8.

------. _Max Weber_. Englewood Cliffs, N.J.: Prentice-Hall, 1970.

Young, James P. _The Politics of Affluence_. San Francisco: Chandler, 1968.

Yorburg, Betty. _Utopia and Reality_. New York: Columbia University Press, 1969.

Znaniecki, Florian. _Social Role of the Man of Knowledge_. New York: Columbia University Press, 1940.

Index

About the Author

Nathan Liebowitz is Adjunct Associate Professor of Sociology at Pace University. He is currently Educational Coordinator in the Mayor's Office for the Handicapped in New York City. He is the author of the *New York Hospital-Cornell Medical Center Graduate Staff Manual* and *Deregulation and Interstate Banking* and co-writer and editor of the *Impact of Phoenix House Therapeutic Model in Treating Drug Addiction* and *Math Anxiety and the Effectiveness of Its Management in American Universities.*